*The What, Where, When, How & Why
of Gardening in Missouri*

Missouri
GARDENER'S
GUIDE

MICHAEL MILLER

COOL
SPRINGS
PRESS

Miller, Michael
    Missouri Gardener's Guide: the what, where, when, how & why of gardening in Missouri / Michael Miller

    p.   cm.
    Includes bibliographical references (p.   ) and index.
    ISBN 1-888608-50-1
    1. Landscape plants -- Missouri 2. Landscape gardening -- Missouri
    3. Gardening -- Missouri I. Title
635.9--dc20
Mill

Cool Springs Press, Inc.
2020 Fieldstone Parkway
Suite 900210
Franklin, Tennessee 37069

First printing 1998
Printed in the United States of America
10 9 8 7 6 5 4 3 2

Horticultural Nomenclature Editor: Robert F. Polomski,
    Extension Consumer Horticulturist, Clemson University

On the cover (clockwise from top left): Trumpet Vine, Sweet William, Europeana Rose,
    Narcissus mix

Visit the Cool Springs Press website at: www.coolspringspress.com

DEDICATION

For the one I love, Tracy Ann, who keeps me company and my feet on the ground; for my parents Rex and Jane and my grandmothers Maggie and Dorothy, whose caring and guidance enabled me to appreciate the outdoors; and for my sister Teri, brothers Tom and Kevin, friends, neighbors, teachers, and community, who were all influential in my nature-loving childhood.

A C K N O W L E D G M E N T S

I WOULD LIKE TO ACKNOWLEDGE Mother Nature who gives me a breathtakingly beautiful, diverse, ever-changing environment that is both challenging and rewarding.

Thanks to the many individual gardeners, garden clubs, wholesale and retail nurseries, park systems, the Universities of Missouri and Illinois Extension Services, Powell Gardens, and the Missouri Botanical Garden, who provided me with interpretation, education, understanding, and insight over the past twenty-one years.

Roger Waynick and the staff of Cool Springs Press allowed me this opportunity to share the knowledge I have acquired and my adventures in the landscape. Jan Keeling and the editorial staff kept me from getting lost in the wordy woods.

Thanks to all, from beginners to Master Gardeners, who have shared with me information about the outdoors.

Missouri

GARDENER'S GUIDE

CONTENTS

INTRODUCTION

M ISSOURI LIES AT THE HEART OF AMERICA, in a place
rich in natural beauty. All schoolchildren learn the names
and history of its two major riverways, the Mississippi and the
Missouri. But natives also know the green banks along its many
smaller waterways and treasure the quiet forests and sunny
meadows that mark their shores. We walk Missouri's timbered
ridges, gaze across its rolling plains of tall grass, and climb to the
top of its rocky river bluffs, always with a sense of gratitude that so
many of nature's gifts are here for us to share.

The deep affinity Missourians have for nature is evident in the
staggering number of people who visit the state's national, state, and
local parks and two major botanical gardens each year. From the
Mark Twain National Forest and Ozark National Scenic Riverways in
mountainous southern Missouri to the national wildlife refuge near
Mound City in the north, natives and visitors to Missouri find ample
opportunity to enjoy a magnificent variety of natural environments.
This same love of the outdoors is seen in Missouri's thriving garden
nursery industry, which strives to be responsive to the public's growing interest in residential landscapes and gardens. A walk through
any town or a drive along country roads reveals the joy Missourians
take in surrounding their homes and businesses with bright flowers,
graceful trees, and fragrant shrubs and vines, all plantings that make
nature's beauty a part of their everyday lives.

Anyone who sets out to establish a healthy and beautiful residential landscape in Missouri will have to spend a fair amount of time
learning about which plants will do best in different locations. There
are vastly different climates and soils in Missouri, from the wind-
blown open plains in the state's far northwest corner to the rich
black soils of the southeastern river lowlands, from the rolling hills
and dales of Missouri's northeast to the lakes region of the south-

west. All across the state there are important differences in prevailing temperatures, precipitation levels, sunlight, humidity, winds, and soil composition, and all serious gardeners eventually become experts on these subjects within the scope of their own backyards.

Becoming well acquainted with weather is a part of any gardener's education. Weather directly affects the hardiness of plants, which respond to fluctuations of heat and cold, rain and drought, freeze and thaw. Climatic extremes weaken plants and reduce their ability to withstand other environmental influences. Most gardeners quickly learn that mulch will help modify the shock of high or low temperatures, that consistent supplemental watering will remedy drought, and that a well-prepared soil will buffer an excess of rain. Experienced gardeners also learn the characteristics of their macro- (regional), meso- (local), and micro- (individual landscape) climates. Information about the macro- and mesoclimates provides broad outlines for plant selection and successful planting. Information about the microclimate is based on a series of seasonal site evaluations, data on an individual site's temperatures, and exposure to sun, winds, rain, ice, and snow throughout the year. When this specific information is carefully gathered and properly understood, it provides the gardener with the best possible tools for managing a healthy landscape of enduring beauty.

Experienced gardeners also become connoisseurs of soil. They do a careful site evaluation to determine its specific soil structure, the nutrient and organic levels, the pH (relative chemical) level, and the nature of the landscape's subterranean insect and animal life. Soil is truly a living and ever-changing environment, and mastering it is a matter of learning how the climatic factors mentioned above affect the soil, how it is changed by plant root growth, by the seasonal loss of leaves, needles, and flowers, and by animal and insect activity both above and below the surface. A soil sample can be professionally tested to discover the levels of all the soil's components, and this information can be used to make needed modifications. Given Missouri's extremes of climate, complete soil preparation is recommended, even if the test seems to indicate otherwise.

Learning all of the special information that makes a landscape unique is both a challenge and a joy, and brings many enduring rewards in the long and healthy lives of your plants. This guide offers help in choosing plants that will meet your design needs and do best in Missouri's various environments, as well as tips on where and how to plant the various species described.

Most Common Mistakes

Use this list of most commonly made mistakes in the landscape as a checklist to help you avoid the unhappiness that results from the decline or death of plants on which you may have spent much time, money, and energy.

1) Improper site evaluation. (Result: You choose the wrong plants for the site.)

2) Inadequate soil preparation prior to plant installation. (Result: Your plants are not healthy and you do not see the aesthetic impact you desired.)

3) Purchasing plants without an appreciation for their growth, habit, and size. (Result: You spend much more time than you anticipated in care and maintenance of the plants.)

4) Misdiagnosis of a plant problem. (Result: The remedy you apply does nothing to solve the problem or makes the predicament worse.)

5) Lack of attention and inconsistent care given to newly installed plants. (Result: The possibly expensive plant that looked so good in the nursery center and so beautiful in gardening books declines and maybe dies.)

BOTANICAL NOMENCLATURE: UNDERSTANDING PLANT NAMES

Many people know what a dogwood should look like and would have no problem picking one out at a garden center or nursery. However, buying a plant based simply on its common name can lead to problems. For example, the Missouri dogwood and the variegated leaf dogwood have the same common name, but they have different growth habits and cultural and care requirements. Labeling plants with their botanical names may seem cumbersome, but it is really the only way for garden centers to help you be sure that you are purchasing the right plant for your landscape needs.

Let's take a look at the botanical names of these two dogwoods. All plants have a series of Latin names that are intended to identify their relationship to other plants (the same is true of animals—take *Homo sapiens sapiens*, for instance). The Missouri dogwood has the family name *Cornaceae*. Its genus is *Cornus*, and its species is *florida*. It is a variety of *florida* that has been given the name 'Welchii'. Therefore the botanical name for the Missouri dogwood is *Cornaceae cornus florida* 'Welchii'. Compare this to the botanical name of the variegated leaf dogwood. It has the same family and genus names— *Cornaceae cornus*—but its species name is *alba*, and its variety name is 'Elegantissma Variegata'. It is certainly acceptable to call both of these plants dogwoods, but when you head for the garden center to purchase a dogwood, knowing its full botanical name will help you get exactly the plant you desire.

PLANT CHARACTERISTICS AT A GLANCE

Each two-page plant entry in this guide offers a box that contains pertinent information about the plant such as its height, bloom period, flower color, and hardiness zones (zones in which the plant is winter hardy). Each plant's light requirements (the amount of sunlight suitable for the plant's needs) are indicated by the following symbols:

Full Sun   Partial Shade   Shade

BENEFICIAL CHARACTERISTICS

Some of the beneficial characteristics of many of the plants are also indicated by symbols:

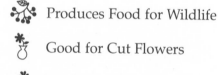

 Attracts Butterflies   Produces Food for Wildlife

 Attracts Hummingbirds   Good for Cut Flowers

 Produces Edible Fruit   Long Bloom Period

Fragrance    Supports Honeybees

NATIVE PLANT

Each plant that is native to Missouri is marked by the following symbol next to its common name:

Introduction

Did You Know?

Many plant entries end with a "Did You Know?" information box that offers information about the plant's uses, nomenclature, history, or other information that is little known or just plain interesting.

My hope is that you will find the information in this guide easy to use and valuable for gardening in our state of Missouri. May you experience many enjoyable gardening hours!

—Mike Miller

Annuals

WHO CAN RESIST THE EXPLOSION of thrilling color when garden centers first display their annuals each year? Cars slow down, and drivers turn their heads to take in the brilliant flats of pansies, begonias, geraniums, impatiens, marigolds, and numerous other varieties. No other group of plants generates so much excitement in gardeners and nongardeners alike. Annuals begin to grace lawns, window boxes, and office entrances as early as mid to late February with the sale of the first flats of pansies or toadflax and continue to adorn garden settings until a heavy fall frost ends their long season. Careful planning makes it possible to inject gardens with their intense colors from Valentine's Day through Thanksgiving. Specific plants prefer the cooler times of the year and go dormant or die with summer's heat, while others prefer the hotter temperatures.

Plants that are considered annuals in Missouri are close relatives to varieties that are perennials in tropical climates. The true definition of an annual is a plant that will germinate from seed, grow foliage, then flower, and if pollinated will produce seed, sometimes dropping winter-hardy seed and returning the ensuing year. However, annual has come to mean any plant that has picturesque blooms and/or colorful leaves throughout the growing season. This more sweeping definition includes not only the true annuals, but also the tropicals marketed as houseplants which are used in vast numbers in the outdoors and brought indoors during the colder weather.

Most annuals are native to tropical regions of the world, where the soil is highly organic and well drained and plants receive rainfall numerous times daily. Keep these native conditions in mind when considering potential locations and uses for these plants. Consider

Chapter One

how much sun the plants will receive, and at what times during the day. Evaluate the planting site's topography and exposure to winds and rain. Think carefully about how much time you will have to provide adequate care for the plants. Doing this kind of site analysis will enable you to make the best choices in annual plants for your particular garden project.

Annuals are popular because of the instant reward they offer. Within days of installing, these plants usually flourish and make a dramatic impact wherever established. A second reason for their popularity is their successful adaptation to so many diverse situations. No other plants work so well standing alone or massed or in mixed plantings, interplanted with ground covers or perennials, skirting shrubs and trees, draping the edge of a water feature or making something out of a mailbox. Arranged in hanging baskets, they decorate patios, decks, and porches. Thriving in window boxes, they dress up apartment balconies. Planted in pots, they are mobile gardens and can be moved on a whim wherever their cheering color is needed.

Balsam

Impatiens balsamina

Height: 1 to 2 feet
Habit: Upright
Flower Color: Various
Type: Flowering

Light Requirements:

Color photograph on page 242.

The balsam once graced gardens in Victorian England and its nostalgic beauty lends itself to heirloom garden landscapes, but its unique characteristics enable it to work in modern garden settings as well. Though considered to have a branching, candelabra habit, the balsam more than likely will appear as single, thick, succulent stems protruding up to 6 inches from the ground. Each stem is a pedestal for clusters of double flowers, which are bunched near the top. The pastel tones of the inflorescence make the balsam extremely vibrant in a partly shaded landscape, and while this plant can tolerate full sun its aesthetic qualities are diminished in overly bright light. Mass plantings should be tightly bunched so that the lower leaves of plants in the middle and back of the mass will drop from stems. There is a good chance that the balsam will self-seed madly, making it a delightful member of the garden for several years.

WHEN TO PLANT

Plant balsam after the last possible frost, usually mid-May.

WHERE TO PLANT

Balsam does well if planted in well-drained, highly organic soil, and protected from midday sun.

HOW TO PLANT

Delineate the bed. Remove any weeds or undesirable plants by digging or using an herbicide. Spade or rototill the planting area, using caution under trees, mix 6 inches of soil amendments with the existing soil, and rake the surface smooth. Dig a hole three times the width and slightly less than the height of the rootball. Remove the plant from the container, loosening the roots if they are pot bound, place in the hole, backfill, and water thoroughly. Remove flowers

and pinch back ¼ of the stem for a bushier plant. Add 1 to 2 inches of mulch. If planting in a pot, first fill the pot one-quarter full with gravel, then add well-drained potting soil, and follow the preceding planting instructions.

CARE AND MAINTENANCE

Fertilize every 14 days using a water-soluble fertilizer for blooming plants. Pinch back the plants periodically to encourage fuller plant growth. Weed on an as-needed basis. Check the soil regularly, daily in the hottest weather, and water if dry.

ADDITIONAL INFORMATION

Purchase the plants in pots of various sizes or as high-quality seed. Seed can be started indoors in containers or cell packs 6 weeks before outdoor planting, with proper light sources (which can be raised and lowered), bottom heat mats, and a sterile growing medium. Or direct sow the seed after the ground has warmed in mid to late May. A quick formula for determining the proper quantity of plants is to divide the square footage of the bed by one-half the height of the plant and by one-half the width of the plant (as noted on its tag); whichever result is larger is the number of plants you should plant per square foot. To determine the spacing between plants, divide the height and the width of the plant by 2. The lower number which results determines the spacing between plants. For example, for a plant that is 6 inches tall and 8 inches wide, use this formula: 6 divided by 2 equals 3; 8 divided by 2 equals 4. Use the lower number of the two answers (3). That means that planting the plants 3 inches apart is best for impact.

ADDITIONAL SPECIES, CULTIVARS, OR VARIETIES

There are none available.

Begonia

Begonia × Semperflorens-Cultorum

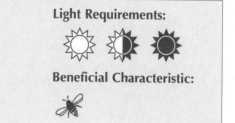

Height: Up to 1 foot
Habit: Mounded
Flower Color: Various
Type: Flowering

Light Requirements:

Beneficial Characteristic:

Color photograph on page 242.

The begonia is nothing short of sensational from the day of planting until it succumbs to the frosts of late fall. Its fat round foliage ranges in color from a polished pure green to a deep tone of bronze. All through the season, it produces more and more red, white, or pink four-petalled flowers. They create a commotion wherever planted, in window boxes, along the front walk, in hanging baskets on the deck, or patio, or by the garage door.

WHEN TO PLANT

Plant begonias in spring after the last frost, usually around mid-May.

WHERE TO PLANT

Plant begonias in well-drained, rich organic soil. If planting under a tree, measure the trunk diameter, multiply by 5, and do not install plants any closer than this distance to trunk.

HOW TO PLANT

Delineate the bed. Remove any weeds or undesirable plants by digging or using an herbicide. Spade or rototill the planting area, using caution under trees, mix 6 inches of soil amendments with the existing soil, and rake the surface smooth. Dig a hole three times the width and slightly less than the height of the rootball. Remove the plant from the container, loosening the roots if they are pot bound, place in the hole, backfill, and water thoroughly. Remove flowers and pinch back 1/4 of the stem for a bushier plant. Add 1 to 2 inches of mulch. If planting in a pot, first fill the pot one-quarter full with gravel, then add well-drained potting soil, and follow the preceding planting instructions.

CARE AND MAINTENANCE

Fertilize every 14 days using a water-soluble fertilizer for blooming plants. Pinch back the plants periodically to encourage fuller plant growth. Weed on an as-needed basis. Check the soil regularly, daily in the hottest weather, and water if dry.

ADDITIONAL INFORMATION

Purchase the plants in pots of various sizes or as high-quality seed. Seed can be started indoors in containers or cell packs 16 weeks before outdoor planting, with proper light sources (which can be raised and lowered), bottom heat mats, and a sterile growing medium. Or direct sow the seed after the ground has warmed in mid to late May. A quick formula for determining the proper quantity of plants is to divide the square footage of the bed by one-half the height of the plant and by one-half the width of the plant (as noted on its tag); whichever result is larger is the number of plants you should plant per square foot. To determine the spacing between plants, divide the height and the width of the plant by 2. The lower number which results determines the spacing between plants. For example, for a plant that is 6 inches tall and 8 inches wide and a bed that is 12 feet square, you should plant 4 plants per square foot (12/3 = 4), and the plants should be spaced 3 inches apart (6/2 = 3).

ADDITIONAL SPECIES, CULTIVARS, OR VARIETIES

Many different varieties of begonias are available. Check to make sure the selected variety will tolerate the sun or shade factor in the proposed planting location.

Did You Know?

Begonias are sometimes referred to as wax begonias because of their exceptionally glossy leaves. There are over 10,000 recorded varieties of begonias; one of the few which is hardy in Missouri is Begonia grandis. Semperflorens *means "ever-flowering."*

Blue Sage

Salvia farinacea

Height: 2 feet
Habit: Upright branching
Flower Color: Blue
Type: Flowering

Color photograph on page 242.

Light Requirements:

Beneficial Characteristics:

Smooth, sleek, and cool, blue sage stands up to the roughest weather summer can bring. Its glossy, pale green foliage is a true beauty asset, each stem sporting slender, 3-inch long, oval leaves. Tall skewers of tiny, sky blue flowers top the stems, attracting bees and beckoning people for a closer look at this winning annual plant.

WHEN TO PLANT

Plant blue sage in the spring after the last frost, usually around mid-May.

WHERE TO PLANT

Blue sage requires well-drained, rich organic soil and exposure to full sun.

HOW TO PLANT

Delineate the bed. Remove any weeds or undesirable plants by digging or using an herbicide. Spade or rototill the planting area, using caution under trees, mix 6 inches of soil amendments with the existing soil, and rake the surface smooth. Dig a hole three times the width and slightly less than the height of the rootball. Remove the plant from the container, loosening the roots if they are pot bound, place in the hole, backfill, and water thoroughly. Remove flowers and pinch back 1/4 of the stem for a bushier plant. Add 1 to 2 inches of mulch. If planting in a pot, first fill the pot one-quarter full with gravel, then add well-drained potting soil, and follow the preceding planting instructions.

CARE AND MAINTENANCE

Fertilize every 14 days using a water-soluble fertilizer for blooming plants. Pinch back the plants periodically to encourage fuller plant growth. Weed on an as-needed basis. Check the soil regularly, daily in the hottest weather, and water if dry.

ADDITIONAL INFORMATION

Purchase the plants in pots of various sizes or as high-quality seed. Seed can be started indoors in containers or cell packs 8 weeks before outdoor planting, with proper light sources (which can be raised and lowered), bottom heat mats, and a sterile growing medium. Or direct sow the seed after the ground has warmed in mid to late May. A quick formula for determining the proper quantity of plants is to divide the square footage of the bed by one-half the height of the plant and by one-half the width of the plant (as noted on its tag); whichever result is larger is the number of plants you should plant per square foot. To determine the spacing between plants, divide the height and the width of the plant by 2. The lower number which results determines the spacing between plants. For example, for a plant that is 6 inches tall and 8 inches wide and a bed that is 12 feet square, you should plant 4 plants per square foot (12/3 = 4), and the plants should be spaced 3 inches apart (6/2 = 3).

ADDITIONAL SPECIES, CULTIVARS, OR VARIETIES

A white flowering variety, *Salvia farinacea* 'Alba', is a nice complement when intermingled with blue.

Did You Know?

Blue sage is a member of the mint family, but does not spread by an underground root system. Species name farinacea *means "mealy" or "starchy" and refers to the texture of the dried, ground-up leaves. Though blue sage is probably a perennial in parts of Missouri, it is labeled an annual and generally considered to be one.*

Cockscomb

Celosia cristata

Height: 1 to 3 feet
Habit: Upright
Flower Color: Various
Type: Flowering

Color photograph on page 242.

Light Requirements:

Beneficial Characteristic:

Cockscomb invigorates any garden with its vivacious hot tints of red, yellow, and orange. It produces several types of bloom shapes, from a flamelike flower to twisted and knurled blossoms. The strong stem that supports the heavy bloom sprouts alternating spear-head-shaped leaves that diminish in size as they climb closer to the flower. Cockscomb plants can bring a little fun into the vegetable plot, strike a pose at the front door, and add a little zip to more conventional plantings. Mix the various blossom colors and shapes to create a kaleidoscope of texture and form. An excellent cutting and drying flower, cockscomb maintains good color for a long time.

WHEN TO PLANT

Plant cockscomb in the spring after the last frost, usually around mid-May.

WHERE TO PLANT

Cockscomb requires a rich, moist, well-drained, organic soil and exposure to full sun.

HOW TO PLANT

Delineate the bed. Remove any weeds or undesirable plants by digging or using an herbicide. Spade or rototill the planting area, using caution under trees, mix 6 inches of soil amendments with the existing soil, and rake the surface smooth. Dig a hole three times the width and slightly less than the height of the rootball. Remove the plant from the container, loosening the roots if they are pot bound, place in the hole, backfill, and water thoroughly. Remove flowers and pinch back 1/4 of the stem for a bushier plant. Add 1 to 2 inches of mulch. If planting in a pot, first fill the pot one-quarter full with gravel, then add well-drained potting soil, and follow the planting instructions.

CARE AND MAINTENANCE

Fertilize every 14 days using a water-soluble fertilizer for blooming plants. Remove side shoots of flowers to ensure larger flower head at top for drying. Weed on an as-needed basis. Check the soil regularly, daily in the hottest weather, and water if dry.

ADDITIONAL INFORMATION

Purchase the plants in pots of various sizes or as high-quality seed. Seed can be started indoors in containers or cell packs 8 weeks before outdoor planting, with proper light sources (which can be raised and lowered), bottom heat mats, and a sterile growing medium. Or direct sow the seed after the ground has warmed in mid to late May. A quick formula for determining the proper quantity of plants is to divide the square footage of the bed by one-half the height of the plant and by one-half the width of the plant (as noted on its tag); whichever result is larger is the number of plants you should plant per square foot. To determine the spacing between plants, divide the height and the width of the plant by 2. The lower number which results determines the spacing between plants. For example, for a plant that is 6 inches tall and 8 inches wide and a bed that is 12 feet square, you should plant 4 plants per square foot (12/3 = 4), and the plants should be spaced 3 inches apart (6/2 = 3).

ADDITIONAL SPECIES, CULTIVARS, OR VARIETIES

Several different varieties are available, all of which differ in their particular flowering habit.

🌿 Did You Know?

Cockscomb is a member of the Amaranth family, and some of its relatives are grown in Asia for their edible green leaves and seeds. The species name cristata *means "comblike" or "crested" and describes the flower configuration. This plant is native to warmer regions of the Americas and Africa.*

Coleus

Solenostemon scutellarioides

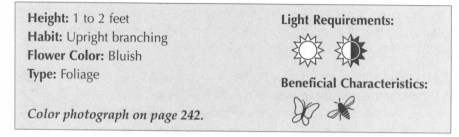

Height: 1 to 2 feet
Habit: Upright branching
Flower Color: Bluish
Type: Foliage

Color photograph on page 242.

Light Requirements:

Beneficial Characteristics:

A mass of coleus plants is a true riot of color that remains "noisy" all through the growing season. The foliage of many varieties with the same name varies uniquely from plant to plant, and therein lies the spontaneous fun of this annual. However, because coleus has an unpredictable look, it is better planted as a large pure stand of coleus instead of being mixed with other annuals or perennials. This unmixed planting controls the "crazier" attributes of coleus, while still allowing the annual to show off its flamboyant beauty. Coleus is very easily propagated by rooting a cutting in a glass of water.

WHEN TO PLANT

Plant coleus in the spring after the last frost, usually around mid-May.

WHERE TO PLANT

Plant coleus in full sun to shade in a rich organic soil that should not be allowed to dry completely.

HOW TO PLANT

Delineate the bed. Remove any weeds or undesirable plants by digging or using an herbicide. Spade or rototill the planting area, using caution under trees, mix 6 inches of soil amendments with the existing soil, and rake the surface smooth. Dig a hole three times the width and slightly less than the height of the rootball. Remove the plant from the container, loosening the roots if they are pot bound, place in the hole, backfill, and water thoroughly. Remove flowers and pinch back 1/4 of the stem for a bushier plant. Add 1 to 2 inches of mulch. If planting in a pot, first fill the pot one-quarter full with gravel, then add well-drained potting soil, and follow the preceding planting instructions.

CARE AND MAINTENANCE

Fertilize every 14 days using a water-soluble fertilizer for blooming plants. Remove flowers immediately when the buds are first noticed to maintain good foliage quantity, size, and color. Pinch back plants periodically to encourage fuller plant growth. Weed on an as-needed basis. Check the soil regularly, daily in the hottest weather, and water if dry.

ADDITIONAL INFORMATION

Purchase the plants in pots of various sizes or as high-quality seed. Seed can be started indoors in containers or cell packs 8 weeks before outdoor planting, with proper light sources (which can be raised and lowered), bottom heat mats, and a sterile growing medium. Or direct sow the seed after the ground has warmed in mid to late May. A quick formula for determining the proper quantity of plants is to divide the square footage of the bed by one-half the height of the plant and by one-half the width of the plant (as noted on its tag); whichever result is larger is the number of plants you should plant per square foot. To determine the spacing between plants, divide the height and the width of the plant by 2. The lower number which results determines the spacing between plants. For example, for a plant that is 6 inches tall and 8 inches wide and a bed that is 12 feet square, you should plant 4 plants per square foot (12/3 = 4), and the plants should be spaced 3 inches apart (6/2 = 3).

ADDITIONAL SPECIES, CULTIVARS, OR VARIETIES

Numerous types of coleus are available, whose foliage color varies from a splattered pattern to a basically solid color with highlights at the edge.

🌿 Did You Know?

Coleus's membership in the mint family is obvious from its flowering structure and habit. It can be grown indoors as a houseplant; some small-leafed hybrids make striking cascades of foliage from hanging baskets. Additional common names include "flame nettle" and "painted leaves."

Flowering Tobacco

Nicotiana alata

Height: Up to 3 feet
Habit: Mounded
Flower Color: Reds, pinks, whites
Type: Flowering

Color photograph on page 242.

Light Requirements:

Beneficial Characteristics:

The trick to getting the most out of flowering tobacco is to plant it near a patio, deck, or window that is left open on cooler summer nights. This is because, after the sun goes down, the new flowers open and release an aroma that is heavenly. The fragrance attracts nocturnal moths for pollination. The pale green, oval-shaped leaves are thick, coarse, and fuzzy and grow up to 10 inches in length, forming a mound close to the ground. Emerging upright from the mound is the stalk, often showing several funnel-shaped flowers that can be 2 or more inches long and 1 inch across at the opening. Closer inspection shows that the throat of the inflorescence is dotted with purplish marks which guide insects to the pollen. This annual offers a great contrast to other plants simply because of its nocturnal bloom time, and its texture, form, and color are impressive when massed in a bed. Mixing the colors and heights of the various flowering tobacco plants creates a lively roller coaster effect.

WHEN TO PLANT

Plant flowering tobacco in the spring after the last frost, usually around mid-May.

WHERE TO PLANT

Flowering tobacco requires rich organic soil which is moist but well drained and full sun or light shade.

HOW TO PLANT

Delineate the bed. Remove any weeds or undesirable plants by digging or using an herbicide. Spade or rototill the planting area, using caution under trees, mix 6 inches of soil amendments with the existing soil, and rake the surface smooth. Dig a hole three times the width and slightly less than the height of the rootball. Remove the plant from the container, loosening the roots if they are pot bound, place in the hole, backfill, and water thoroughly. Remove flowers, pinching back $1/4$ of the stem for a bushier plant. Add 1 to 2 inches of mulch. If planting in a pot, first fill the pot one-quarter full with gravel, then add well-drained potting soil, and follow the planting instructions.

CARE AND MAINTENANCE
Fertilize every 14 days using a water-soluble fertilizer for blooming plants. Remove dead flowers. Pinch back plants periodically to encourage fuller plant growth. Weed on an as-needed basis. Check the soil regularly, daily in the hottest weather, and water if dry.

ADDITIONAL INFORMATION
Purchase the plants in pots of various sizes or as high-quality seed. Seed can be started indoors in containers or cell packs 8 weeks before outdoor planting, with proper light sources (which can be raised and lowered), bottom heat mats, and a sterile growing medium. Or direct sow the seed after the ground has warmed in mid to late May. A quick formula for determining the proper quantity of plants is to divide the square footage of the bed by one-half the height of the plant and by one-half the width of the plant (as noted on its tag); whichever result is larger is the number of plants you should plant per square foot. To determine the spacing between plants, divide the height and the width of the plant by 2. The lower number which results determines the spacing between plants. For example, for a plant that is 6 inches tall and 8 inches wide and a bed that is 12 feet square, you should plant 4 plants per square foot ($12/3 = 4$), and the plants should be spaced 3 inches apart ($6/2 = 3$). A member of the tomato family, this specific plant is native to the warmer climates of South America. Another common name is "Jasmine tobacco," which regards the fact that the flowers open at night and are very fragrant. The species name *alata* means "winged."

ADDITIONAL SPECIES, CULTIVARS, OR VARIETIES
Nicotiana alata 'Grandiflora' has white night-blooming flowers that emit a sweet, powerful fragrance. The newer varieties are usually not fragrant.

French Marigold

Tagetes patula

Height: Up to 1 foot
Habit: Mounded
Flower Color: Orange and yellow
Type: Flowering

Color photograph on page 242.

Light Requirements:

Beneficial Characteristic:

The chubby French marigold makes a cheerful garden bouquet. Its mixture of vibrant summer colors, bold yellows and oranges, is set off by dark green foliage. The heavily dissected leaf frames the two-toned yellow and orange blooms, which can grow up to 2 inches in diameter. Often used to line the edge of a flower bed or vegetable garden, French marigolds also work well mingled with other annuals and perennials, planted en masse as a blanket of rolling color, or plumped in a pot. The deep, rich colors of the entire plant ensure no fade-out during the brightest time of day.

WHEN TO PLANT

Plant French marigolds in the spring after the last frost, usually around mid-May.

WHERE TO PLANT

French marigolds do well in full sun in average to good soil that is well drained.

HOW TO PLANT

Delineate the bed. Remove any weeds or undesirable plants by digging or using an herbicide. Spade or rototill the planting area, using caution under trees, mix 6 inches of soil amendments with the existing soil, and rake the surface smooth. Dig a hole three times the width and slightly less than the height of the rootball. Remove the plant from the container, loosening the roots if they are pot bound, place in the hole, backfill, and water thoroughly. Remove flowers and pinch back 1/4 of the stem for a bushier plant. Add 1 to 2 inches of mulch. If planting in a pot, first fill the pot one-quarter full with gravel, then add well-drained potting soil, and follow the preceding planting instructions.

Care and Maintenance

Fertilize every 14 days using a water-soluble fertilizer for blooming plants. Remove dead flowers. Pinch back plants periodically to encourage fuller plant growth. Weed on an as-needed basis. Check the soil regularly, daily in the hottest weather, and water if dry. Proper care will minimize pest and disease problems.

Additional Information

Purchase the plants in pots of various sizes or as high-quality seed. Seed can be started indoors in containers or cell packs 8 weeks before outdoor planting, with proper light sources (which can be raised and lowered), bottom heat mats, and a sterile growing medium. Or direct sow the seed after the ground has warmed in mid to late May. A quick formula for determining the proper quantity of plants is to divide the square footage of the bed by one-half the height of the plant and by one-half the width of the plant (as noted on its tag); whichever result is larger is the number of plants you should plant per square foot. To determine the spacing between plants, divide the height and the width of the plant by 2. The lower number which results determines the spacing between plants. For example, for a plant that is 6 inches tall and 8 inches wide and a bed that is 12 feet square, you should plant 4 plants per square foot (12/3 = 4), and the plants should be spaced 3 inches apart (6/2 = 3).

Additional Species, Cultivars, or Varieties

Although there is an astronomical number of different marigolds in the market, few close relatives of this specific type are available.

🌿 Did You Know?

French marigolds belong to the huge sunflower family. The species name, patula, *refers to the bushy spreading habit of this plant, which despite its common name is native to Mexico and Guatemala. A long-lived cut flower, French marigolds are perfect for smaller vases.*

Geranium

Pelargonium × hortorum

Height: 1 foot
Habit: Mounded
Flower Color: Pinks, whites, reds
Type: Flowering

Light Requirements:

Color photograph on page 242.

Geraniums are perhaps the most familiar annual plant, but their popularity may fool first-timers into thinking they are easy to raise. The robust stem is thicker than that boasted by most annuals, which means they do not have to be watered as often as other plants. However, regular fertilizing is necessary to capture the full potential of their fantastic balloon-shaped clusters of blooms. The pure and vivid colors of their dense blossoms dominate nearby plantings. Geraniums are best planted in containers, window boxes, pots, and in easily accessed garden spaces, where they can be easily and regularly tended.

WHEN TO PLANT
Plant geraniums in the spring after the last frost, usually around mid-May.

WHERE TO PLANT
Geraniums do well in the full sun in an average to rich organic soil that can be on the drier side.

HOW TO PLANT
Delineate the bed. Remove any weeds or undesirable plants by digging or using an herbicide. Spade or rototill the planting area, using caution under trees, mix 6 inches of soil amendments with the existing soil, and rake the surface smooth. Dig a hole three times the width and slightly less than the height of the rootball. Remove the plant from the container, loosening the roots if they are pot bound, place in the hole, backfill, and water thoroughly. Remove flowers and pinch back 1/4 of the stem for a bushier plant. Add 1 to 2 inches of mulch. If planting in a pot, first fill the pot one-quarter full with

gravel, then add well-drained potting soil, and follow the preceding planting instructions.

CARE AND MAINTENANCE

Fertilize every 14 days using a water-soluble fertilizer for blooming plants. Remove dead flowers. Pinch back plants periodically to encourage fuller plant growth. Weed on an as-needed basis. Check the soil regularly, daily in the hottest weather, and water if dry. Proper care will minimize pest and disease problems.

ADDITIONAL INFORMATION

Purchase the plants in pots of various sizes or as high-quality seed. Seed can be started indoors in containers or cell packs 16 weeks before outdoor planting, with proper light sources (which can be raised and lowered), bottom heat mats, and a sterile growing medium. Or direct sow the seed after the ground has warmed in mid to late May. A quick formula for determining the proper quantity of plants is to divide the square footage of the bed by one-half the height of the plant and by one-half the width of the plant (as noted on its tag); whichever result is larger is the number of plants you should plant per square foot. To determine the spacing between plants, divide the height and the width of the plant by 2. The lower number which results determines the spacing between plants. For example, for a plant that is 6 inches tall and 8 inches wide and a bed that is 12 feet square, you should plant 4 plants per square foot (12/3 = 4), and the plants should be spaced 3 inches apart (6/2 = 3).

ADDITIONAL SPECIES, CULTIVARS, OR VARIETIES

A tremendous number of varieties are available, some grown from cuttings, others from seed. They are distinguished by differences in growth habit, hardiness, leaf shape, and fragrance.

Globe Amaranth

Gomphrena globosa

Height: 1 foot or more
Habit: Mounding
Flower Color: Pinks, reds, whites
Type: Flowering

Color photograph on page 242.

Light Requirements:

Beneficial Characteristics:

A bank of globe amaranth creates a living pointillistic landscape, its small round flowers dancing on the larger green canvas of its foliage. The branching of the stem is comparatively stiff, and the oblong leaves, which can reach 4 inches in length, grow close together, increasing the density of the foliage's color. The globular flower is held by a portion of the bud which peels back as the bloom bursts forth. Globe amaranth is best sited close to view so that the vivid bloom colors are not lost with distance. The mounded growth habit makes it an excellent candidate for a hedge fronting or surrounding other sunny plantings, or it also works well as a contrast beside upright annuals or perennials. Its effects are subtle, not overwhelming, and much of its value lies in its versatile placements.

WHEN TO PLANT

Plant globe amaranth in the spring after the last frost, usually around mid-May.

WHERE TO PLANT

Globe amaranth does well in the full sun in an average to good soil that is well drained.

HOW TO PLANT

Delineate the bed. Remove any weeds or undesirable plants by digging or using an herbicide. Spade or rototill the planting area, using caution under trees, mix 6 inches of soil amendments with the existing soil, and rake the surface smooth. Dig a hole three times the width and slightly less than the height of the rootball. Remove the plant from the container, loosening the roots if they are pot bound, place in the hole, backfill, and water thoroughly. Remove flowers

and pinch back ¹/₄ of the stem for a bushier plant. Add 1 to 2 inches of mulch. If planting in a pot, first fill the pot one-quarter full with gravel, then add well-drained potting soil, and follow the preceding planting instructions.

CARE AND MAINTENANCE

Fertilize every 14 days using a water-soluble fertilizer for blooming plants. Remove dead flowers. Pinch back plants periodically to encourage fuller plant growth. Weed on an as-needed basis. Check the soil regularly, daily in the hottest weather, and water if dry.

ADDITIONAL INFORMATION

Purchase the plants in pots of various sizes or as high-quality seed. Seed can be started indoors in containers or cell packs 8 weeks before outdoor planting, with proper light sources (which can be raised and lowered), bottom heat mats, and a sterile growing medium. Or direct sow the seed after the ground has warmed in mid to late May. A quick formula for determining the proper quantity of plants is to divide the square footage of the bed by one-half the height of the plant and by one-half the width of the plant (as noted on its tag); whichever result is larger is the number of plants you should plant per square foot. To determine the spacing between plants, divide the height and the width of the plant by 2. The lower number which results determines the spacing between plants. For example, for a plant that is 6 inches tall and 8 inches wide and a bed that is 12 feet square, you should plant 4 plants per square foot (12/3 = 4), and the plants should be spaced 3 inches apart (6/2 = 3).

ADDITIONAL SPECIES, CULTIVARS, OR VARIETIES

G. globosa 'Gnome' is a dwarf cultivar. The many varieties exhibit marked differences in color.

Impatiens

Impatiens wallerana

Height: 6 inches to 2 feet

Habit: Spreading

Flower Color: Various

Type: Flowering

Light Requirements:

Color photograph on page 242.

Impatiens bring a welcome taste of the tropics into the midwestern gardens and lawns of Missouri. They have incredible drought tolerance. These plants make an exuberantly bright impact as soon as they are planted in shady spaces, and their brilliance lasts uninterrupted for the entire growing season. The pure green, fleshy, multibranched stems support a large number of alternating elliptical leaves whose spacing accentuates the roundish, somewhat flat-topped growth habit and allows the brilliant blooms full exposure. Solitary on the stem, the blossom sometimes grows as large as 2 inches in diameter and is always eye-catching. Impatiens work well in any shade unless it is very dense—beside the house, under trees, trimming a walk, or making a colorful transition between sun-loving plants and shady beds.

WHEN TO PLANT

Plant impatiens in the spring after the last frost, usually around mid-May.

WHERE TO PLANT

Impatiens must be protected from midday sun and require well-drained, moist, rich organic soil.

HOW TO PLANT

Delineate the bed. Remove any weeds or undesirable plants by digging or using an herbicide. Spade or rototill the planting area, using caution under trees, mix 6 inches of soil amendments with the existing soil, and rake the surface smooth. Dig a hole three times the width and slightly less than the height of the rootball. Remove the plant from the container, loosening the roots if they are pot bound, place in the hole, backfill, and water thoroughly. Remove flowers

and pinch back ¼ of the stem for a bushier plant. Add 1 to 2 inches of mulch. If planting in a pot, first fill the pot one-quarter full with gravel, then add well-drained potting soil, and follow the preceding planting instructions.

CARE AND MAINTENANCE

Fertilize every 14 days using a water-soluble fertilizer for blooming plants. Remove dead flowers. Pinch back plants periodically to encourage fuller plant growth. Weed on an as-needed basis. Check the soil regularly, daily in the hottest weather, and water if dry.

ADDITIONAL INFORMATION

Purchase the plants in pots of various sizes or as high-quality seed. Seed can be started indoors in containers or cell packs 8 weeks before outdoor planting, with proper light sources (which can be raised and lowered), bottom heat mats, and a sterile growing medium. Or direct sow the seed after the ground has warmed in mid to late May. A quick formula for determining the proper quantity of plants is to divide the square footage of the bed by one-half the height of the plant and by one-half the width of the plant (as noted on its tag); whichever result is larger is the number of plants you should plant per square foot. To determine the spacing between plants, divide the height and the width of the plant by 2. The lower number which results determines the spacing between plants. For example, for a plant that is 6 inches tall and 8 inches wide and a bed that is 12 feet square, you should plant 4 plants per square foot (12/3 = 4), and the plants should be spaced 3 inches apart (6/2 = 3).

ADDITIONAL SPECIES, CULTIVARS, OR VARIETIES

Numerous types are available. They differ in height, color, and occasionally in foliage color.

Pansy

Viola × wittrockiana

Height: 6 inches
Habit: Mounding
Flower Color: Various
Type: Flowering—cool season

Light Requirements:

Color photograph on page 242.

Pansies are essential to spring and fall gardens, where they frequently are used to outline other plantings with a richly colored fringe. The heavily branched stems are covered with small, elliptical-shaped leaves of medium green color. The flower stem looks like a spearhead breaking the ground. Upon reaching the prescribed height, the pansy's bloom uncurls and exposes the most daring alliance of colors on any single flower known to nature. Pansies are particularly useful for filling in gaps and providing color at the beginning and close of the growing season.

WHEN TO PLANT

Plant pansies in early spring and in the fall when available.

WHERE TO PLANT

Plant pansies in the full sun in moist, rich organic soil that is well drained.

HOW TO PLANT

Delineate the bed. Remove any weeds or undesirable plants by digging or using an herbicide. Spade or rototill the planting area, using caution under trees, mix 6 inches of soil amendments with the existing soil, and rake the surface smooth. Dig a hole three times the width and slightly less than the height of the rootball. Remove the plant from the container, loosening the roots if they are pot bound, place in the hole, backfill, and water thoroughly. Remove flowers and pinch back 1/4 of the stem for a bushier plant. Add 1 to 2 inches of mulch. If planting in a pot, first fill the pot one-quarter full with gravel, then add well-drained potting soil, and follow the preceding planting instructions.

Care and Maintenance

Fertilize every 14 days using a water-soluble fertilizer for blooming plants. Remove dead flowers. Pinch back plants periodically to encourage fuller plant growth. Weed on an as-needed basis. Check the soil regularly, daily in the hottest weather, and water if dry.

Additional Information

Purchase the plants in pots of various sizes. A quick formula for determining the proper quantity of plants is to divide the square footage of the bed by one-half the height of the plant and by one-half the width of the plant (as noted on its tag); whichever result is larger is the number of plants you should plant per square foot. To determine the spacing between plants, divide the height and the width of the plant by 2. The lower number which results determines the spacing between plants. For example, for a plant that is 6 inches tall and 8 inches wide and a bed that is 12 feet square, you should plant 4 plants per square foot (12/3 = 4), and the plants should be spaced 3 inches apart (6/2 = 3).

Additional Species, Cultivars, or Varieties

Several additional types are available, which differ in flower size and color.

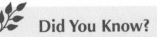

Did You Know?

Pansies belong to the violet family and result from crossing three other species. If planted in fall, pansies will winter over in many situations and return to complement bulbs and other spring bloomers.

Periwinkle

Catharanthus roseus

Height: Up to 1 foot
Habit: Mounded
Flower Color: Rosy pink
Type: Flowering

Light Requirements:

Color photograph on page 242.

The beauty of the periwinkle's star-shaped flowers is perfectly com-
plemented by its glistening, dark green foliage, which is etched by
pale green veins. This annual works well in garden settings that range
from formal landscape plantings to highly informal driveway beds and
mail box plantings. As the flower buds unfurl, they resemble an umbrella
which separates into 5 overlapping petals encircling a very dark reddish center. Because the periwinkle does not produce any pollen or
nectar, it is an excellent choice for use around sunny seating areas.

WHEN TO PLANT
Plant periwinkles in spring after the last frost, usually in mid-May.

WHERE TO PLANT
Periwinkles require full sun and a rich organic soil that can be on the
dry side.

HOW TO PLANT
Delineate the bed. Remove any weeds or undesirable plants by
digging or using an herbicide. Spade or rototill the planting area,
using caution under trees, mix 6 inches of soil amendments with the
existing soil, and rake the surface smooth. Dig a hole three times the
width and slightly less than the height of the rootball. Remove the
plant from the container, loosening the roots if they are pot bound,
place in the hole, backfill, and water thoroughly. Remove flowers
and pinch back 1/4 of the stem for a bushier plant. Add 1 to 2 inches
of mulch. If planting in a pot, first fill the pot one-quarter full with
gravel, then add well-drained potting soil, and follow the preceding
planting instructions.

CARE AND MAINTENANCE

Fertilize every 14 days using a water-soluble fertilizer for blooming plants. Pinch back plants periodically to encourage fuller plant growth. Weed on an as-needed basis. Check the soil regularly, daily in the hottest weather, and water if dry.

ADDITIONAL INFORMATION

Purchase the plants in pots of various sizes or as high-quality seed. Seed can be started indoors in containers or cell packs 8 weeks before outdoor planting, with proper light sources (which can be raised and lowered), bottom heat mats, and a sterile growing medium. Or direct sow the seed after the ground has warmed in mid to late May. A quick formula for determining the proper quantity of plants is to divide the square footage of the bed by one-half the height of the plant and by one-half the width of the plant (as noted on its tag); whichever result is larger is the number of plants you should plant per square foot. To determine the spacing between plants, divide the height and the width of the plant by 2. The lower number which results determines the spacing between plants. For example, for a plant that is 6 inches tall and 8 inches wide and a bed that is 12 feet square, you should plant 4 plants per square foot (12/3 = 4), and the plants should be spaced 3 inches apart (6/2 = 3).

ADDITIONAL SPECIES, CULTIVARS, OR VARIETIES

Catharanthus roseus 'Albus' has white flowers. 'Pretty in White', 'Pretty in Pink', and 'Pretty in Red' are wonderful varieties.

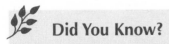

Did You Know?

This species is native to Madagascar and India; its species name, roseus, *refers to the rose-colored flowers. Periwinkles have medicinal properties, but are poisonous to cattle if eaten by them. The origin of an additional common name, "old maid," is not certain.*

Petunia

Petunia × hybrida

Height: 6 inches to 1 foot
Habit: Spreading
Flower Color: Various
Type: Flowering

Color photograph on page 243.

Light Requirements:

Beneficial Characteristic:

The petunia is an old-fashioned plant that has not lost its popularity over its long history. When planted en masse, they spread out over the landscape like a bright quilt, a patchwork array of exceptional color and texture. The smaller, smooth-edged leaves alternate along the stem, but often are not noticed because of the large (up to 5-inch) upturned, trumpet-shaped flowers. Improved inflorescence has resulted in a stronger fragrance and veined or splattered petals that effectively direct pollinators into the throat of the flower. Petunias make a fantastic foreground plant for taller or upright growing annuals or sun perennials and are a favorite choice for hanging baskets and patio pots. Petunias can be divided into two groups: grandiflora and multiflora. Grandiflora, or "large-flowered," petunias can be further divided into three groups: single, double, and California giants. Multiflora, or "many-flowered," petunias do not have ruffles or fringes as the grandifloras do, but they tend to be vigorous, good for use where you want color all summer long. There are double multifloras and single multifloras.

WHEN TO PLANT
Plant petunias in the spring after the last frost, usually in mid-May.

WHERE TO PLANT
Petunias do well in full sun and in rich organic, well-drained soil.

HOW TO PLANT
Delineate the bed. Remove any weeds or undesirable plants by digging or using an herbicide. Spade or rototill the planting area, using caution under trees, mix 6 inches of soil amendments with the existing soil, and rake the surface smooth. Dig a hole three times the width and slightly less than the height of the rootball. Remove the plant from the container, loosening the roots if they are pot bound,

place in the hole, backfill, and water thoroughly. Remove flowers, pinching back $^1/_4$ of the stem for a bushier plant. Add 1 to 2 inches of mulch. If planting in a pot, first fill the pot one-quarter full with gravel, then add well-drained potting soil, and follow the planting instructions.

CARE AND MAINTENANCE

Fertilize every 14 days using a water-soluble fertilizer for blooming plants. Pinch back plants periodically to encourage fuller plant growth. Weed on an as-needed basis. Check the soil regularly, daily in the hottest weather, and water if dry. Proper care will minimize pest and disease problems.

ADDITIONAL INFORMATION

Purchase the plants in pots of various sizes or as high-quality seed. Seed can be started indoors in containers or cell packs 8 weeks before outdoor planting, with proper light sources (which can be raised and lowered), bottom heat mats, and a sterile growing medium. Or direct sow the seed after the ground has warmed in mid to late May. A quick formula for determining the proper quantity of plants is to divide the square footage of the bed by one-half the height of the plant and by one-half the width of the plant (as noted on its tag); whichever result is larger is the number of plants you should plant per square foot. To determine the spacing between plants, divide the height and the width of the plant by 2. The lower number which results determines the spacing between plants. For example, for a plant that is 6 inches tall and 8 inches wide and a bed that is 12 feet square, you should plant 4 plants per square foot (12/3 = 4), and the plants should be spaced 3 inches apart (6/2 = 3). Petunias belong to the nightshade family, which includes tomatoes, potatoes, eggplant, and tobacco. Most relatives are native to areas of South America.

ADDITIONAL SPECIES, CULTIVARS, OR VARIETIES

Many types are available and new ones show up each year. The changes involve flower configuration, size, and overall growth habit. Some excellent grandiflora varieties are 'Old Glory' (red), 'Tangerine' (orange), and 'Glacier' (white). Multiflora types include 'Blue Joy' (blue), 'Starfive' (bicolor), and 'Summer Sun' (yellow).

Snapdragon

Antirrhinum majus

Height: 1 to 3 feet
Habit: Upright
Flower Color: Various
Type: Flowering

Color photograph on page 243.

Light Requirements:

Beneficial Characteristics:

Snapdragons are planted in the spring, but the best flowering and color comes in late summer and fall with cooler weather. The extraordinary blooms are well worth the wait. Each stalk supports a large number of blossoms, whose weight causes the stalk to bend toward the ground. When this bending occurs, the flowers continue to point upward and remain off the ground. The hues and tones of this annual are very inviting to pollinators, and just a few minutes' observation is certain to yield the amusing spectacle of a bee opening the trap door of the flower to retrieve the pollen inside. While not always the easiest to grow, the snapdragon makes an excellent cutting flower.

WHEN TO PLANT

Plant snapdragons in the spring after the last frost, usually in mid-May.

WHERE TO PLANT

Snapdragons do well in full sun and in rich organic, well-drained soil.

HOW TO PLANT

Delineate the bed. Remove any weeds or undesirable plants by digging or using an herbicide. Spade or rototill the planting area, using caution under trees, mix 6 inches of soil amendments with the existing soil, and rake the surface smooth. Dig a hole three times the width and slightly less than the height of the rootball. Remove the plant from the container, loosening the roots if they are pot bound, place in the hole, backfill, and water thoroughly. Remove flowers and pinch back 1/4 of the stem for a bushier plant. Add 1 to 2 inches of mulch. If planting in a pot, first fill the pot one-quarter full with gravel, then add well-drained potting soil, and follow the preceding planting instructions.

CARE AND MAINTENANCE

Fertilize every 14 days using a water-soluble fertilizer for blooming plants. Remove dead flowers and pinch back plants periodically to encourage fuller plant growth. Taller varieties may have to be staked to prevent falling. Weed on an as-needed basis. Check the soil regularly, daily in the hottest weather, and water if dry.

ADDITIONAL INFORMATION

Purchase the plants in pots of various sizes or as high-quality seed. Seed can be started indoors in containers or cell packs 6 weeks before outdoor planting, with proper light sources (which can be raised and lowered), bottom heat mats, and a sterile growing medium. Or direct sow the seed after the ground has warmed in mid to late May. A quick formula for determining the proper quantity of plants is to divide the square footage of the bed by one-half the height of the plant and by one-half the width of the plant (as noted on its tag); whichever result is larger is the number of plants you should plant per square foot. To determine the spacing between plants, divide the height and the width of the plant by 2. The lower number which results determines the spacing between plants. For example, for a plant that is 6 inches tall and 8 inches wide and a bed that is 12 feet square, you should plant 4 plants per square foot (12/3 = 4), and the plants should be spaced 3 inches apart (6/2 = 3).

ADDITIONAL SPECIES, CULTIVARS, OR VARIETIES

These cool-season annuals come in many varieties, which are differentiated by plant height and color.

🌿 Did You Know?

The common name refers to the fact that the flower somewhat resembles a dragon's head, and when the back of the flower is gently squeezed, the front will open as if two jaws are parting. This annual is native to the Mediterranean region.

Spider Flower

Cleome hassleriana

Height: 3 feet or more
Habit: Upright
Flower Color: Pink and white
Type: Flowering

Color photograph on page 243.

Light Requirements:

Beneficial Characteristics:

Bouncing and weaving in the slightest breeze, this plant brings to mind a spider dancing on its own silken threads. Spider flower rises above all other annuals on a very strong stem which has compound palm-shaped leaves with stickers at their base. The foliage arrangement is equally spaced along the entire length of the stem, with the lower leaves being the largest. The flowers, occupying the top quarter of the long stem, emerge pink and almost immediately begin to fade to white. The flowers are wind pollinated for the most part and produce a tremendous amount of seed. If allowed to fall, the seed will winter over and germinate the following spring, or it can be gathered and dispersed in new locations the ensuing May. Children are especially delighted to find spider flower in the garden.

WHEN TO PLANT
Plant spider flowers in the spring after the last frost, usually in mid-May.

WHERE TO PLANT
Spider flowers do well in full sun or light shade, in dry or well-drained soil that is average to better in organic content.

HOW TO PLANT
Delineate the bed. Remove any weeds or undesirable plants by digging or using an herbicide. Spade or rototill the planting area, using caution under trees, mix 6 inches of soil amendments with the existing soil, and rake the surface smooth. Dig a hole three times the width and slightly less than the height of the rootball. Remove the plant from the container, loosening the roots if they are pot bound, place in the hole, backfill, and water thoroughly. Remove flowers

and pinch back $^1/_4$ of the stem for a bushier plant. Add 1 to 2 inches of mulch. If planting in a pot, first fill the pot one-quarter full with gravel, then add well-drained potting soil, and follow the preceding planting instructions.

CARE AND MAINTENANCE

Fertilize every 14 days using a water-soluble fertilizer for blooming plants. Remove dead flowers. Pinch back plants only on installation. Weed on an as-needed basis. Check the soil regularly, daily in the hottest weather, and water if dry. Proper care will minimize pest and disease problems.

ADDITIONAL INFORMATION

Purchase the plants in pots of various sizes or as high-quality seed. Seed can be started indoors in containers or cell packs 6 weeks before outdoor planting, with proper light sources (which can be raised and lowered), bottom heat mats, and a sterile growing medium. Or direct sow the seed after the ground has warmed in mid to late May. A quick formula for determining the proper quantity of plants is to divide the square footage of the bed by one-half the height of the plant and by one-half the width of the plant (as noted on its tag); whichever result is larger is the number of plants you should plant per square foot. To determine the spacing between plants, divide the height and the width of the plant by 2. The lower number which results determines the spacing between plants. For exam-ple, for a plant that is 6 inches tall and 8 inches wide and a bed that is 12 feet square, you should plant 4 plants per square foot (12/3 = 4), and the plants should be spaced 3 inches apart (6/2 = 3).

ADDITIONAL SPECIES, CULTIVARS, OR VARIETIES

There are none available.

Toadflax

Linaria marocanna

Height: 1 foot
Habit: Upright
Flower Color: Pale purple with yellow
Type: Flowering—cool season

Light Requirements:

Color photograph on page 243.

The pastel flowers of toadflax are highlighted by dots of color that pulsate in bright spring sunshine. The leaves on the tall stems are narrow and add a fine visual texture to any planting. A cool season annual, toadflax can play a number of different roles in the spring landscape. It accents early spring flowering bulbs, works well with perennials, and offers a curiosity for anyone passing by the front gate. It is an uncommon, under-utilized plant whose time has come.

WHEN TO PLANT
Plant toadflax in early spring.

WHERE TO PLANT
Toadflax does well in full sun in a well-drained soil; it can be placed under a canopy of deciduous trees that have not yet leafed out.

HOW TO PLANT
Delineate the bed. Remove any weeds or undesirable plants by digging or using an herbicide. Spade or rototill the planting area, using caution under trees, mix 6 inches of soil amendments with the existing soil, and rake the surface smooth. Dig a hole three times the width and slightly less than the height of the rootball. Remove the plant from the container, loosening the roots if they are pot bound, place in the hole, backfill, and water thoroughly. Remove flowers and pinch back 1/4 of the stem for a bushier plant. Add 1 to 2 inches of mulch. If planting in a pot, first fill the pot one-quarter full with gravel, then add well-drained potting soil, and follow the preceding planting instructions.

CARE AND MAINTENANCE
Fertilize every 14 days using a water-soluble fertilizer for blooming

plants. Remove dead flowers and pinch back plants periodically to encourage fuller plant growth. Weed on an as-needed basis. Check the soil regularly, daily in the hottest weather, and water if dry.

ADDITIONAL INFORMATION

Purchase the plants in pots of various sizes or as high-quality seed. Seed can be started indoors in containers or cell packs 8 weeks before outdoor planting, with proper light sources (which can be raised and lowered), bottom heat mats, and a sterile growing medium. Or direct sow the seed after the ground has warmed in mid to late May. A quick formula for determining the proper quantity of plants is to divide the square footage of the bed by one-half the height of the plant and by one-half the width of the plant (as noted on its tag); whichever result is larger is the number of plants you should plant per square foot. To determine the spacing between plants, divide the height and the width of the plant by 2. The lower number which results determines the spacing between plants. For example, for a plant that is 6 inches tall and 8 inches wide and a bed that is 12 feet square, you should plant 4 plants per square foot (12/3 = 4), and the plants should be spaced 3 inches apart (6/2 = 3).

ADDITIONAL SPECIES, CULTIVARS, OR VARIETIES

There are none available.

Did You Know?

Toadflax is a member of the snapdragon family and is native to Morocco. Sometimes it is referred to as a "spurred snapdragon" due to the flower configuration. Macro in the species name means "big," but no part of this annual would be considered large.

Yellow Cosmos

Cosmos sulphureus

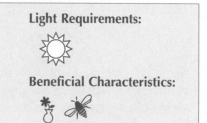

Height: 2 to 3 feet
Habit: Upright
Flower Color: Yellow and orange
Type: Flowering

Color photograph on page 243.

Light Requirements:

Beneficial Characteristics:

Cosmos is a phenomenal late-flowering annual, with blooms like bright stars buoyed up on clouds of misty green foliage. Breaking the ground in mid to late spring with very fine textured leaves, the plant gradually rises to a substantial height before the flower buds begin to form. When the buds pop open, they reveal bright flowers with paper thin petal rays, some blossoms growing up to 3 inches across. Cosmos creates an activity center for pollinating insects. The seeds drop to the ground, promising the chance of a magnificent return the following year.

WHEN TO PLANT

Plant cosmos in the spring after the last frost, usually around mid-May.

WHERE TO PLANT

Plant cosmos in full sun, in average or better soil that is well drained and can be on the dry side.

HOW TO PLANT

Delineate the bed. Remove any weeds or undesirable plants by digging or using an herbicide. Spade or rototill the planting area, using caution under trees, mix 6 inches of soil amendments with the existing soil, and rake the surface smooth. Dig a hole three times the width and slightly less than the height of the rootball. Remove the plant from the container, loosening the roots if they are pot bound, place in the hole, backfill, and water thoroughly. Remove flowers and pinch back 1/4 of the stem for a bushier plant. Add 1 to 2 inches of mulch. If planting in a pot, first fill the pot one-quarter full with gravel, then add well-drained potting soil, and follow the preceding planting instructions.

CARE AND MAINTENANCE

Fertilize every 14 days using a water-soluble fertilizer for blooming plants. Remove dead flowers. Pinch back plants periodically to encourage fuller plant growth. Weed on an as-needed basis. Check the soil regularly, daily in the hottest weather, and water if dry.

ADDITIONAL INFORMATION

Purchase the plants in pots of various sizes or as high-quality seed. Seed can be started indoors in containers or cell packs 8 weeks before outdoor planting, with proper light sources (which can be raised and lowered), bottom heat mats, and a sterile growing medium. Or direct sow the seed after the ground has warmed in mid to late May. A quick formula for determining the proper quantity of plants is to divide the square footage of the bed by one-half the height of the plant and by one-half the width of the plant (as noted on its tag); whichever result is larger is the number of plants you should plant per square foot. To determine the spacing between plants, divide the height and the width of the plant by 2. The lower number which results determines the spacing between plants. For example, for a plant that is 6 inches tall and 8 inches wide and a bed that is 12 feet square, you should plant 4 plants per square foot (12/3 = 4), and the plants should be spaced 3 inches apart (6/2 = 3).

ADDITIONAL SPECIES, CULTIVARS, OR VARIETIES

Some double-flowered types are available.

Did You Know?

A member of the sunflower family, cosmos is a relative which is native to Mexico. A bank of cosmos makes a great stopping-off place for butterflies migrating south for the winter. The species name sulphureus *means "yellow," which is one color cosmos blooms in.*

Zinnia

Zinnia elegans

Height: 1 to 2 feet
Habit: Upright branching
Flower Color: Various
Type: Flowering

Color photograph on page 243.

Light Requirements:

Beneficial Characteristics:

The zinnia is the boutonniere of the summer, the bright decoration that shows the garden has put on its party clothes. This plant's lance-shaped leaves can grow to 5 inches in length, but are widely spaced on the stem, giving the plant an airy texture and making the large colorful blooms seem to float above the ground like party balloons. The inflorescence invites insect pollinators and hummingbirds, and the long stems reach around and into nearby plantings, holding out their bright corsages. A long-lived flower, the zinnia is excellent for cutting and using in arrangements.

WHEN TO PLANT

Plant zinnias in the spring after the last frost, usually in mid-May.

WHERE TO PLANT

Zinnias require full sun and do well in average or better soil. Because of their height and reaching habit, they are best placed in the background.

HOW TO PLANT

Delineate the bed. Remove any weeds or undesirable plants by digging or using an herbicide. Spade or rototill the planting area, using caution under trees, mix 6 inches of soil amendments with the existing soil, and rake the surface smooth. Dig a hole three times the width and slightly less than the height of the rootball. Remove the plant from the container, loosening the roots if they are pot bound, place in the hole, backfill, and water thoroughly. Remove flowers and pinch back 1/4 of the stem for a bushier plant. Add 1 to 2 inches of mulch. If planting in a pot, first fill the pot one-quarter full with gravel, then add well-drained potting soil, and follow the preceding planting instructions.

CARE AND MAINTENANCE

Fertilize every 14 days using a water-soluble fertilizer for blooming plants. Remove dead flowers and pinch back plants periodically to encourage fuller plant growth. Weed on an as-needed basis. Check the soil regularly, daily in the hottest weather, and water if dry. A powdery mildew that may occur on the leaves is extremely difficult to control.

ADDITIONAL INFORMATION

Purchase the plants in pots of various sizes or as high-quality seed. Seed can be started indoors in containers or cell packs 6 weeks before outdoor planting, with proper light sources (which can be raised and lowered), bottom heat mats, and a sterile growing medium. Or direct sow the seed after the ground has warmed in mid to late May. A quick formula for determining the proper quantity of plants is to divide the square footage of the bed by one-half the height of the plant and by one-half the width of the plant (as noted on its tag); whichever result is larger is the number of plants you should plant per square foot. To determine the spacing between plants, divide the height and the width of the plant by 2. The lower number which results determines the spacing between plants. For example, for a plant that is 6 inches tall and 8 inches wide and a bed that is 12 feet square, you should plant 4 plants per square foot ($12/3 = 4$), and the plants should be spaced 3 inches apart ($6/2 = 3$).

ADDITIONAL SPECIES, CULTIVARS, OR VARIETIES

Zinnia angustifolia produces an excellent orange-colored flower. It is a lower growing variety with gray-green foliage and does not require deadheading.

Did You Know?

The zinnia is a member of the sunflower family. Few disk flowers appear with the ray flowers. Petals may be cupped, giving a tighter, more formal look to the bloom. The species name, elegans, *means "beautiful" or "elegant."*

Bulbs

B ULBS—THE HOMELY GARDEN STAPLE coveted by knowing gardeners—guarantee a variety of beautiful and exotic flowers throughout the growing season. Their exact location is sometimes nearly forgotten until an old spring favorite once again pokes its green fingers through the thawing earth, or the appearance of a tropical variety signals that summer has arrived.

Bulbs are a collection of subterranean roots and stems originally found in various parts of the globe. Early European explorers gathered bulbs on their travels to distant lands and carried them back home where they were planted in palace gardens and nurtured in royal greenhouses. Interest in these exotic plants eventually raised the status of bulbs to a horticultural pinnacle in Europe during the seventeenth century. Today, gardeners perpetuate this reverence for bulbs in their carefully orchestrated, formal and informal arrangements of showy bulb plantings.

Formal bulb plantings utilize straight lines and specific patterns that mimic architectural features. To accomplish a formal arrangement, use large numbers of fewer bulb varieties, making sure they have the same or sequential bloom periods. Minimize variations in spacing, color, height, and frilliness of flowers. Even though the guidelines for informal plantings are looser and allow the gardener more freedom from every perspective, some pointers are helpful. Plant no fewer than five of the same type of bulb in close proximity. Select bulbs that will provide the most extended bloom sequence. And, finally, plant some new varieties each year. Informal plantings let you improvise and satisfy spontaneous whims for new colors and textures, and any bulb "mistakes" you make can be easily corrected or rearranged. Be sure to scatter clusters of bulbs among annuals, perennials, and ground covers, and near shrubs or trees. Remember

Chapter Two

to reduce the number of colors and varieties in smaller planting spaces to prevent the creation of too much visual stimulation.

Bulbs are divided into five separate categories: (1) true bulbs, like daffodils, contain a miniature plant inside; (2) corms, like crocus stems, function as modified storage units, each with a tunic, basal plate, and eye on top; (3) tubers, like caladiums, are similar to corms but have no tunic or basal plate; (4) tuberous roots, like dahlias, are swollen roots that grow downward; and (5) rhizomes, like cannas, are thickened segmented roots that grow laterally. In this chapter, the term "bulb" will be used in a broad sense to include all of the 5 storage organs just described.

Traditional methods of creating new bulb varieties involve cross-pollinating, field-testing, and assessing the production of necessary quantities, all of which can take up to twenty years. Nontraditional methods have occasionally sped up the process. Herbicides such as Surflan are sometimes used to create mutations.

Bulbs are considered to be the fast food of the plant world—just drop one in a hole and up pops a beautiful flower each year. But while most bulbs are quite tough and durable, they do even better with some attention after planting. Most benefit from regular fertilizing and from watering during dry spells. Some varieties do best when dug up and stored indoors over the winter. And others will provide a wealth of new blossoms if divided when they become overgrown.

Bulbs are a reliable source of gardening pleasure whether aligned in neat geometric shapes in a formal garden, sprinkled mid-lawn, planted in a terrace pot, or forced indoors to cure mid-winter doldrums. They occupy a special place in our imagination, perhaps best indicated by the fact that a child's first drawing of a flower is so very often the spring blossom produced by the tulip bulb.

Autumn Crocus

Colchicum autumnale

Height: Over 6 inches
Flower Color: Various
Bloom Period: Fall
Type: Hardy
Color photograph on page 243.

Light Requirements:

The fall crocus comes as a last-minute surprise to remind us of all the colorful new life that follow winters. This small flower has several aspects that make it a unique addition to any garden; it should be planted in a minimum cluster of ten in close proximity to provide the maximum impact. The foliage, which numbers between three and eight leaves, is a narrow straplike blade that emerges in the spring and can reach 10 inches in length. As the heat of late spring and early summer climbs, the leaf goes into dormancy below ground. Several months later, depending on the weather, up shoots a bud. This unexpected guest in the garden is the "inflorescence." As it opens, it boasts up to four flowers and sometimes one will be a double. Closer inspection reveals a cuplike blossom shape similar to the spring crocus, with colors ranging from white to deepening shades of purple, and soft yellow highlights at the center. Forgotten, unexpected, the autumn crocus is always a welcome surprise as colors dim elsewhere in the fall garden.

WHEN TO PLANT
Plant in late summer to early fall.

WHERE TO PLANT
Autumn crocus bulbs do well in rich, organic, fertile soil that is well drained. Place well away from any woody plants whose aggressive roots may compete for nutrients and moisture. Siting where there is afternoon shade can extend the bloom period.

HOW TO PLANT
Delineate the bed. Dig up any undesired plants or remove them with an herbicide. Spade or rototill the area, using caution under trees. Then blend 6 inches of organic matter and bonemeal with the existing soil and level the area. Dig a hole twice the diameter of the bulb.

Place the bulb at the bottom of the hole, narrow end pointed up. Backfill the hole, firm soil, water thoroughly, and add 1 to 2 inches of mulch. When planting bulbs at random and not in a bed, prepare each hole as described. Multiple bulbs placed in a large single hole should not touch. If planting in a container for forcing indoors, use one that is a minimum of 6 inches in diameter and well-drained potting mix. Place bulbs 2/3 of the way into the pot, backfill, firm soil, and water. Store in a cold location (but do not allow to freeze) for a minimum of 8 weeks, then set the plant in a sunny location and water thoroughly.

CARE AND MAINTENANCE

Bulbs benefit from watering if dry through entire growing season, until leaves are brown. Spring-flowering bulbs can be fertilized one of two ways. Try a single fall application when planting of Bulb Booster™ fertilizer; or incorporate bonemeal into the planting area along with an application of 8-8-8 or 10-10-10 in the fall, repeating this procedure when the shoots emerge in spring. Foliage feeds the bulb and should not be removed until it dies back. Pest and disease problems are minimal. Do not dig up bulbs to divide. When plants begin to show signs of decline, plant new bulbs.

ADDITIONAL INFORMATION

Bulbs can be purchased at garden centers or by mail order. At garden centers select the largest and firmest bulbs which are not sprouting, and store in a dark, cool, dry location in a paper bag. If ordering by mail, ask about size, time of shipment, and planting instructions. Bulbs forced indoors and planted outdoors may take several years to begin flowering again. Bonemeal nutrients remain in the soil for many years and do not require frequent reapplication. Do not use manure to solve disease problems.

ADDITIONAL SPECIES, CULTIVARS, OR VARIETIES

There are none available.

Caladium

Caladium × hortulanum

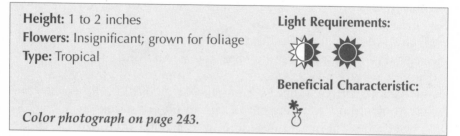

Height: 1 to 2 inches
Flowers: Insignificant; grown for foliage
Type: Tropical

Light Requirements:

Beneficial Characteristic:

Color photograph on page 243.

Caladiums always demand attention whether captured in a pot, thriving in the shade of the back porch, or gracefully skirting the trunk of a tree. Rising up from the ground on long stems, the foliage first resembles a spear point, which then unrolls over the next few days. The caladium's rather small heart-shaped leaf positions itself toward the brightest light and increases in size ever so slightly each day until reaching maturity. The vividly painted leaf, which can increase to 8 inches long and 6 inches wide, bobs on the stem with each ripple of wind. Depending on the particular variety, the caladium's colors range from pure white accented with green veins, to splattered reds, roses, and pinks, each unparalleled. Caladiums provide a colorful accent that works well in any size and style of landscape.

WHEN TO PLANT
Plant in late spring to early summer.

WHERE TO PLANT
Caladiums require rich, organic, fertile soil that is well drained. When planting bulbs around a tree, measure the trunk's diameter, multiply by five, and do not install bulbs any closer to trunk than this distance. Siting in afternoon shade will minimize leaf scorch.

HOW TO PLANT
Delineate the bed. Dig up any undesired plants or remove them with an herbicide. Spade or rototill the area, using caution under trees. Then blend 6 inches of organic matter and bonemeal with the existing soil and level the area. Dig a hole 3 or more times the diameter of the bulb. Place the bulb at the bottom at the bottom of the hole, narrow end pointed up. Backfill the hole, firm soil, and water thoroughly. If bulbs have been sprouted indoors in a container, do not

plant outside any deeper than currently growing. When planting bulbs at random and not in a bed, prepare each hole as described. Multiple bulbs placed in a large single hole should not touch. If planting in a container, use one that is a minimum of 12 inches in diameter and well-drained potting mix. Place bulbs $1/3$ of the way into the pot, backfill, firm soil, and water thoroughly.

CARE AND MAINTENANCE

Caladiums benefit from watering if dry through entire growing season. Remove bulbs after frost has killed leaves, allow the soil to dry, then shake off excess soil and discard any spotted, moldy, or undersized bulbs. Store bulbs in a dark, cool, dry location in a box or paper bag with vermiculite. In mid-spring pot bulbs indoors to get a jump on summer planting. Use heating cables or mats for bottom heat to end the dormancy period more quickly, but do not set outdoors until air temperature remain in the upper 70s Fahrenheit. Pests and diseases are not a problem.

ADDITIONAL INFORMATION

Bulbs can be purchased at garden centers or by mail order. At garden centers select largest and firmest bulbs which are not sprouting, and store in a dark, cool, dry location in a paper bag. Caladium bulbs are also available growing in nursery pots. If ordering by mail, ask about size, time of shipment, and planting instructions. Bonemeal nutrients remain in the soil for many years and do not require frequent reapplication. Do not use manure to solve disease problems.

ADDITIONAL SPECIES, CULTIVARS, OR VARIETIES

There are none available.

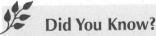 **Did You Know?**

The caladium is a mixed hybrid that resulted from crossing several varieties, one which is native to Brazil. The roots or fruits are edible.

Canna

Canna × generalis

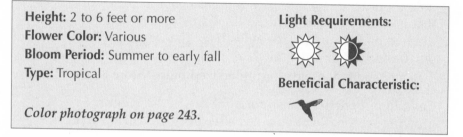

Height: 2 to 6 feet or more
Flower Color: Various
Bloom Period: Summer to early fall
Type: Tropical

Light Requirements:

Beneficial Characteristic:

Color photograph on page 243.

The botanical equivalent of the ugly duckling turned swan, the ugly canna bulb, a flattish rhizome with big bulging knots, evolves into a majestic plant, often towering over the gardener. The fleshy green or intense red stem stands proudly upright, with large simple leaves alternating along its length. The leaves, which are often as large as 1 foot long by 8 inches wide at the foot of the canna, decrease in size nearer its head. Crowned by an exquisite flower, the canna attracts hummingbirds and pollinating insects. Its small, roundish fruits are protected by a bristly capsule. A tropical native, the canna can be grown in larger pots or scattered for dramatic effect among annuals or perennials in any landscape.

WHEN TO PLANT
Plant in late spring to early summer.

WHERE TO PLANT
Cannas require rich, organic, fertile soil that is well drained. Choosing a site that receives afternoon shade will extend the length of bloom, but taller varieties will lean or flop with too much shade.

HOW TO PLANT
Delineate the bed. Dig up any undesired plants or remove them with an herbicide. Spade or rototill the area, using caution under trees. Then blend 6 inches of organic matter and bonemeal with the existing soil and level the area. Dig a hole 3 or more times the diameter of the bulb. Place the bulb horizontally at the bottom of the hole. Backfill the hole, firm soil, water thoroughly, and add 1 to 2 inches of mulch. When planting bulbs at random and not in a bed, prepare each hole as described. Multiple bulbs placed in a large single hole should not touch. If planting in a container, use one that is a mini-

mum of 20 inches in diameter and well-drained potting mix. Place bulbs $1/3$ of the way into the pot, backfill, firm soil, and water thoroughly.

CARE AND MAINTENANCE

Cannas benefit from watering if dry through entire growing season. Remove the bulbs after frost has killed the leaves, allow soil to dry, then shake off excess soil and discard any spotted, moldy, or undersized bulbs. Store bulbs in a dark, cool, dry location in a box or paper bag with vermiculite. In mid-spring pot bulbs indoors to get a jump on summer planting. Use heating cables or mats as bottom heat to end the dormancy period more quickly, but do not set outdoors until air temperature remains in the upper 70s Fahrenheit. Pests and diseases are not a problem.

ADDITIONAL INFORMATION

Bulbs can be purchased at garden centers or by mail order. At garden centers select the largest and firmest bulbs which are not sprouting, and store in a dark, cool, dry location in a paper bag. Caladium bulbs are also available growing in nursery pots. If ordering by mail, ask about size, time of shipment, and planting instructions. Bonemeal nutrients remain in the soil for many years and do not require frequent reapplication. Do not use manure to solve disease problems.

ADDITIONAL SPECIES, CULTIVARS, OR VARIETIES

Many are available, some with yellow striped foliage, others with larger flowers, and some shorter in height.

Did You Know?

The canna is the only genus of the family, making it a truly unique plant. Although the leaf is very wide, the plant is a monocot, meaning it is related to the grasses rather than the broadleaf plants. This hybrid results from cross-pollinating plants in their tropical habitats.

Crocus

Crocus spp.

Height: 6 inches
Flower Color: Various
Bloom Period: Spring
Type: Hardy

Light Requirements:

Color photograph on page 243.

The crocus paints subtle pastel color across spring lawns. These plants can be clustered to highlight a walk or drive, dotted in among other blooming bulbs, and mixed with favorite garden perennials, spring annuals, or shrubbery. Struck by direct sun, crocus petals fully open outward, inviting bees in for nectar. But when clouds shadow the flowers, they snap shut, sometimes trapping the unsuspecting—and now wildly buzzing—bees inside. The grasslike leaves spring way from the stem, fully exposing the velvety colors of the blossoms. The crocus is a sure bet and a good bulb to give children for their first planting experience.

WHEN TO PLANT
Plant in late fall to early winter.

WHERE TO PLANT
The crocus requires rich, organic, fertile soil that is well drained. When planting bulbs around a tree, measure the trunk's diameter, multiply by five, and do not install bulbs any closer to the trunk than this distance. Siting in afternoon shade can extend the bloom period.

HOW TO PLANT
Delineate the bed. Dig up any undesired plants or remove them with an herbicide. Spade or rototill the area, using caution under trees. Then blend 6 inches of organic matter and bonemeal with the existing soil and level the area. Dig a hole 3 or more times the diameter of the bulb. Place the bulb at the bottom of the hole, narrow end pointed up. Backfill the hole, firm soil, water thoroughly, and add 1 to 2 inches of mulch. When planting bulbs at random and not in a bed, prepare each hole as described. Multiple bulbs placed in a large single hole should not touch. If planting in a container for forcing

indoors, use one that is a minimum of 6 inches in diameter and well-drained potting mix. Place bulbs 1/3 of the way into the pot, backfill, firm soil, and water thoroughly. Store in a cold location (but do not allow to freeze) for a minimum of 8 weeks, then set the plant in a sunny location and water thoroughly.

CARE AND MAINTENANCE

Crocuses benefit from watering if dry through the entire growing season, until the leaves are brown. Foliage on hardy bulbs should remain until at least until 50 percent brown, so if bulbs are planted in the lawn, do not mow over until mid-May—leaves will be adding energy for next year. Pest and disease problems are minimal, except for problems controlling wildlife that attempt to dig up bulbs or eat the foliage.

ADDITIONAL INFORMATION

Bulbs can be purchased at garden centers or by mail order. At garden centers select the largest and firmest bulbs which are not sprouting, and store in a dark, cool, dry location in a paper bag. If ordering by mail, ask about size, time of shipment, and planting instructions. Bulbs forced indoors and planted outdoors may take several years to begin flowering again. Bonemeal nutrients remain in the soil for many years and do not require frequent reapplication. Do not use manure to solve disease problems.

ADDITIONAL SPECIES, CULTIVARS, OR VARIETIES

There are none available.

🌿 Did You Know?

Today's crocus is the hybrid cross of many different species which are members of the iris family and found throughout the Mediterranean region of the world. The harvested and dried flower parts of a close relative of the crocus are the source of the highly prized yellow food flavoring, saffron.

Daffodil

Narcissus spp.

Height: 6 inches to 2 feet
Flower Color: White, yellow (new varieties
  include pale pink and orangish)
Bloom Period: Spring
Type: Hardy
Color photograph on page 243.

Light Requirements:

Beneficial Characteristic:

Many gardeners consider daffodils, jonquils, and narcissus the brilliant stars of the spring stage. Their best-loved status is hard to dispute. The large number of daffodil varieties and their subtle differences made it necessary in 1950 to revise their system of horticultural classification. The dark green foliage, which sometimes grows taller than the flower stalk, provides a rich contrast to the clear colors of the tumbling cup-and-saucer-shaped blossoms. With some planning, any landscape will benefit from planting masses or small clusters of these extraordinary bulbs.

WHEN TO PLANT
Plant in late fall to early winter.

WHERE TO PLANT
Daffodils require rich, organic, fertile soil that is well drained. When planting bulbs around a tree, measure the trunk's diameter, multiply by five, and do not install bulbs any closer to the trunk than this distance. Siting in afternoon shade can extend the bloom period.

HOW TO PLANT
Delineate the bed. Dig up any undesired plants or remove them with an herbicide. Spade or rototill the area, using caution under trees. Then blend 6 inches of organic matter and bonemeal with the existing soil and level the area. Dig a hole 3 or more times the diameter of the bulb. Place the bulb at the bottom of the hole, narrow end pointed up. Backfill the hole, firm soil, water thoroughly, and add 1 to 2 inches of mulch. When planting bulbs at random and not in a bed, prepare each hole as described. Multiple bulbs placed in a large single hole should not touch. If planting in a container for forcing indoors, use one that is a minimum of 6 inches in diameter and well-

drained potting mix. Place bulbs $1/3$ of the way into the pot, backfill, firm soil, and water thoroughly. Store in a cold location (but do not allow to freeze) for a minimum of 8 weeks, then set the plant in a sunny location and water thoroughly.

CARE AND MAINTENANCE

Daffodils benefit from watering if dry through the entire growing season, until the leaves are brown. Foliage on hardy bulbs should remain, unfolded or twisted, until they are at least until 50 percent brown; the leaves are adding energy for next year. Pest and disease problems are minimal.

ADDITIONAL INFORMATION

Bulbs can be purchased at garden centers or by mail order. At garden centers, select the largest and firmest bulbs which are not sprouting, and store in a dark, cool, dry location in a paper bag. Do not expect flowering for several years if bulbs are undersized. If ordering by mail, ask about size, time of shipment, and planting instructions. Bulbs forced indoors and planted outdoors may take several years to begin flowering again. Bonemeal nutrients remain in the soil for many years and do not require frequent reapplication. Do not use manure to solve disease problems.

ADDITIONAL SPECIES, CULTIVARS, OR VARIETIES

The number of new varieties and cultivars available each year when added to the current selection is astronomical— and means a lot of fun!

Did You Know?

The daffodil, like many other celebrities of the spring landscape, is a member of the amaryllis family. The bulbs are nonpalatable, meaning that wildlife will not eat them.

Dahlia

Dahlia hybrids

Height: 1 to 4 feet
Flower Color: Various
Bloom Period: Late summer
Type: Tropical

Color photograph on page 243.

Light Requirements:

Beneficial Characteristics:

A truly remarkable member of the sunflower family, the dahlia's bright coloration reflects the "fiesta attitude" of its Latin American and South American homeland. At first appearance, there is little sign of beauty in the dahlia bulb's dangling mass of tuberous roots. But with a little extra care, the unbranched stem gradually reaches for the sun, sprouting compound featherlike leaves arranged either oppositely or in a whorl. Some of the flower heads are enormous. The vivid flowers emerge late in the summer, their size, colors, and ray or disk petal shapes differing with each variety, and all are an invitation to celebrate a beautiful end of the season.

WHEN TO PLANT
Plant in late spring to early summer.

WHERE TO PLANT
Dahlias require rich, organic, fertile soil that is well drained. When planting bulbs around a tree, measure the trunk's diameter, multiply by five, and do not install bulbs any closer to the trunk than this distance.

HOW TO PLANT
Delineate the bed. Dig up any undesired plants or remove them with an herbicide. Spade or rototill the area, using caution under trees. Then blend 6 inches of organic matter and bonemeal with the existing soil and level the area. Dig a hole 6 inches deep, place roots over a small mound in the bottom of the hole, backfill, firm soil, water thoroughly, and add 1 to 2 inches of mulch. Space plants 3 to 4 inches apart. When planting bulbs at random and not in a bed, prepare each hole as described. Multiple bulbs placed in a large single hole should not touch. If planting in a container, use one that is a

minimum of 20 inches in diameter and well-drained potting mix. Place bulbs ⅓ of the way into the pot, backfill, firm soil, and water thoroughly.

CARE AND MAINTENANCE
Dahlias benefit from monthly fertilizing with a lower analysis balanced food. Water to maintain a consistent level of moisture through the entire growing season. If multiple stems emerge, remove all but one. Pinch off some flower buds to get maximum-size flowers, remove some leaves to increase air circulation, and shade the plants from the midday sun. Remove bulbs with stalks after frost has killed the leaves, allow soil to dry, shake off excess soil, and discard any undersized, moldy, or spotted bulbs. Store bulbs, not touching one another, in a dark, cool, dry location. Dahlias can be potted up indoors in mid-spring to get a jump on summer planting. Use heating cables or mats as bottom heat to speed up breaking of dormancy. Do not set outdoors until air temperatures remain in the upper 70s Fahrenheit. Watch for aphids, cutworms, and the fungus/bacteria botrytis.

ADDITIONAL INFORMATION
Bulbs can be purchased at garden centers or by mail order. At garden centers, select the largest and firmest bulbs which are not sprouting, and store in a dark, cool, dry location in a paper bag. If ordering by mail, ask about size, time of shipment, and planting instructions. Bonemeal nutrients remain in the soil for many years and do not require frequent reapplication. Do not use manure to solve disease problems.

ADDITIONAL SPECIES, CULTIVARS, OR VARIETIES
There are twelve different groups of dahlias available, categorized according to flower configuration.

Elephant Ears

Colocasia esculenta

Height: 2 to 3 feet
Flowers: Insignificant; grown for
  its foliage
Type: Tropical
Color photograph on page 244.

Light Requirements:

This plant gets its name from its amazingly huge, coarsely textured, heart-shaped leaves that have a waxy gray-blue sheen. One of the few bulbs that can grow equally well in a well-drained or constantly wet soil, elephant ears work well in beds, patio containers, or water gardens and create a striking visual effect wherever grown, especially when tossed by the wind. The bigger the bulb, which resembles a de-prickled pineapple, the more impressive the size of the foliage. Only a few of the gigantic leaves emerge through the summer, but they retain their color and proud shape until the first frost of fall.

WHEN TO PLANT

Plant in late spring to early summer.

WHERE TO PLANT

Elephant ears do well in rich, organic, fertile soil that can range from well drained to standing water of a few inches.

HOW TO PLANT

Delineate the bed. Dig up any undesired plants or remove them with an herbicide. Spade or rototill the area, using caution under trees. Then blend 6 inches of organic matter and bonemeal with the existing soil and level the area. Dig a hole 6 inches deep, place roots over a small mound in the bottom of the hole, backfill, firm soil, water thoroughly, and add 1 to 2 inches of mulch. When planting bulbs at random and not in a bed, prepare each hole as described. Multiple bulbs placed in a large single hole should not touch. If planting in a container, use one that is a minimum of 20 inches in diameter and well-drained potting mix. Place bulbs $1/3$ of the way into the pot, backfill, firm soil, and water thoroughly.

CARE AND MAINTENANCE

Elephant ears benefit from watering to keep very moist through the entire growing season. Remove bulbs after frost has killed leaves, allow soil to dry, shake off excess soil, discard any spotted, moldy, or undersized bulbs, and store in a dark, cool, dry location in a box or paper bag with vermiculite. Pot up indoors, mid-spring to get a jump on summer planting. Use heating cables or mats as bottom heat to speed up breaking of dormancy and do not set outdoors until air temperatures remain in the upper 70s Fahrenheit. Pests and diseases are not a problem.

ADDITIONAL INFORMATION

Bulbs can be purchased at garden centers or by mail order. At garden centers, select the largest and firmest bulbs which are not sprouting, and store in a dark, cool, dry location in a paper bag. Bulbs are also available growing in nursery pots. If ordering by mail, ask about size, time of shipment, and planting instructions. Bonemeal nutrients remain in the soil for many years and do not require frequent reapplication. Do not use manure to solve disease problems.

ADDITIONAL SPECIES, CULTIVARS, OR VARIETIES

Look for *Colocasia antiquorum* 'Illustris', the black-leaf taro, and *Colocasia* 'Black Magic', the black-leaf elephant ear. *C. fontanesii* is the black-stem elephant ear. *Colocasia* 'Burgundy Stem' is the violet-stem taro.

Did You Know?

The elephant ear is a member of the aroid or arum family with caladiums, pothos, and philodendrons. The species name esculenta *means "edible," and in their native homelands young shoots are harvested and blanched for winter food. In Hawaii the root is ground up to make poi.*

Giant Flowering Onion

Allium giganteum

Height: 3 feet or more **Flower Color:** Bright lavender **Bloom Period:** Spring **Type:** Hardy *Color photograph on page 244.*	**Light Requirements:** ☀ **Beneficial Characteristics:**

This bulb produces a plant that seems a lovely visitor from another world. When growth first appears in early spring, you'll think a pale blue-green sea star has washed up on your garden shore. The leaves continue to elongate, reaching up to 1½ feet long and nearly 2 inches wide. The stem shoots rocketlike from the foliage center, a swelling spear point at the tip, and soon a 6-inch iridescent lavender globe bursts into bloom. Nothing exceeds its botanical fireworks. Cut and dried, the blossom makes a silverish globe to use in seasonal arrangements.

WHEN TO PLANT
Plant in late fall to early winter.

WHERE TO PLANT
Allium requires rich, organic, fertile soil that is well drained. When planting bulbs around a tree, measure the trunk's diameter, multiply by five, and do not install bulbs any closer to the trunk than this distance. Siting in afternoon shade can extend the bloom period.

HOW TO PLANT
Delineate the bed. Dig up any undesired plants or remove them with an herbicide. Spade or rototill the area, using caution under trees. Then blend 6 inches of organic matter and bonemeal with the existing soil and level the area. Dig a hole 3 or more times the diameter of the bulb. Place the bulb at the bottom of the hole, narrow end pointed up. Backfill the hole, firm soil, water thoroughly, and add 1 to 2 inches of mulch. When planting bulbs at random and not in a bed, prepare each hole as described. Multiple bulbs placed in a large single hole should not touch. If planting in a container for forcing indoors, use one that is a minimum of 6 inches in diameter and well-

drained potting mix. Place bulbs ²/₃ of the way into the pot, backfill, firm soil, and water thoroughly. Store in a cold location (but do not allow to freeze) for a minimum of 8 weeks, then set the plant in a sunny location and water thoroughly.

CARE AND MAINTENANCE

Allium benefits from watering if dry through the entire growing season, until the leaves are brown. Foliage on hardy bulbs should remain, unfolded or twisted, until at least 50 percent are brown; the leaves are adding energy for next year. Pest and disease problems are minimal.

ADDITIONAL INFORMATION

Bulbs can be purchased at garden centers or by mail order. If purchasing at a garden center, select the largest and firmest bulbs, with none sprouting, and store in a dark, cool, dry location in a paper bag. If ordering by mail, ask about size, time of shipment, and planting instructions. Bonemeal nutrients remain in the soil for many years and do not require frequent reapplication. Do not use manure to solve disease problems.

ADDITIONAL SPECIES, CULTIVARS, OR VARIETIES

There are none available.

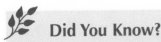 **Did You Know?**

This plant is a member of the amaryllis family, which includes all the other ornamental and edible relatives of the onion. The name giganteum *refers to the flower size and is clearly well deserved. The flower stalk, when cut, will bleed a red sap, giving an eerie quality to this already unique plant.*

Gladiolus

Gladiolus × hortulanus

Height: 1 to 3 feet
Flower Color: Various
Bloom Period: Summer
Type: Tropical

Light Requirements:

Color photograph on page 244.

Beneficial Characteristic:

Glads are one of the most glamorous cutting flowers, whose long stalks continue to open in colorful sequence long after most other plants are added to the compost pile. The flower's colors and size, which can be up to 5 inches across, make a spectacular showing in the garden, and mass planting will provide cut flowers for every room in the house. Flowers open up from the bottom to the top. The sword-like foliage, which bunches at the ground, introduces unique texture and form to the landscape. Simple to plant, gladiolas provide an exceptionally healthy return on your gardening investment.

WHEN TO PLANT

Begin in late spring, then stagger plantings at 2-week intervals to have continuous blooms throughout the summer. Do not plant after mid-July.

WHERE TO PLANT

Glads require rich, organic, fertile soil that is well drained. Siting where there is afternoon shade will extend the length of bloom, but taller varieties will lean or flop if there is too much shade or if planting is too shallow. To prevent disease problems, do not repeat the planting location each year.

HOW TO PLANT

Delineate the bed. Dig up any undesired plants or remove them with an herbicide. Spade or rototill the area, using caution under trees. Then blend 6 inches of organic matter and bonemeal with the existing soil and level the area. Dig a hole 3 or more times the diameter of the bulb. Place the bulb at the bottom of the hole, narrow end pointed up. Backfill the hole, firm soil, water thoroughly, and add 1 to 2 inches of mulch. Allow 5 to 6 inches between bulbs. When planting bulbs at random and not in a bed, prepare each hole as described. Multiple bulbs placed in a large single hole should not touch. If planting in a container, use one that is a minimum of 20 inches in diameter and well-drained potting mix. Place bulbs 2/3 of the way into the pot, backfill, firm soil, and water thoroughly.

CARE AND MAINTENANCE

Glads benefit from watering if dry throughout the growing season. Varieties that are 2 feet or taller must be staked. Pot up indoors mid-spring to get a jump on summer planting. Use heating cables or mats as bottom heat to speed up breaking of dormancy, and do not set outdoors until air temperatures remain in the upper 70s Fahrenheit. Discard the bulb after flowering. Watch for aphids. Diseases can be avoided by not siting in the same location every year.

ADDITIONAL INFORMATION

Bulbs can be purchased at garden centers or by mail order. At garden centers, select the largest, at least $1^1/_2$ inches in diameter, and firmest bulbs; store them in a dark, cool, dry location in a paper bag. Bulbs should be in the ground up to 90 days before flowering. If ordering by mail, ask about size, time of shipment, and planting instructions. Bonemeal nutrients remain in the soil for many years and do not require frequent reapplication. Do not use manure to solve disease problems.

ADDITIONAL SPECIES, CULTIVARS, OR VARIETIES

Many different varieties, grouped according to height and flower size, are available.

Did You Know?

A member of the iris family, this hybrid is the result of several crosses of plants which were first gathered in Southeast Africa. Tips on cutting: Cut as the first flower opens, smash the bottom inch of the stalk to allow for greater water absorption, and place the stem in cool water.

BULBS

Glory-of-the-Snow

Chionodoxa luciliae

Height: Depends on variety
Flower Color: Pale blue
Bloom Period: Spring
Type: Hardy
Color photograph on page 238.

Light Requirements:

This blue star-shaped flower with its snowy white center spreads out among neighboring plantings like a rich carpet of captured snowflakes. Each bulb produces more than a single 5- or 6-petaled flower, and so the gaps between individually planted bulbs are easily filled. The low-growing, dark green foliage may emerge early, while there is still a chance of snow, and after bloom is nearly obscured by the flowers.

WHEN TO PLANT

Plant in late spring to early winter, and replenish the colony every 3 to 4 years.

WHERE TO PLANT

Glory-of-the-snow require rich, organic, fertile soil that is well drained. When planting bulbs around a tree, measure the trunk's diameter, multiply by five, and do not install bulbs any closer to trunk than this distance. Siting in afternoon shade can extend the bloom period.

HOW TO PLANT

Delineate the bed. Dig up any undesired plants or remove them with an herbicide. Spade or rototill the area, using caution under trees. Then blend 6 inches of organic matter and bonemeal with the existing soil and level the area. Dig a hole 3 or more times the diameter of the bulb. Place the bulb at the bottom of the hole, narrow end pointed up. Backfill the hole, firm soil, water thoroughly, and add 1 to 2 inches of mulch. When planting bulbs at random and not in a bed, prepare each hole as described. Multiple bulbs placed in a large single hole should not touch. If planting in a container for forcing indoors, use one that is a minimum of 6 inches in diameter and well-

drained potting mix. Place bulbs $^2/_3$ of the way into the pot, backfill, firm soil, and water thoroughly. Store in a cold location (but do not allow to freeze) for a minimum of 8 weeks, then set the plant in a sunny location and water thoroughly.

CARE AND MAINTENANCE

Glory-of-the-snow benefit from watering if dry through the entire growing season, until the leaves are brown. Foliage should not be cut off, but allowed instead to go completely brown and die; the leaves are adding energy for next year. Pest and disease problems are minimal.

ADDITIONAL INFORMATION

Bulbs can be purchased at garden centers or by mail order. At garden centers select the largest and firmest bulbs, with none sprouting; store them in a dark, cool, dry location in a paper bag. If ordering by mail, ask about size, time of shipment, and planting instructions. Bulbs forced indoors and planted outdoors may take several years to begin flowering again. Bonemeal nutrients remain in the soil for many years and do not require frequent reapplication. Do not use manure to solve disease problems.

ADDITIONAL SPECIES, CULTIVARS, OR VARIETIES

Chionodoxa luciliae 'Alba' is a white-flowering variety, and *Chionodoxa luciliae* 'Tmoli' flowers a bit later in the season.

Did You Know?

This member of the lily family is found naturally in the mountainous regions of the islands of Crete and Cyprus, as well as in Asia Minor. Other close relatives include asparagus, hosta, and the Missouri native wildflower false Solomon's seal.

BULBS

Grape Hyacinth

Muscari spp.

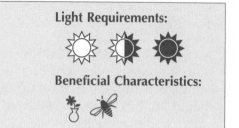

Height: Up to 1 foot
Flower Color: Purplish blue
Bloom Period: Spring
Type: Hardy

Color photograph on page 244.

Light Requirements:

Beneficial Characteristics:

A great player in the spring garden, grape hyacinths mingle especially well with other spring-flowering bulbs and plants with blooms of lighter shades of color. The paler shades make a striking contrast for the grape hyacinth's rich royal purple flowerets and its medium-green spiky leaves that weave through surrounding foliage. The flower spike is launched from the center of the foliage, and positioned neatly along the stalk are smaller-than-a-pea, roundish flowers, each with a tiny opening. The purple hue and sweet fragrance attract early spring bees whose repeated attempts to get through the tiny door for pollen can be very entertaining.

WHEN TO PLANT
Plant in late fall to early winter.

WHERE TO PLANT
Grape hyacinths require rich, organic, fertile soil that is well drained. When planting bulbs around a tree, measure the trunk's diameter, multiply by five, and do not install bulbs any closer to the trunk than this distance. Siting in afternoon shade can extend the bloom period.

HOW TO PLANT
Delineate the bed. Dig up any undesired plants or remove them with an herbicide. Spade or rototill the area, using caution under trees. Then blend 6 inches of organic matter and bonemeal with the existing soil and level the area. Dig a hole 3 or more times the diameter of the bulb. Place the bulb at the bottom of the hole, narrow end pointed up. Backfill the hole, firm soil, water thoroughly, and add 1 to 2 inches of mulch. When planting bulbs at random and not in a bed, prepare each hole as described. Multiple bulbs placed in a large

single hole should not touch. If planting in a container for forcing indoors, use one that is a minimum of 6 inches in diameter and well-drained potting mix. Place bulbs 2/3 of the way the pot, backfill, firm soil, and water thoroughly. Store in a cold location (but do not allow to freeze) for a minimum of 8 weeks, then set the plant in a sunny location and water thoroughly. Grape hyacinths benefit from watering if dry through the entire growing season, until leaves are brown. Foliage should not be cut off, but allowed instead to go completely brown and die; leaves are adding energy for next year. Pest and disease problems are minimal.

ADDITIONAL INFORMATION

Bulbs can be purchased at garden centers or by mail order. At garden centers, select the largest and firmest bulbs, with none sprouting; store in a dark, cool, dry location in a paper bag. If ordering by mail, ask about size, time of shipment, and planting instructions. Bulbs forced indoors and planted outdoors may take several years to begin flowering again. Bonemeal nutrients remain in the soil for many years and do not require frequent reapplication. Do not use manure to solve disease problems.

ADDITIONAL SPECIES, CULTIVARS, OR VARIETIES

A white-flowered variety is *Muscari azureum* 'Album'.

Did You Know?

The common name refers to the flower stalk configuration and grapelike shape of the individual blooms. This species is the result of the hybridizing of several members of this genus which are found in the Mediterranean and Southeast Asian regions of the world.

Snowdrops

Galanthus nivalis

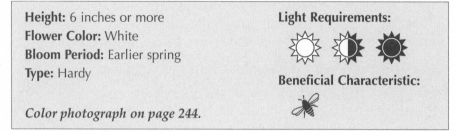

Height: 6 inches or more
Flower Color: White
Bloom Period: Earlier spring
Type: Hardy

Color photograph on page 244.

Light Requirements:

Beneficial Characteristic:

When these bulbs are clustered together in a mass of ten or more, the flowers they produce resemble a small bank of spring snow. The bulb sends up two relatively short, dark green, straplike leaves. At the same time, the flower bud opens to reveal an unusual flower spike. It resembles a miniature street light hung upside down, with some portion of the lamp tinted green and the remainder a glowing white. Snowdrops provide accent when sited among evergreen groundcovers, dotted with other bulbs or perennials, or standing as a solitary armful.

WHEN TO PLANT
Plant in late fall to early winter.

WHERE TO PLANT
Snowdrops require rich, organic, fertile soil that is well drained. When planting bulbs around a tree, measure the trunk's diameter, multiply by five, and do not install bulbs any closer to the trunk than this distance. Siting in afternoon shade can extend the bloom period.

HOW TO PLANT
Delineate the bed. Dig up any undesired plants or remove them with an herbicide. Spade or rototill the area, using caution under trees. Then blend 6 inches of organic matter and bonemeal with the existing soil and level the area. Dig a hole 3 or more times the diameter of the bulb. Place the bulb at the bottom of the hole, narrow end pointed up. Backfill the hole, firm soil, water thoroughly, and add 1 to 2 inches of mulch. When planting bulbs at random and not in a bed, prepare each hole as described. Multiple bulbs placed in a large single hole should not touch. If planting in a container for forcing indoors, use one that is a minimum of 6 inches in diameter and well-

drained potting mix. Place bulbs ²/₃ of the way into the pot, backfill, firm soil, and water thoroughly. Store in a cold location (but do not allow to freeze) for a minimum of 8 weeks, then set the plant in a sunny location and water thoroughly.

CARE AND MAINTENANCE

Snowdrops benefit from watering if dry through entire growing season, until leaves are brown. Foliage should not be cut off, but allowed instead to go completely brown and die; leaves are adding energy for next year. Pest and disease problems are minimal.

ADDITIONAL INFORMATION

Bulbs can be purchased at garden centers or by mail order. At garden centers, select the largest and firmest bulbs, with none sprouting; store them in a dark, cool, dry location in a paper bag. If ordering by mail, ask about size, time of shipment, and planting instructions. Bulbs forced indoors and planted outdoors may take several years to begin flowering again. Bonemeal nutrients remain in the soil for many years and do not require frequent reapplication. Do not use manure to solve disease problems.

ADDITIONAL SPECIES, CULTIVARS, OR VARIETIES

Galanthus nivalis 'Flore Pleno' is a double-flowered variety. *G. n.* 'Sam Arnott' is the best double-flowered variety.

Did You Know?

Like many of the smaller bulbs, snowdrops belong to the amaryllis family, whose other members are a source of food and seasonings. This particular plant is native to Europe. The species name, nivalis, *means "snowy white."*

Snowflake

Leucojum aestivum

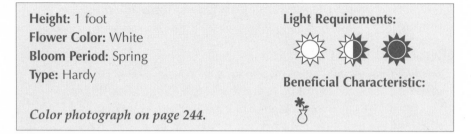

Height: 1 foot
Flower Color: White
Bloom Period: Spring
Type: Hardy

Color photograph on page 244.

Light Requirements:

Beneficial Characteristic:

Snowflakes are small in relation to other bulbs, but this late-spring bloomer makes a big impression. The narrow blade of bright green foliage breaks ground as a single point, sometimes reaching 18 inches, then the individual leaves split from one another, forming the center focal point. Simultaneously surging up is the flower stalk, upright with a slight bend at the top. Hanging from the top is the white bell-shaped flower spike, delicate, eye-catching, a suspended snowflake.

WHEN TO PLANT

Plant in late fall or early winter.

WHERE TO PLANT

Snowflakes require rich, organic, fertile soil that is well drained. When planting bulbs around a tree, measure the trunk's diameter, multiply by five, and do not install bulbs any closer to trunk than this distance. Siting in afternoon shade can extend the bloom period.

HOW TO PLANT

Delineate the bed. Dig up any undesired plants or remove them with an herbicide. Spade or rototill the area, using caution under trees. Then blend 6 inches of organic matter and bonemeal with the existing soil and level the area. Dig a hole 3 or more times the diameter of the bulb, or about 3 inches wide. Place the bulb at the bottom of the hole, narrow end pointed up. Backfill the hole, firm soil, water thoroughly, and add 1 to 2 inches of mulch. When planting bulbs at random and not in a bed, prepare each hole as described. Multiple bulbs placed in a large single hole should not touch. If planting in a container for forcing indoors, use one that is a minimum of 6 inches in diameter and well-drained potting mix. Place bulbs 2/3 of the way

into the pot, backfill, firm soil, and water thoroughly. Store in a cold location (but do not allow to freeze) for a minimum of
8 weeks, then set the plant in a sunny location and water thoroughly.

CARE AND MAINTENANCE

Snowflakes benefit from watering if dry through entire growing season, until leaves are brown. Foliage should not be cut off, but allowed instead to go completely brown and die. Leaves are adding energy for next year. Pest and disease problem are minimal.

ADDITIONAL INFORMATION

Bulbs can be purchased at garden centers or by mail order. At garden centers, select the largest and firmest bulbs, with none sprouting; store them in a dark, cool, dry location in a paper bag. If ordering by mail, ask about size, time of shipment, and planting instructions. Bulbs forced indoors and planted outdoors may take several years to begin flowering again. Bonemeal nutrients remain in the soil for many years and do not require frequent reapplication. Do not use manure to solve disease problems.

ADDITIONAL SPECIES, CULTIVARS, OR VARIETIES

Look for *L. Gravetye* 'Giant', *L. vernum* (spring snowflake), and *L. autumnale*.

🌿 Did You Know?

A member of the amaryllis family, which includes onions and daffodils, the snowflake is native to Central and Southern Europe. The species name aestivum *refers to summer. Sometimes this bulb is called summer snowflake because it can bloom in later spring.*

Tulip

Tulipa spp.

Height: 6 to 18 inches **Flower Color:** Various **Boom Period:** Spring **Type:** Hardy *Color photograph on page 244.*	**Light Requirements:** **Beneficial Characteristic:**

Conjure up an image of spring and you see magnificent tulips, fairy pots of yellow gold, cups of ivory white, goblets of winey red, or pint-size urns of pastel pink strewn across the landscape. Peer into their deep centers to see even more exquisite patterns of color. Tulips vibrate with color under the cloudy spring skies and pulsate vividly when spotlighted by the sun. The basal rosette of green leaves supports a fine thin stem that bends gracefully with the weight of its bold flower.

WHEN TO PLANT

Plant late fall into early winter.

WHERE TO PLANT

Tulips require rich, organic, fertile soil that is well drained. When planting bulbs around a tree, measure the trunk's diameter, multiply by five, and do not install bulbs any closer to trunk than this distance. Siting in afternoon shade can extend the bloom period.

HOW TO PLANT

Delineate the bed. Dig up any undesired plants or remove them with an herbicide. Spade or rototill the area, using caution under trees. Then blend 6 inches of organic matter and bonemeal with the existing soil and level the area. Dig a hole 3 or more times the diameter of the bulb. Place the bulb at the bottom of the hole, narrow end pointed up. Backfill the hole, firm soil, water thoroughly, and add 1 to 2 inches of mulch. When planting bulbs at random and not in a bed, prepare each hole as described. Multiple bulbs placed in a large single hole should not touch. If planting in a container for forcing indoors, use one that is a minimum of 6 inches in diameter and well-drained potting mix. Place bulbs 2/3 of the way into the pot, backfill, firm soil, and water thoroughly. Store in a cold location (but do not allow to freeze) for a minimum of 8 weeks, then set the plant in a sunny location and water thoroughly.

Care and Maintenance

Tulips benefit from watering through entire growing season, until leaves are brown. Foliage should remain, unfolded or twisted, until at least 50 percent are brown, and then the foliage can be removed. Pest and disease problems are minimal, except that wildlife will attempt to dig up or eat foliage.

Additional Information

Bulbs can be purchased at garden centers or by mail order. At garden centers, select the largest and firmest bulbs, with none sprouting; store in a dark, cool, dry location in a paper bag. If ordering by mail, ask about size, time of shipment, and planting instructions. Bulbs forced indoors and planted outdoors may take several years to begin flowering again. Bonemeal nutrients remain in the soil for many years and do not require frequent reapplication. Do not use manure to solve disease problems.

Additional Species, Cultivars, or Varieties

Tulipa greigii is an early-flowering species, shorter in stature and with reddish stripes on the foliage until the flowers fade. Mid-season bloomer *Tulipa* 'Triumph' is available in numerous colors.

Did You Know?

A member of the lily family, today's tulip bulbs are the result of extensive hybridizing over hundreds of years. The only color of tulip which has not yet been developed is any shade of blue. The original bulb is native to Turkey and its flower has little resemblance to today's tulips.

Winter Aconite

Eranthis hyemalis

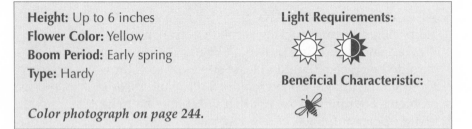

Height: Up to 6 inches
Flower Color: Yellow
Boom Period: Early spring
Type: Hardy

Color photograph on page 244.

Light Requirements:

Beneficial Characteristic:

Often the first sign of spring that greets the hungry gardener peering from a frosted window or taking a hopeful stroll around the yard is a glowing yellow blossom of the winter aconite. Its whorl of dark green leaves makes a perfectly round saucer to hold the single cup-shaped flower, usually only an inch in diameter but still a powerfully sunny omen of spring.

WHEN TO PLANT

Plant in late fall to early winter. It must be in the ground 2 or more months prior to the anticipated bloom period.

WHERE TO PLANT

The winter aconite requires rich, organic, fertile soil that is well drained but evenly moist. If planting around a tree, measure the trunk's diameter, multiply by five, and do not install bulbs any closer to tree than this distance.

HOW TO PLANT

Delineate the bed. Dig up any undesired plants or remove them with an herbicide. Spade or rototill the area, using caution under trees. Then blend 6 inches of organic matter and bonemeal with the existing soil and level the area. Dig a hole 3 or more times the diameter of the bulb, or about 3 inches. Place the bulb at the bottom of the hole, narrow end pointed up. Backfill the hole, firm soil, water thoroughly, and add 1 to 2 inches of mulch. When planting bulbs at random and not in a bed, prepare each hole as described. Multiple bulbs placed in a large single hole should not touch.

CARE AND MAINTENANCE

The plants will benefit from watering if dry through the entire growing season, until the leaves are brown. Foliage on hardy bulbs should remain, unfolded or twisted, until at least 50 percent are brown; leaves are adding energy for next year. Pest and disease problems are minimal.

ADDITIONAL INFORMATION

Bulbs can be purchased at garden centers or by mail order. At garden centers, select the largest and firmest bulbs. Although a bulb will appear as a small piece of dirt, make sure that it is not sprouting, and store in a dark, cool, dry location in a paper bag. If ordering by mail, ask about size, time of shipment, and planting instructions. Bonemeal nutrients remain in the soil for many years and do not require frequent reapplication. Do not use manure to solve disease problems.

ADDITIONAL SPECIES, CULTIVARS, OR VARIETIES

There are none available.

Did You Know?

The winter aconite is a member of the buttercup family which includes columbine and clematis. This particular plant is native to Southern Europe and has migrated through most of the continent. The species name, hyemalis, means "of winter."

CHAPTER THREE

Flowering Trees

THERE IS A CHINESE PROVERB that says, "Keep a green tree in your heart and perhaps the singing bird will come." It is a good philosophy and solid gardening advice as well, especially if the tree you keep is an ornamental variety that serves as a bird habitat. The most popular ornamental trees are usually recognized for their beautiful flowers, but they are valued by landscapers for other qualities as well. They also provide dramatic foliage color, unique branching habits, and striking bark textures. Their flowers attract butterflies and their fruits bring birds. They establish focal points and supply numerous design uses, from shading a walk, to sheltering a patio, to framing a garage, back porch, or gazebo. In all these ways, they gracefully unify the architectural and horticultural elements of a landscape. Their beauty and usefulness are sure to win them a permanent place in your heart.

Careful planning and installation and consistent care will enhance the glorious possibilities and qualities of the ornamental tree. Prior to making any purchase, consider the function of the tree in the projected location. Remember that the ultimate selection will be a powerful focal point that dramatically changes the existing view. Complete a site analysis of the designated area, determining the amount of sun exposure, what the neighboring plantings are and how they will change in size, the topography, exposure to winds, drainage, and future planned use for the area. Take a close look at each candidate, considering its mature height and width, outline or shape, branching habit, blooming season, fruit, whether or not the tree suckers and where, and whether the root system is aggressive. Will bees and other insects cause problems when the tree is in

Chapter Three

flower? Are the fruits persistent, and do they attract birds? All of this information will help you determine whether an ornamental tree will work in a specific landscape location.

Flowering trees provide benefits as soon as they are planted. Their standing and girth make any setting more dynamic regardless of the season. A way to make their visual drama even greater is to site the same variety in different settings. Many varieties of evergreen trees are considered ornamental, but they have not been included here because their seasonal changes are far less pronounced.

Chinese or Kousa Dogwood

Cornus kousa

Height and Width: 20 by 15 feet, and larger
Bloom Period: Late spring
Flower Color: Milky white
Type: Deciduous tree
Zones: 4 through 8
Color photograph on page 244.

Light Requirements:

Beneficial Characteristic:

The young Chinese dogwood is a rather awkward, top heavy tree which matures into an elegant ornamental. Its trunk and perpendicular growing branches are covered with earth-colored peeling bark. The limbs reach far and wide, their dark green leaves dramatically highlighting the soft white flowers which open from late May to early June. In late summer, berry-like fruits appear. The tree's final performance is a reddish maroon fall foliage which can persist for several weeks before the last leaf has fallen.

WHEN TO PLANT

Plant this tree in the spring before dormancy has broken while the buds are tight to reduce the amount of maintenance required during the first year. If planting after the leaves have emerged, protect the tree from wind burn during transport.

WHERE TO PLANT

The ideal location is sunny with some protection from the harshest winter winds. A well-drained, rich organic soil is essential.

HOW TO PLANT

Dig a hole three times the width and slightly less than the height of the rootball to provide the best drainage. Mix 6 inches of organic matter with the existing soil; add no fertilizer. Loosen the roots of a pot-bound tree prior to installation. After positioning a balled and burlapped tree in the hole, cut all twine and fold down burlap. Backfill the hole, firm the soil around the root system, water immediately and thoroughly, and add 2 to 3 inches of mulch. If larger trees are staked, keep wires loose to allow for movement.

CARE AND MAINTENANCE

Prevent any drought stress for several years after planting. Fertilize the second year after installation and every 3 years thereafter. Remove any staking wires after 1 year. Prune mid-summer to avoid cutting off next year's buds. There are very few pest or disease problems.

ADDITIONAL INFORMATION

Select a tree that is 4 to 8 feet tall, has a strong trunk with no open wounds, and numerous flexible branches which can appear from the ground to the top depending on the individual specimen. The flower buds are plump on the ends of the twigs; the leaf buds have more of a pointed shape. These trees are available container grown or balled and burlapped; the rootball should be approximately 3 inches in diameter for every foot of height. Companion plantings to consider are primrose, liveforever, switch grass, winter creeper, daffodils, and yellow false cypress.

ADDITIONAL SPECIES, CULTIVARS, OR VARIETIES

Cornus kousa var. *chinensis* 'Milky Way' provides even more flowers. The flowers of the *Cornus kousa* 'Moonbeam' can grow to 7 inches in diameter.

 Did You Know?

The Chinese dogwood is a member of the unique family that features only dogwoods. This native to the Far East has been used in that part of the world for centuries in temple gardens and residential landscapes. Discovered by European travelers in the mid 1800s, the Chinese dogwood was carried home for use in specialty gardens.

Donald Wyman Crabapple

Malus 'Donald Wyman'

Height and Width: 20 by 25 feet
Bloom Period: Mid-spring
Flower Color: White
Type: Deciduous tree
Zones: 4 through 7
Color photograph on page 244.

Light Requirements:

Beneficial Characteristic:

Crabapples reward those who tend them with their impressive height, abundance of flowers, and vibrant red fruits. In spring the buds swell with a pale pinkish-reddish cast and then burst into pure white blossoms. Almost immediately, the fruits for which this tree is named begin to form. The "apples" grow to a mature size of less than 1/2 inch in diameter. They turn a deep red color and persist through much of the winter providing a welcome feast for birds. The Donald Wyman crabapple is one of the best varieties both for its aesthetic qualities and its resistance to fungus problems. Its bumpy and scarred gray bark highlights the shimmery, dark green foliage.

WHEN TO PLANT

The best times to plant this tree are in the fall or the early spring before the buds open.

WHERE TO PLANT

This tree requires no particular soil type or depth, but full sun and a well-drained site are essential.

HOW TO PLANT

Dig the planting hole three times the width of the rootball for better lateral root growth and faster establishment. The depth of hole should ensure that, when the tree is placed in the hole, its crown is higher than the surrounding ground. There is no need to add amendments or fertilizer in the planting hole. Place balled and burlapped trees in the hole, remove the rope, and fold burlap downward. For containerized trees, loosen roots if pot bound before placing the tree into the hole. Backfill the hole, firm the soil around the roots, water immediately and thoroughly, and cover the planting area with 2 to 3 inches of mulch. If the tree is staked, make the wiring loose enough to allow for tree movement. Prune only dead or damaged branches.

CARE AND MAINTENANCE

Monitor rainfall and supplement as needed for 2 years after planting. Fertilize the second year after installation and every 3 years thereafter. Remove any staking wires after 1 year. There are minimal pest or disease problems. Little pruning is needed; if necessary, prune within 3 months of petal drop.

ADDITIONAL INFORMATION

Select a tree that is either container grown or balled and burlapped, 12 feet tall or less, with a straight trunk and numerous branches, their spread greater than the their height. The limbs should be heavily budded and flexible. The rootball should be approximately 3 inches in diameter for every foot of height. Companion plantings to consider are the purple leaf sand cherry, coneflower, daylily, fountain grass, and Dutch white clover.

ADDITIONAL SPECIES, CULTIVARS, OR VARIETIES

The number of available types of crabapples is enormous. The main criteria to consider when selected one is its resistance to disease problems, particularly apple scab, fireblight, powdery mildew, and cedar apple rust. Resistant varieties include *Malus* 'Autumn Glory', 'Beauty', 'Coral Cascade', or a dwarf 'Tina'.

Did You Know?

'Donald Wyman' is an improved variety of crabapple, all of which are members of the extensive rose family. Its parents were discovered in the fields and meadows of the Midwest by the English in the early 1700s, and transported back across the Atlantic for royal collector gardens. The seeds are sterile and will not germinate.

Fringetree

Chionanthus virginicus

Height and Width: 15 by 10 feet
Bloom Period: Late spring
Flower Color: White
Type: Deciduous tree
Zones: 3 through 9
Color photograph on page 244.

Light Requirements:

Beneficial Characteristic:

The fringetree has many outstanding characteristics, including its lovely fragrance, unusual flowering habit, textures that range from fine to medium to coarse depending on the season, and an adaptability to growing conditions. Its large, floppy, pale to medium green leaves are widely spaced on the branches, a configuration that allows the white cloudlike flowering plenty of room to float between the limbs. In fall the leaves turn a straw-yellow hue that offers a beautiful contrast to the small dark blue fruit and the tree's gray bark. The fringetree is usually a bonus wherever planted, but in some settings its impressive blossoms may overpower nearby plantings.

WHEN TO PLANT

Plant the fringetree from early to mid-spring, before the leaf buds have opened.

WHERE TO PLANT

A fringetree will do well in any type of soil or drainage and is best appreciated if planted in a spot near any seating or viewing area.

HOW TO PLANT

While the fringetree does not require a richer or an especially well-drained soil, the health of the tree is usually improved when attention is given to both of these conditions. If the planting spot is unimproved, follow these steps. Remove competing vegetation by digging or with a safe herbicide. Spade or rototill the area and mix 6 inches of organic matter with the existing soil, but do not add fertilizer. Dig a hole three times the width and slightly less than height of the rootball to achieve the best drainage. The root system is fibrous, so carefully remove the tree from the container or carefully cut the balling ropes and fold down the burlap. Backfill the hole and firm the soil around the root system, water immediately and thoroughly, and add 2 to 3 inches of mulch. Prune only dead or damaged branches.

CARE AND MAINTENANCE
Prevent any drought stress for several years after planting. Fertilize the second year after installation and every 3 years thereafter. Remove any staking wires after 1 year. There are very few pest or disease problems.

ADDITIONAL INFORMATION
The best height for planting is the available one, but check for pliable limbs and robust small buds all up and down the trunk. Fringetrees are available in containers or balled and burlapped, and their shapes range from shrublike to treelike, from messy to neat tight. Choose whatever is appealing for your purposes. The rootball should be approximately 3 inches diameter for every foot of height. Companion plantings to consider are the red twig dogwood, lily of the valley, snakeroot, Japanese blood grass, and lilyturf.

ADDITIONAL SPECIES, CULTIVARS, OR VARIETIES
There are none available.

🌿 Did You Know?

The earliest existing records show that fringetrees were discovered by settlers in the American lowlands and carried back to England in the mid-1700s. This member of the olive family is still considered by the English to be one of the most spectacular North American trees.

'Cherokee Princess' Dogwood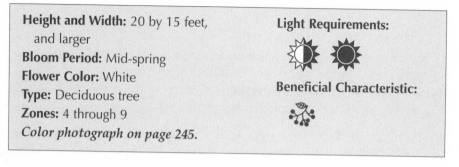

Cornus florida 'Cherokee Princess'

Height and Width: 20 by 15 feet, and larger	**Light Requirements:**
Bloom Period: Mid-spring	
Flower Color: White	**Beneficial Characteristic:**
Type: Deciduous tree	
Zones: 4 through 9	
Color photograph on page 245.	

Flowering dogwood is one of the ornamentals most commonly found in the woods, parks, and landscapes. Cherokee Princess dogwood has all the top temperament and structural aspects of the native dogwood, only at a much younger age. This means its wonderfully rustic knurled trunks are thicker and fuller at an earlier age, and that it soon produces an abundance of unforgettably pure white flowers. Its medium-green summer foliage is open, allowing light to filter through and creating a dappled shade pattern. Its fall colors vary within the world of red.

WHEN TO PLANT

Plant dogwood cultivars in the spring before they have flowered. If planted after flowering, their care requirements increase considerably.

WHERE TO PLANT

Plant in very well-drained, highly organic soil, wherever you want to create a focal point.

HOW TO PLANT

Dig the planting hole three times the width and slightly less than the height of the rootball. Provide the best drainage for the tree and a high organic content by mixing 6 inches of organic matter with the existing soil. Do not add fertilizer. Place balled and burlapped trees in the hole, remove the rope, and fold burlap downward. For containerized trees, loosen roots if pot bound before placing the tree into the hole. Backfill the hole, firm the soil around the roots, water immediately and thoroughly, and cover the planting area with 2 to 3 inches of mulch. If the tree is staked, make the wiring loose enough to allow for tree movement. Prune only dead or damaged branches.

CARE AND MAINTENANCE

Prevent any drought stress for several years after planting. Fertilize the second year after installation and every 3 years thereafter. Remove any staking wires after 1 year. Prune during dormancy to create the desired habit. There are no major pest or disease problems as long as the tree's general health is maintained.

ADDITIONAL INFORMATION

Select a tree that is 4 to 10 feet tall with no open wounds. Branching can start at the ground and continue to the top, or run anywhere in between. Flower buds are small round buttons on the ends of the twigs; the leaf buds are pointed. These trees are available in containers or balled and burlapped; the rootball should be approximately 3 inches in diameter for every foot of height. Companion plantings to consider include creeping jenny, canna, impatiens, red twig dogwood, and blue bells.

ADDITIONAL SPECIES, CULTIVARS, OR VARIETIES

Improved varieties of dogwoods include the red-flowering *Cornus florida* 'Cherokee Chief' and white-flowering *Cornus florida* 'Pendula'.

 Did You Know?

This tree improves on the well-known native dogwood which is found at the edge of the woods throughout the Eastern portion of this country.

Improved Flowering Pear

Pyrus calleryana 'Aristocrat'

Height and Width: 40 by 20 feet, and larger
Bloom Period: Spring
Flower Color: White
Type: Deciduous tree
Zones: 4 through 8
Color photograph on page 245.

Light Requirements:

The ascending branches of this tree, which tightly hug its brown-toned trunk, support some of the most beautiful early spring flowers. As the flowers begin to drop, glossy dark green leaves emerge. The foliage transforms in autumn to an unmatched red maroon blaze of leaves which persists until very late in the season. The 'Aristocrat' flowering pear has all of these characteristics but also a wider angle between the trunk and branches of which reduces the chance of storm damage. A wave or ripple in the shiny leaf adds to its polished appearance. Though the actual number of flowers produced by an improved tree may be less than the unimproved flowering pear, the difference is not noticeable to the eye.

WHEN TO PLANT

The leaves hang on the improved flowering pears very late in the fall. Once they have turned brown and before the buds open in the spring is the time to plant.

WHERE TO PLANT

Improved flowering pear requires full sun and a well-drained site.

HOW TO PLANT

Dig the planting hole three times the width and slightly less than the height of the rootball. Do not add amendments or fertilizer to the planting hole. Place balled and burlapped trees in the hole, remove the rope, and fold burlap downward. For containerized trees, loosen roots if pot bound before placing the tree into the hole. The tree's crown should be slightly higher than the surrounding ground. Back-fill the hole, firm the soil around the roots, water immediately and thoroughly, and cover the planting area with 2 to 3 inches of mulch. If the tree is staked, make the wiring loose enough to allow for tree movement. Prune only dead or damaged branches.

CARE AND MAINTENANCE

Monitor rainfall and supplement as needed for 2 years after planting. Fertilize the second year after installation and every 3 years thereafter. Remove any staking wires after 1 year. There are minimal pest or disease problems, although improved flowering pear is more susceptible to fireblight than the standard Bradford pear. Little pruning is needed; if necessary, prune within 3 months of petal drop.

ADDITIONAL INFORMATION

Select a tree that is 12 feet or less in height, with a straight trunk and numerous ascending branches. The limbs should be flexible with a large number of closely positioned buds. The rootball should be approximately 3 inches in diameter for every foot of height. Container- grown or balled and burlapped trees are both equally easy to install. Companion plantings to consider are sweet William, hosta, ribbon grass, myrtle, elephant ears, and yew.

ADDITIONAL SPECIES, CULTIVARS, OR VARIETIES

There are several types of the improved flowering pear: a slower growing type is *Pyrus calleryana* 'Redspire'; or for a narrower planting area, use *Pyrus calleryana* 'Whitehouse'.

Did You Know?

Native to China, this member of the rose family is a relatively recent introduction to the world of landscape plants. However it has quickly become one of the most popular ornamental trees and is often planted with little consideration for its mature height and width.

Redbud

Cercis canadensis

Height and Width: 20 by 20 feet, and larger
Bloom Period: Early spring
Flower Color: Pale purple
Type: Deciduous tree
Zones: 4 through 9
Color photograph on page 245.

Light Requirements:

Several unique characteristics of the redbud combine to help it make a very strong landscape statement. Its extremely open branching habit arises from a twisting trunk whose very dark gray bark reveals a cinnamon-red-orange coloration at each split or crack in the bark. The blossoms erupt randomly throughout on the branches, and their pale purple color is unequaled in nature. When the leaf buds first open, they are a pale purple hue until the heart-shaped leaf unfurls in a moderate shade of green. The fall foliage color is not spectacular, but the dark brown pea pods that dangle where flowers bloomed offer an eye-catching element in the autumn landscape.

WHEN TO PLANT
It is best to plant redbuds in late fall to early spring before the buds break.

WHERE TO PLANT
Redbuds are happiest in full sun, and the soil must be well drained.

HOW TO PLANT
Dig the planting hole three times the width and slightly less than the height of the rootball. Do not add amendments or fertilizer to the planting hole. Place balled and burlapped trees in the hole, remove the rope, and fold burlap downward. For containerized trees, loosen roots if pot bound before placing the tree into the hole. The tree's crown should be slightly higher than the surrounding ground. Backfill the hole, firm the soil around the roots, water immediately and thoroughly, and cover the planting area with 2 to 3 inches of mulch. If the tree is staked, make the wiring loose enough to allow for tree movement. Prune only dead or damaged branches.

CARE AND MAINTENANCE

Monitor rainfall and supplement as needed for 2 years after planting. Fertilize the second year after installation and every 3 years thereafter. Remove any staking wires after 1 year. Watch for bot canker, verticillium, and a few insects, and control as needed. Very little pruning should be needed.

ADDITIONAL INFORMATION

Select a tree that is 10 feet or less in height, either single or multi-trunked, with a sparse and open branching habit and zigzag patterning with buds at each turn. The limbs should be stiffly flexible and ascending. The rootball should be approximately 3 inches in diameter for every foot of height. Redbuds are available grown in containers or balled and burlapped. Companion plantings to consider are creeping juniper, winter aconite, autumn crocus, flowering tobacco, and rose verbena.

ADDITIONAL SPECIES, CULTIVARS, OR VARIETIES

An amazing redbud with white flowers is the *Cercis canadensis* var. *alba*. Another, *Cercis canadensis* 'Forest Pansy', has purplish leaves until mid-summer.

Did You Know?

A member of the bean family, the redbud's seeds germinate quite easily, making it a good tree for educating children about plant growth. The heart-shaped foliage is a reliable thermometer: during the hottest part of a summer day, the leaves wilt, only to recover their shape at sundown.

Red Japanese Maple

Acer palmatum 'Bloodgood'

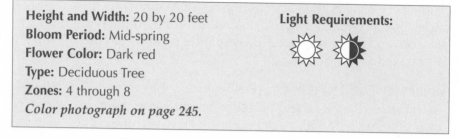

Height and Width: 20 by 20 feet
Bloom Period: Mid-spring
Flower Color: Dark red
Type: Deciduous Tree
Zones: 4 through 8
Color photograph on page 245.

Light Requirements:

Few trees rival the Japanese maple for grace and commanding presence. Wherever it grows, it dominates the field of view as though it were placed on a pedestal. Many factors contribute to its powerful impact on landscapes. While the bark is a very dark shade of grayish brown, the thickness of the foliage makes it nearly invisible even at close range. The tree is made up of a massive amount of limbs, which become quite narrow and willowy at their apex. Their bouncy movement is delightful to watch when the foliage is present, and remains eye-catching even after leaf drop. Finally, its deep maroon foliage is mesmerizing, and unlike many of its relatives, the Japanese maple holds this intense hue through the entire growing season.

WHEN TO PLANT

The best time to plant Japanese maples is in the spring before the leaf buds open. If purchase occurs after the foliage is developing, take care to protect the leaves from wind burn during transport.

WHERE TO PLANT

This tree requires a richly organic, well-drained soil. The red-leafed Japanese maple commands and deserves trophy status, so put it in a worthy location.

HOW TO PLANT

Remove competing vegetation from planting site by digging or with a safe herbicide. Dig a hole three times the width and slightly less than the height of the rootball. Mix 6 inches of organic matter with the existing soil, but add no fertilizer. If planting a container-grown tree, loosen pot-bound roots prior to installation. After positioning a balled and burlapped tree in the hole, cut the rope and fold down the burlap. Backfill the hole, firm the soil around the root system, water immediately and thoroughly, and add 2 to 3 inches of mulch over the top. Prune only dead or damaged branches.

CARE AND MAINTENANCE
Monitor rainfall and supplement as needed for 2 years after planting. Fertilize the second year after installation and every 3 years thereafter. Prune during the summer to minimize bleeding. There are no major pest or disease problems.

ADDITIONAL INFORMATION
The red-leafed Japanese maple has several different and equally exciting trunk configurations; select one with a minimal amount of dead twigs. The perpendicular branching should be limber and full of tiny buds. Trees are available in containers or balled and burlapped; the rootball should be approximately 5 inches diameter for every foot of height. Available sizes range from 1 to 6 feet. Companion plantings to consider are bugle weed, grape hyacinth, periwinkle, yellow false cypress, and columbine.

ADDITIONAL SPECIES, CULTIVARS, OR VARIETIES
A beautiful red cut-leaf variety is the *Acer palmatum* var. *dissectum* 'Ever Red' and a spectacular green one is *Acer palmatum* var. *dissectum* 'Waterfall'.

🌿 Did You Know?
For centuries this native to the Orient has been planted in Chinese and Japanese gardens. If was first brought to England in the early 1800s. The winged seeds hang on through much of the fall, gradually turning red. A close relative is the full moon maple which has a slightly different leaf structure.

Serviceberry

Amelanchier arborea

Height and Width: 20 by 10 feet, and larger
Bloom Period: Early spring
Flower Color: White
Type: Deciduous Tree
Zones: 4 through 9
Color photograph on page 245.

Light Requirements:

Beneficial Characteristics:

Probably the least well known native ornamental tree, one scattered through the valleys and woods of the Midwest, is the serviceberry. The serviceberry's trunk and branches are not particularly attractive on their own, but this ornamental plays a bit of hide and seek and provides seasonal surprises. In spring its flock of white flowers, which hang like bells, signal that winter is over. The pollinated flowers mature in summer into small, round, dark red fruit that draw hungry birds. The growing season culminates in a show of numerous shades of fall color.

WHEN TO PLANT

The best time to select and plant serviceberries is late winter or early spring.

WHERE TO PLANT

Serviceberries do well in a sunny or shady location that has a highly organic, well-drained soil.

HOW TO PLANT

Dig the planting hole three times the width and slightly less than the height of the rootball. Mix 6 inches of organic matter with the existing soil, but add no fertilizer. Place balled and burlapped trees in the hole, remove the rope, and fold burlap downward. For containerized trees, loosen roots if pot bound before placing the tree into the hole. Backfill the hole, firm the soil around the roots, water immediately and thoroughly, and cover the planting area with 2 to 3 inches of mulch. If the tree is staked, make the wiring loose enough to allow for tree movement. Prune only dead or damaged branches.

Care and Maintenance

Prevent any drought stress for several years after planting. Fertilize the second year after installation and every 3 years thereafter. Remove any staking wires after 1 year. There are minimal pest and disease problems.

Additional Information

Serviceberries get their strength and disposition from the twisted and natural trunk, so select a tree accordingly, making certain that there are no open wounds. The branches are most likely to be growing only on the top half of the tree. Pointed buds are found along the very gentle and somewhat frail looking limbs. Trees are available in containers or balled and burlapped; the rootball should be approximately 3 inches in diameter for every foot of height. Select tree size according to availability. Companion plantings to consider are columbine, snowball bush, spider flower, grape hyacinth, and creeping jenny.

Additional Species, Cultivars, or Varieties

Consider using the *Amelanchier arborea* 'Autumn Sunset' for a site near a hardscape or structure that may reflect or produce extra heat in the summer.

FLOWERING TREES

Did You Know?

Although it was first described in the mid 1700s, the serviceberry remains an almost unknown native tree because it is so difficult to propagate and thus very few plants are available. The hiplike fruits of this member of the rose family member are very attractive to birds.

Tricolor Beech

Fagus sylvatica 'Purpurea Tricolor'

Height and Width: 20 by 20 feet, and larger
Bloom Period: Mid-spring
Flower Color: Pale green
Type: Deciduous tree
Zones: 4 through 7
Color photograph on page 245.

Light Requirements:

Refined, mysterious, and never conspicuous, the tricolor beech is an elegant addition to any landscape. Its equally spaced perpendicular limbs climb to the top of a grayish, rather smooth trunk, producing a distinguished pyramidal shape. The architectural impact of this ornamental tree is even more pronounced over winter when the branches are bare. The foliage that unfurls from pointed leaf buds in the spring in a remarkable mixture of variegated rose-red and pink makes the tricolor beech seem to be a kind of hybrid tree-flower that quietly blooms all season long.

WHEN TO PLANT

The best time of year to plant the tricolor beech is in the spring before dormancy has broken, when the buds are still tight. If planting after the leaves emerge, protect the foliage from wind burn during transport.

WHERE TO PLANT

Plant tricolor beech in a deep, rich, well-drained organic soil. The aesthetic impact of the foliage is best if the tree is protected from the afternoon sun which can cause leaf scorch.

HOW TO PLANT

If the planting spot is unimproved, follow these steps. Remove competing vegetation by digging or with a safe herbicide. Spade or rototill the area and mix 6 inches of organic matter with the existing soil, but do not add fertilizer. If the soil was previously amended and is easily worked, there is no need to make these improvements. Dig a hole three times the width and slightly less than height of the rootball to achieve the best root growth and drainage. If planting a container-grown tree, loosen pot-bound roots prior to installation. After positioning a balled and burlapped tree in the hole, remove the rope and fold down the burlap. Backfill the hole and firm the soil around the root system, water immediately and thoroughly, and add 2 to 3 inches of mulch. Prune only dead or damaged branches.

CARE AND MAINTENANCE

Prevent any drought stress for several years after planting. Fertilize the second year after installation and every 3 years thereafter. Remove any staking wires after 1 year. Prune during the summer to minimize bleeding. There are minimal pest and disease problems.

ADDITIONAL INFORMATION

Select a tree that is 3 to 6 feet tall with a single trunk and no open wounds. The flexible branching can begin near the ground and move all the way up the trunk. The leaf buds are long and pointed. Choose either a container grown or balled and burlapped tree, according to size preference. The rootball should be approximately 3 inches in diameter for every foot of height. Companion plantings to consider are glory-of-the-snow, impatiens, yews, celandine poppy, and lady's mantle.

ADDITIONAL SPECIES, CULTIVARS, OR VARIETIES

Many different types of beech trees with colorful foliage are on the market. A cascading type is *Fagus sylvatica* 'Purpurea Pendula'. A more compact grower is *Fagus sylvatica* 'Purpurea Nana'.

Did You Know?

The tricolor beech has been grown in Europe for several centuries because its lumber is prized for furniture and cabinetry. The nuts produced by this tree are used to supplement livestock feed. The tricolor beech is a natural mutation that was discovered in Europe in the late 1800s, when cuttings were taken and cultivation began.

Washington Hawthorn N

Crataegus phaenopyrum

Height and Width: 20 by 20 feet, and larger
Bloom Period: Late spring
Flower Color: White
Type: Deciduous tree
Zones: 3 through 7
Color photograph on page 245.

Light Requirements:

Beneficial Characteristic:

There is no season when the Washington hawthorn disappoints. In spring, its single trunk or cluster of mini-trunks is spangled with leaf and flower buds. By early June, it is blanketed with fully developed green foliage and spotted with the creamy white flowers that are beginning to emerge. Soon bees arrive and do their summer work, turning the flower sprays into bunches of ripe red fruit by mid to late September. The leaves turn a warm shade of yellowish-orange ranging to red in the fall, and in winter the Washington hawthorne shows off its dark pitted bark against a white bank of snow. This ornamental works well as a free-standing tree, or when planted in a grove, and makes an effective screen or barrier.

WHEN TO PLANT

It is best to install Washington hawthorn in late fall through the early spring, allowing it plenty of time to become established before summer.

WHERE TO PLANT

The Washington hawthorn requires full sun and a well-drained soil. Site with caution because of its thorns.

HOW TO PLANT

Dig the planting hole three times the width and slightly less than the height of the rootball. Do not add amendments or fertilizer to the hole prior to installation. Place balled and burlapped trees in the hole, remove the rope, and fold burlap downward. For containerized trees, loosen roots if pot bound before placing the tree into the hole. Backfill the hole, firm the soil around the roots, water immediately and thoroughly, and cover the planting area with 2 to 3 inches of mulch. If the tree is staked, make the wiring loose enough to allow for tree movement. Prune only dead or damaged branches.

CARE AND MAINTENANCE
Monitor rainfall and supplement as needed for 2 years after planting. Fertilize the second year after installation and every 3 years thereafter. Remove any staking wires after 1 year. There are minimal pest and disease problems. Very little pruning should be needed.

ADDITIONAL INFORMATION
Select a containerized or balled and burlapped tree that is 10 feet or less in height with a thick single trunk or a cluster of smaller ones; either trunk formation will provide the same outline. The branching should be numerous, rigid, and very thorny, with buds equally spaced along the entire length. The rootball should be approximately 3 inches in diameter for every foot of height. Companion plantings to consider are bleeding heart, Japanese blood grass, Hall's honeysuckle, and snowdrops.

ADDITIONAL SPECIES, CULTIVARS, OR VARIETIES
There are none available.

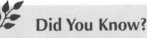

Did You Know?

A member of the rose family, the hawthorn is the state tree and flower of Missouri. It offers an excellent, well-protected spot for many birds to nest. Growing a hawthorn tree from seed is a long-term project; seeds can take up to two years to germinate.

CHAPTER FOUR

Ground Covers

THE FINISHING TOUCHES GIVEN to a well-tailored suit, a holiday table, or a beautifully appointed room are often so subtle they go unnoticed except for an enhanced overall look. The same is true for the group of plants which provide finishing touches to gardens and landscapes: the ground covers. While they are sometimes regarded merely as a living mulch or as outdoor carpeting, ground covers actually have a landscape design value that is hard to overstate. They create harmony and rhythm between diverse plants and structures, and work in the brightest sun as well as the deepest shade. Beyond their diverse textural and color contributions, ground covers also visually and physically cool down areas, retain soil moisture, reduce erosion, and offer habitats for insects, birds, and wildlife. Technically, ground covers include lawns, living plants, and nonliving or inorganic materials. Here we will concentrate on traditional living ground covers.

One of the greatest virtues of ground covers is the tasteful solution they frequently provide to various landscape problems. For example, when older plantings die and are removed, the ground cover quickly steps in to cover the empty area. They also help fill in gaps when plants are pruned back and provide visual and physical support to newly installed plants. The best ground cover solution to a landscape problem is directly related to the growth habit of the ground cover's root system and its evergreen quality. Though several different ground covers may thrive in numerous sites, careful analysis of the location and specific candidate plants is crucial. Factors to keep in mind are the desired aesthetic effect, proximity to structures, topography, drainage, exposure, and existing plantings. Be sure to know the soil profile and what improvements may be needed, depending on the short-term and long-term cultural requirements for establishing the ground cover.

Chapter Four

Unlike other types of plants, many varieties of ground covers cannot be mixed in close proximity. Selecting one ground cover that is evergreen and interplanting it with another type that is herbaceous is an excellent way to achieve variety without creating visual chaos. Establishing a number of stands of the same type of ground cover can be equally rewarding. When choosing a site for ground covers, be aware that foot traffic in that area must be limited. Once a ground cover is established, it requires a minimum amount of care.

Ground covers provide a visual and a physical stair step between all other aspects of the landscape. They link lawn to trees, front walk to house, the wet shady side of yard to its sunnier expanse. They make these connections, and many others, quietly or with a punch, depending on the variety and the gardener's whim.

Bishop's Weed

Aegopodium podograria 'Picta'

Flower Color: White
Bloom Period: Late spring
Type: Herbaceous
Zones: 4 through 8
Color photograph on page 245.

Light Requirements:

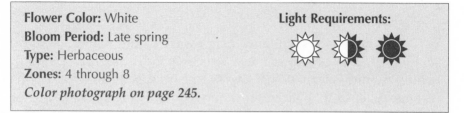

From mid-spring until the fall night-time temperatures become quite cold, bishop's weed spreads a green and white blanket over the landscape. Glowing in the moonlight, accenting the shade during the day, and highlighting other sunny plantings, this ground cover offers an attractive transition between many different environments. The green and white markings on the leaves simultaneously create repetition and visual rhythm, both essential qualities a successful design. Late in the summer, bishop's weed makes a humble offering of flowers in a spray of white blossoms. Companion plantings to consider are pfitzers and techy arborvitae.

WHEN TO PLANT

Plant bishop's weed in the spring and in the early fall.

WHERE TO PLANT

Bishop's weed does well in rich, organic, fertile soil that is well drained and sited in sun to deeper shade. If planting under a tree, multiply the trunk's diameter by three, and do not install the plants any closer than this distance to the trunk.

HOW TO PLANT

Keep plants well-watered prior to installation. Delineate the bed, removing undesirable plants by digging or with an herbicide. Rototill or spade the soil to a depth of 6 to 8 inches, using caution under trees, and mix 6 inches of amendments with the existing soil before raking the bed smooth. Dig a hole three times the diameter of the root ball. Pinch back the flowers and one-quarter of the stem. Remove the plant from the pot and loosen the roots if pot bound. Place the plant at a depth slightly higher than previously grown, backfill the hole, firm the soil, and water thoroughly. Place 1 inch of mulch around the plants.

CARE AND MAINTENANCE

This plant benefits from twice-monthly fertilizing with a balanced food during the growing season, but apply none after mid-August. Water if the growing season is dry, that is if there is less than 1 inch of water in a 10-day period. If possible, water evergreen types in the winter. Mow in the mid-summer if the foliage has browned; new growth will emerge and be fuller. Trim or cut back as needed to control growth. Weeds will be a problem for up to 5 years in a new planting area; careful use of herbicides or hand digging are the only real solutions. Geotextile weed barriers can be used but they slow establishment times. Pests and diseases are not problematic.

ADDITIONAL INFORMATION

These plants are available in pots ranging from 1 pint to 1 gallon. The only advantage to larger plants is that they require less care and take a shorter time to infill. The rough formula for determining how long it will take 1-pint plants to cover an area of ground is: 1 year if planted 6 inches apart, 2 years if planted 9 inches apart, 3 or more years if planted 12 inches apart. Inspect the plants before purchasing for consistent leaf color and size.

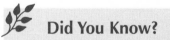

ADDITIONAL SPECIES, CULTIVARS, OR VARIETIES

There are none available.

🌿 Did You Know?

Bishop's weed grows by an underground root system and is a member of the carrot family, which also includes dill and other plants grown for food, flavoring, and medicinal purposes. It is native to Europe and Asia. Another common name, "snow on the mountain," indicates the overall white coloration of the leaf.

Bugle Weed

Ajuga reptans

Flower Color: Blue
Bloom Period: Spring
Type: Semi-evergreen
Zones: 4 through 9

Color photograph on page 245.

Light Requirements:

Beneficial Characteristics:

B ugle weed seems ready to leap its nursery container in the spring, so eager is this colorful ground cover to spread out in larger spaces. Its heavily textured and numerous leaves create immediate impact whether planted as a pure stand or used as an underplanting for perennials, trees, and shrubs. Its spectacular stalks of iridescent blue, bugle-shaped flowers shoot straight up from the base of the foliage, lasting longer during cooler weather. Companion plantings to consider are barberry and the redbud tree.

WHEN TO PLANT

Plant bugle weed in the spring and early fall.

WHERE TO PLANT

Good drainage is essential, and this plant does well in average to rich organic soil. If planting under a tree, multiply the trunk's diameter by three, and do not install plants any closer than this distance to the trunk.

HOW TO PLANT

Keep plants well watered prior to installation. Delineate the bed, removing undesirable plants by digging or with an herbicide. Rototill or spade the soil to a depth of 6 to 8 inches, using caution under trees, and mix 6 inches of amendments with the existing soil before raking the bed smooth. If planting in a sloped area, use erosion netting. Dig a hole three times the diameter of the root ball. Pinch back the flowers and one-quarter of the stem. Remove the plant from the pot and loosen the roots if pot bound. Place the plant at a depth slightly higher than previously grown, backfill the hole, firm the soil, and water thoroughly. Place 1 inch of mulch around the plants.

Care and Maintenance

This plant benefits from twice-monthly fertilizing with a balanced food during the growing season, but apply none after mid-August. Water if the growing season is dry, that is, if there is less than 1 inch of water in a 10-day period. Mow over in the late fall to remove any leaf debris that may have collected. Trim or cut back in the spring or fall to control growth. Weeds will be a problem for up to 5 years in a new planting area; careful use of herbicides or hand digging are the only real solutions. Geotextile weed barriers can be used, but they slow establishment times. Remove 1-foot-square sections of established bugle weed every spring to prevent crown rot. Other diseases and pests are not problematic.

Additional Information

Bugle weed is available in pots ranging from 2¹/₄-inch cell packs to 1-gallon containers. The only advantage to larger plants is that they require less care and take a shorter time to infill. The rough formula for determining how long it will take 2¹/₄-inch plants to cover an area of ground is: 2 or more years if planted 6 inches apart, 3 or more years if planted 9 inches apart, and 5 years or more if planted 12 inches apart. Inspect the plants for consistent leaf color and size.

Additional Species, Cultivars, or Varieties

Ajuga pyramidalis 'Metallica Crispa' has a very crinkled, glossy leaf when grown in the full sun and is not an aggressive spreader. *Ajuga reptans* 'Burgundy Glow' has a variegated, tri-colored leaf.

Did You Know?

Bugle weed is a member of the mint family. The species name reptans *means "creeping" and refers to this plant's growth habit.*

Chameleon Plant

Houttuynia cordata

Flower Color: White **Bloom Period:** Summer **Type:** Herbaceous **Zones:** 4 through 8 *Color photograph on page 245.*	**Light Requirements:**

Just like the changeable creature for which it is named, the chameleon plant demands a second look. Its alternating, tri-colored leaves—green, highlighted by milky white and pale red—create a visual charge. The leaves can grow as large as 3 inches wide and 3 inches long, a size that helps this plant fill in quickly and more than adequately fulfills the need for color during the growing season. Because chameleon plant can reach a height of 15 inches, it is very useful in distant plantings where physical and textural background uplift is always a plus. Its tolerance for wet soil also makes it a good candidate for plantings in lower terrains where water sometimes collects. Chameleon plant is best used in a larger area where there are no other herbaceous plants. Companion plantings to consider are bald cypress and red twig dogwood.

WHEN TO PLANT
Plant chameleon plant in the spring and early fall.

WHERE TO PLANT
Chameleon plant does well in rich, organic, fertile soil which can have any moisture level except very dry or constant standing water.

HOW TO PLANT
Keep plants well watered prior to installation. Delineate the bed, removing undesirable plants by digging or with an herbicide. Rototill or spade the soil to a depth of 6 to 8 inches, using caution under trees, and mix 6 inches of amendments with the existing soil before raking the bed smooth. If planting in a sloped area, use erosion netting. Dig a hole three times the diameter of the root ball. Pinch back the flowers and one-quarter of the stem. Remove the plant from the pot and loosen the roots if pot bound. Place the plant

at a depth slightly higher than previously grown, backfill the hole, firm the soil, and water thoroughly. Place 1 inch of mulch around the plants.

CARE AND MAINTENANCE
This plant benefits from twice-monthly fertilizing with a balanced food during the growing season, but apply none after mid-August. Water to ensure no periods of extreme drought; the minimum amount of water allowed is 1 inch in a 10-day period. Mow over in the late fall to remove any leaf debris that may have collected. Trim or cut back in the spring or fall to control growth. Weeds will be a problem for up to 5 years in a new planting area; careful use of herbicides or hand digging are the only real solutions. Geotextile weed barriers can be used, but they slow establishment times. Pests and diseases are not problematic.

ADDITIONAL INFORMATION
Chameleon plant is available in pots ranging from 2¹/4-inch cell packs to 1-gallon containers. The only advantage to larger plants is that they require less care and take a shorter time to infill. The rough formula for determining how long it will take 2¹/4-inch plants to cover an area of ground is: 2 or more years if planted 6 inches apart, 3 or more years if planted 9 inches apart, and 5 years or more if planted 12 inches apart. Inspect the plants for consistent leaf color and size.

ADDITIONAL SPECIES, CULTIVARS, OR VARIETIES
There are none available.

Did You Know?
Chameleon plant belongs to the lizard's tail family, named for the spike habit of their flower, which is native to moist valleys and mountains from Japan south to Java and Nepal. The species name, cordata, *means "heart-shaped," which is the leaf configuration.*

Creeping Jenny

Lysimmachia nummularia

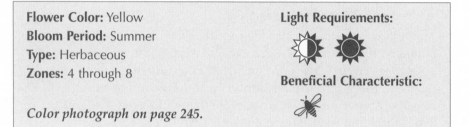

Flower Color: Yellow

Bloom Period: Summer

Type: Herbaceous

Zones: 4 through 8

Color photograph on page 245.

Light Requirements:

Beneficial Characteristic:

Creeping Jenny provides a living landscape carpet. It rarely reaches an inch in height, slowly spreading to embrace any tree, shrub, perennial, or annual that is planting in its path. Its linear growth habit is interrupted only by the tiny, solitary, bright yellow flowers that stand about an inch above the nearly perfectly circular leaves. This ground cover works well as an edging for other plantings or along walks and patios. It requires minimal care while supplying a subtle and tasteful finishing touch to many landscape settings. Companion plantings to consider are snowball bush, Japanese maple, and globe arborvitae.

WHEN TO PLANT

Plant creeping Jenny in the spring and early fall.

WHERE TO PLANT

Creeping Jenny does well in evenly moist, rich organic soil which is well drained. If planting under a tree, multiply the trunk's diameter by three and do not install plants any closer to trunk than this distance.

HOW TO PLANT

Keep plants well watered prior to installation. Delineate the bed, removing undesirable plants by digging or with an herbicide. Rototill or spade the soil to a depth of 6 to 8 inches, using caution under trees, and mix 6 inches of amendments with the existing soil before raking the bed smooth. If planting in a sloped area, use erosion netting. Dig a hole three times the diameter of the root ball. Pinch back the flowers and one-quarter of the stem. Remove the plant from the pot and loosen the roots if pot bound. Place the plant at a depth slightly higher than previously grown, backfill the hole, firm the soil, and water thoroughly. Place 1 inch of mulch around the plants.

CARE AND MAINTENANCE
This plant benefits from twice-monthly fertilizing with a balanced food during the growing season, but apply none after mid-August. Water to ensure no periods of extreme drought, that is, if there is less than 1 inch of water in a 10-day period. Mow over in the late fall to remove any leaf debris that may have collected. Trim or cut back in the spring or fall to control growth. Weeds will be a problem for up to 5 years in a new planting area; careful use of herbicides or hand digging are the only real solutions. Geotextile weed barriers can be used, but they slow establishment times. Pests and diseases are not problematic.

ADDITIONAL INFORMATION
Creeping Jenny is available in pots ranging from 2^1/$_4$-inch cell packs to 1-gallon containers. The only advantage to larger plants is that they require less care and take a shorter time to infill. The rough formula for determining how long it will take 2^1/$_4$-inch plants to cover an area of ground is: 2 or more years if planted 6 inches apart, 3 or more years if planted 9 inches apart, and 5 years or more if planted 12 inches apart. Inspect the plants for consistent leaf color and size.

ADDITIONAL SPECIES, CULTIVARS, OR VARIETIES
Lysimmachia nummularia 'Aurea' is a yellowed-leafed variety.

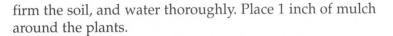

Did You Know?

Creeping Jenny belongs to the primrose family, which includes several plants that are grown commercially for use in home aquariums, but not the plant found in Missouri whose common name is "primrose." This ground cover is native to Europe and over time has naturalized in various areas of the eastern United States.

Creeping Juniper

Juniperus horizontalis

Flowers: Insignificant

Type: Coniferous evergreen

Zones: 3 through 9

Color photograph on page 245.

Light Requirements:

Creeping juniper offers a perfect solution for steep hillsides that seem impossible to maintain, rock formations that cry out for planted trimmings, or flat areas that are exposed to very direct sun. Its coarse, spreading texture mimics and follows all the contours of the planting space, and its form is noncompetitive, meaning that nearby structures or plantings are made to look even more dynamic. Its coloration is unlike most other evergreens, and the hues change in tone with the coming and going of the winter season.

WHEN TO PLANT

Creeping juniper is so tough and durable that it can be planted at any time of the year except when the ground is frozen.

WHERE TO PLANT

Plant creeping juniper in any type of soil, from dry and poor to organic and moist. The site must be well drained, with no standing water ever.

HOW TO PLANT

Keep plants well watered prior to installation. Delineate the bed, removing undesirable plants by digging or with an herbicide. Rototill or spade the soil to a depth of 6 to 8 inches, using caution under trees, and mix 6 inches of amendments with the existing soil before raking the bed smooth. If planting in a sloped area, use erosion netting. Dig a hole three times the diameter of the root ball. Pinch back the flowers and one-quarter of the stem. Remove the plant from the pot and loosen the roots if pot bound. Place the plant at a depth slightly higher than previously grown, backfill the hole, firm the soil, and water thoroughly. Place 1 inch of mulch around the plants.

CARE AND MAINTENANCE

This plant benefits from monthly fertilizing with a tree and shrub food during the growing season, from May to August. Water to ensure no periods of extreme drought, that is, if there is less than 1 inch of water in a 10-day period. If possible, water in the winter also. Trim, prune, or cut back in the spring or fall to control growth. Weeds will be a problem for up to 5 years in a new planting area; careful use of herbicides or hand digging are the only real solutions. Geotextile weed barriers can be used, but they slow establishment times. Pests and diseases are not problematic.

ADDITIONAL INFORMATION

Creeping juniper is available in pots ranging from 1 to 5-gallon containers. The only advantage to larger plants is that they require less care and take a shorter time to infill. Inspect the plants for consistent leaf color and basically symmetrical growth.

ADDITIONAL SPECIES, CULTIVARS, OR VARIETIES

Juniperus horizontalis 'Blue Chip' is a steel-blue variety that provides more texture because it does not spread flat on the ground.

Did You Know?

Creeping juniper is native to the North American eastern seashore, where it is found growing in the cracks of cliffs. The species name, horizontalis, *refers to the plant's low-reaching, armlike growing habit. An oil squeezed from the blue berries (cones) of some species is used in the making of gin.*

Creeping Phlox

Phlox subulata

Flower Color: Various
Bloom Period: Spring
Type: Evergreen
Zones: 4 through 8

Color photograph on page 246.

Light Requirements:

Beneficial Characteristic:

Once you've seen a stand of creeping phlox burst into color in the spring, you'll watch for it eagerly each year. A massive amount of intense pure color flows across the entire planting when it blooms, completely obscuring the foliage. Creeping phlox works well on a steep, dry slope that is difficult to mow, in a specialty rock garden, or along the top of a wall. It is most deeply enjoyed during spring, and the cooler the early spring temperatures, the longer the flowering cycle will last. After bloom, the foliage remains green until the end of the growing cycle, conforming to the rock or wall or shrub shapes it embraces. Companion plantings to consider are yews and Japanese blood grass.

WHEN TO PLANT

Plant creeping phlox in the spring and into early summer. If you can resist the temptation to enjoy the color immediately, it is best to plant this ground cover after it has finished flowering.

WHERE TO PLANT

Creeping phlox requires well-drained soil; the soil profile and nutrient level can be average or better.

HOW TO PLANT

Keep plants well watered prior to installation. Delineate the bed, removing undesirable plants by digging or with an herbicide. Rototill or spade the soil to a depth of 6 to 8 inches, using caution under trees, and mix 6 inches of amendments with the existing soil before raking the bed smooth. If planting in a sloped area, use erosion netting. Dig a hole three times the diameter of the root ball. Pinch back the flowers and one-quarter of the stem. Remove the plant from the pot and loosen the roots if pot bound. Place the plant

at a depth slightly higher than previously grown, backfill the hole, firm the soil, and water thoroughly. Place 1 inch of mulch around the plants.

CARE AND MAINTENANCE

This plant benefits from one fertilizing with a balanced food during the growing season; apply none after mid-August. Water only if there is an extended drought, a period longer than 14 days without 1 inch of rain; if possible, water in the winter if extremely dry. Trim or cut back in the spring or fall to control growth. Divide the plants every 4 to 5 years to maintain the blooming quality. Weeds will be a problem for up to 5 years in a new planting area; careful use of herbicides or hand digging are the only real solutions. Geotextile weed barriers can be used, but they slow establishment times. Pests and diseases are not problematic.

ADDITIONAL INFORMATION

Creeping phlox is available in pots ranging from 2^1/$_4$-inch cell packs to 1-gallon containers. The only advantage to larger plants is that they require less care and take a shorter time to infill. The rough formula for determining how long it will take 2^1/$_4$-inch plants to cover an area of ground is: 2 or more years if planted 6 inches apart, 3 or more years if planted 9 inches apart, and 5 years or more if planted 12 inches apart. Inspect the plants for consistent leaf color and size.

ADDITIONAL SPECIES, CULTIVARS, OR VARIETIES

Phlox subulata 'Candystripe' has a flower that is white and pink striped.

Did You Know?

Creeping phlox is a member of the very small phlox family, most members of which are found in North America. It is native to the sunny mountain faces in the northeast. The species name subulata *refers to the slender, sharply pointed shape of the foliage.*

Crown Vetch

Coronilla varia

Flower Color: Pink
Bloom Period: Summer into fall
Type: Herbaceous
Zones: 4 through 8

Color photograph on page 246.

Light Requirements:

Beneficial Characteristics:

The long reach of crown vetch makes this magnificent ground cover a plant that is strictly for large expanses of landscape where maintenance may be difficult or impossible. The surface coverage for an individual mature plant can be up to 36 square feet. Underground modified stems, which serve the function of roots, are responsible for the aggressive growth habit. This underground network stabilizes the soil and prevents erosion. As growth continues, crown vetch becomes one of the main players in a natural or rusticated setting. It provides an important source of pollen and nectar for bees and butterflies, and at a mature height of 2 feet it offers a sanctuary for small wildlife. The foliage dies back to the ground in the late fall and early winter. This ground cover is well suited to a dry, unimproved, rocky hillside, the edge of a pond, or an open area ready to be naturalized. Companion plantings to consider are the upright juniper and crabapple.

WHEN TO PLANT
Plant crown vetch in the spring or fall, using either seed or sprouted seedlings.

WHERE TO PLANT
Crown vetch requires full sun in a well-drained, poor to average soil.

HOW TO PLANT
Keep plants well watered prior to installation. Do not remove any planting from the area where the crown vetch is to be established, and do not disturb the surface with any type of rototilling or spading. Spread the crown vetch seed or plant seedlings among existing plant material. If the area is sloped, use erosion netting. Place 1 inch of mulch around the plants.

CARE AND MAINTENANCE

This plant benefits from one fertilizing with a balanced food during growing season, none after mid August. Water if the growing season is dry, that is, less than 1 inch of water in a 10-day period. Mow in the late fall, if possible, to remove any leaf debris that may have collected. Pest and disease problems are minimal.

ADDITIONAL INFORMATION

Space seedlings 2 feet apart. The seeding rate is $^1/_2$ pound per 1000 square feet. Before seeding, cover the area with inoculate, a powdery black nitrogen fixative.

ADDITIONAL SPECIES, CULTIVARS, OR VARIETIES

There are none available.

Did You Know?

Crown vetch belongs to the pea family. It captures nitrogen from the air and stores it in root nodules. As a result, if crown vetch is incorporated into the soil, a process called green manuring, the soil's nutrient level is improved. The genus name, Coronilla, *means "crown" and describes the flower configuration.*

Dead Nettle

Lamium maculatum

Flower Color: Pinkish purple
Bloom Period: Summer
Type: Herbaceous
Zones: 4 through 8
Color photograph on page 246.

Light Requirements:

Dead nettle flows easily into the gaps that lie between perennials, shrubs, and trees in the shade garden. It smoothes the lines of other plantings, allowing the eye to move uninterrupted over the landscape. The heart-shaped foliage supports a spiky cluster of flowers, so delicate in hue that their color almost disappears in the shade. In midsummer, the inflorescence adds a new accent of color. This ground cover works well whether planted in a small colony or installed over a large area.

WHEN TO PLANT
Plant dead nettle in the spring or early fall.

WHERE TO PLANT
Dead nettle does well in a well-drained soil which can be either moist and organic in composition or be on the dry side. The best growth will occur in richer soils. If planting under a tree, multiply the trunk's diameter by three and do not install plants any closer than this distance to the trunk.

HOW TO PLANT
Keep plants well watered prior to installation. Delineate the bed, removing undesirable plants by digging or with an herbicide. Rototill or spade the soil to a depth of 6 to 8 inches, using caution under trees, and mix 6 inches of amendments with the existing soil before raking the bed smooth. If planting in a sloped area, use erosion netting. Dig a hole three times the diameter of the root ball. Pinch back the flowers and one-quarter of the stem. Remove the plant from the pot and loosen the roots if pot bound. Place the plant at a depth slightly higher than previously grown, backfill the hole, firm the soil, and water thoroughly. Place 1 inch of mulch around the plants.

CARE AND MAINTENANCE

This plant benefits from twice-monthly fertilizing with a balanced food during the growing season, but apply none after mid-August. Water to ensure no periods of extreme drought, that is, if there is less than 1 inch of water in a 10-day period. Mow over in the late fall to remove any leaf debris that may have collected. Trim or cut back in the spring or fall to control growth. Weeds will be a problem for up to 5 years in a new planting area; careful use of herbicides or hand digging are the only real solutions. Geotextile weed barriers can be used, but they slow establishment times. Pests and diseases are not problematic.

ADDITIONAL INFORMATION

Dead nettle is available in pots ranging from $2^1/4$-inch cell packs to 1-gallon containers. The only advantage to larger plants is that they require less care and take a shorter time to infill. The rough formula for determining how long it will take $2^1/4$-inch plants to cover an area of ground is: 2 or more years if planted 6 inches apart, 3 or more years if planted 9 inches apart, and 5 years or more if planted 12 inches apart. Inspect the plants for consistent leaf color and size.

ADDITIONAL SPECIES, CULTIVARS, OR VARIETIES

Lamium maculatum 'White Nancy' and *Lamium maculatum* 'Beacon Silver' are two improved varieties that offer more color and differing coloration on the leaf.

Did You Know?

Dead nettle is a member of the mint family which spreads by underground rhizomes. Native to parts of Northern Africa, Europe, and Asia, it has become naturalized in areas of the United States.

Dutch White Clover

Trifolium repens

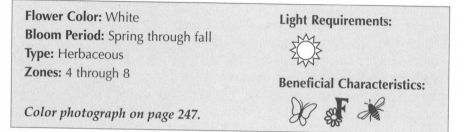

Flower Color: White
Bloom Period: Spring through fall
Type: Herbaceous
Zones: 4 through 8

Light Requirements:

Color photograph on page 247.

Beneficial Characteristics:

A field of Dutch white clover is a fine sight to behold. The horizontal growth habit of this plant, and the white flowers that float above its bright green foliage, accentuate all the minor dips and major changes in the topography, creating a rolling feel to the land. This ground cover is extraordinarily useful. It eliminates the necessity of mowing, except for once a year, and provides a sea of pollen for honey bees. It also stabilizes hillsides and slopes. The textural aspect of the entire planting is coarse, while individual plants offer a fine look and feel. Among its virtues are the enjoyment children, and adults as well, will have searching for a four-leaf clover and the good luck this discovery is certain to bring. Companion plantings to consider are inkberry and Norway spruce.

WHEN TO PLANT

Plant Dutch white clover in the spring whether growing from seed or sprouted seedlings.

WHERE TO PLANT

Dutch white clover requires full sun in a well-drained, poor to average soil.

HOW TO PLANT

Keep the plants well watered prior to installation. Delineate the area where Dutch white clover is to be established, but do not remove any planting or disturb the surface with any rototilling or spading. Spread seed or plant seedlings among existing plant material. If planting in a sloped area, use erosion netting. Place 1 inch of mulch around the plants.

CARE AND MAINTENANCE

This plant benefits from one fertilizing with a balanced food during the growing season, with none applied after mid-August. Water if the growing season is dry, that is, if there is less than 1 inch of water in a 10-day period. Mow in the late fall, if possible, to remove any leaf debris that may have collected. Pest and disease problems are minimal.

ADDITIONAL INFORMATION

If installing plants, space 2 feet apart. The seeding rate is 1/2 pound per 1000 square feet. Before spreading seed, cover the planting area with inoculate, a black powdery nitrogen fixative.

ADDITIONAL SPECIES, CULTIVARS, OR VARIETIES

There are none available.

 Did You Know?

Dutch clover is a member of the pea family. It captures nitrogen from the air, stores it in root nodules, and then, if incorporated into the soil, will boost the nutrients. The genus name, Trifolium, *means "three leaflets," and the species name,* repens, *refers to the plants creeping growth habit.*

English Ivy

Hedera helix

Flower Color: Greenish
Bloom Period: Summer
Type: Broadleaf Evergreen
Zones: 4 through 8
Color photograph on page 247.

Light Requirements:

nglish ivy may make you think of manor homes or gothic academic courtyards, but the cool and tranquil effect of this ground cover benefits nearly any home or landscape style. The coarseness of English ivy works with foreground, mid-ground, and background sitings, and the color is such a deeply rich green that almost any other planting pales in comparison and makes an interesting contrast. English ivy usually does not flower or produce fruit when growing along the ground, except occasionally in a very mature planting. Consider planting it around crimson king maple or burning bush.

WHEN TO PLANT
Plant English ivy in the spring or early fall.

WHERE TO PLANT
English ivy does well in average to rich, fertile, organic, well drained soil from light to deep shade. If planting under a tree, multiply the trunk's diameter by three and do not install plants any closer to the trunk than this distance.

HOW TO PLANT
Keep plants well watered prior to installation. Delineate the bed, removing undesirable plants by digging or with an herbicide. Rototill or spade the soil to a depth of 6 to 8 inches, using caution under trees, and mix 6 inches of amendments with the existing soil before raking the bed smooth. If planting in a sloped area, use erosion netting. Dig a hole three times the diameter of the root ball. Pinch back the flowers and one-quarter of the stem. Remove the plant from the pot and loosen the roots if pot bound. Place the plant at a depth slightly higher than previously grown, backfill the hole, firm the soil, and water thoroughly. Place 1 inch of mulch around the plants.

Care and Maintenance

This plant benefits from monthly fertilizing with a balanced food during the growing season; apply none after mid-August. Water if the growing season is dry, that is, if there is less than 1 inch of water in a 10-day period. If possible, water in the winter also. Mow in the late fall to remove any leaf debris that may have collected and to encourage fuller plantings. Trim, prune, or cut back in the spring or fall to control growth. Clinging roots along the stem enable English ivy to climb almost any surface; prune as needed. Weeds will be a problem for up to 5 years in a new planting area; careful use of herbicides or hand digging are the only real solutions. Geotextile weed barriers can be used, but they slow establishment times. Pests and diseases are not problematic.

Additional Information

English ivy is available in pots ranging from 2¼-inch cell packs to 1-gallon containers. The only advantage to larger plants is that they require less care and take a shorter time to infill. The rough formula for determining how long it will take 2¼-inch plants to cover an area of ground is: 2 or more years if planted 6 inches apart, 3 or more years if planted 9 inches apart, and 5 years or more if planted 12 inches apart. Inspect the plants for consistent leaf color and size.

Additional Species, Cultivars, or Varieties

Hedera helix 'Bulgaria' is drought resistant and *Hedera helix* 'Thorndale' has foliage with distinctive, lighter colored veins.

🌿 Did You Know?

English ivy belongs to the ginseng family, some members of which are used in rice paper production and others for medicine. Though naturalized in the United States, this ground cover is native to Northern Africa, Europe, and Asia. Many of the variegated forms, although hardy, will revert to solid green leaves after a period of time.

Hall's Honeysuckle

Lonicera japonica 'Halliana'

Flower Color: White
Bloom Period: June through October
Type: Evergreen
Zones: 4 through 9

Color photograph on page 247.

Light Requirements:

Beneficial Characteristics:

Some care must be exercised in selecting a good spot for planting Hall's honeysuckle, since it grows very rapidly, quickly becomes fully established. Its coarsely textured, dense mat of foliage moves through and around low-lying obstacles, and confronted with a fence or wall, this nonclinging plant will wind and twist into itself until enough support is created to allow it to move upward and over the barrier. The cool-colored, glossy foliage glistens in the sun. Pure white, extremely fragrant flowers appear above the foliage, attracting bees. As they age, the flowers yellow and then produce a fruit that is highly attractive to birds.

WHEN TO PLANT

Plant Hall's honeysuckle in the spring and again in the early fall.

WHERE TO PLANT

Hall's honeysuckle is tolerant of poor to richly organic soils and should be sited in well drained spot. If planting under a tree, multiply the trunk's diameter by three and do not install plants any closer than this distance to the trunk.

HOW TO PLANT

Keep plants well watered prior to installation. Delineate the bed, removing undesirable plants by digging or with an herbicide. Rototill or spade the soil to a depth of 6 to 8 inches, using caution under trees, and mix 6 inches of amendments with the existing soil before raking the bed smooth. If planting in a sloped area, use erosion netting. Dig a hole three times the diameter of the root ball. Pinch back the flowers and one-quarter of the stem. Remove the plant from the pot and loosen the roots if pot bound. Place the plant

at a depth slightly higher than previously grown, backfill the hole, firm the soil, and water thoroughly. Place 1 inch of mulch around the plants.

CARE AND MAINTENANCE
This plant benefits from twice-monthly fertilizing with a balanced food during the growing season, with none applied after August. Water if the growing season is dry, that is, if there is less than 1 inch of water in a 10-day period. If possible, water in the winter also. In late fall, mow to remove any leaf debris that may have collected and to encourage fuller plantings. Trim, prune, or cut back in the spring or fall to control growth. Weeds will be a problem for up to 5 years in a new planting area; careful use of herbicides or hand digging are the only real solutions. Geotextile weed barriers can be used, but they slow establishment times.

ADDITIONAL INFORMATION
Hall's honeysuckle is available in pots ranging from 2$\frac{1}{4}$-inch cell packs to 1-gallon containers. The only advantage to larger plants is that they require less care and take a shorter time to infill. The rough formula for determining how long it will take 2$\frac{1}{4}$-inch plants to cover an area of ground is: 2 or more years if planted 6 inches apart, 3 or more years if planted 9 inches apart, and 5 years or more if planted 12 inches apart. Check plants for consistent leaf color and size.

ADDITIONAL SPECIES, CULTIVARS, OR VARIETIES
Lonicera japonica 'Aureo-reticulata' has a variegated foliage and wants full sun; a purplish green-leafed variety is *Lonicera japonica* 'Purpurea'.

Did You Know?
Hall's honeysuckle was introduced into cultivation in the very early 1800s. The species name, japonica, *indicates the plant is native to the Orient and, more specifically, to Japan.*

Lilyturf
Liriope spicata

Flower Color: Pale blue
Bloom Period: Late summer
Type: Herbaceous
Zones: 4 through 9

Light Requirements:

Beneficial Characteristics:

Color photograph on page 247.

Lilyturf became available in garden centers only in the last quarter century, but has quickly moved to the top of the list of ground covers in high demand. It closely and consistently hugs the profile of the landscape, emphasizing any and all topographic peculiarities and provides astonishing animation, especially when stirred by wind. Its dark green foliage glistens in the sun, and the bluish flowers and black fruits add to this plant's beauty. Lilyturf is effective at controlling soil erosion. It grows right up to the trunks of large trees, and sets the stage as well for large perennials, shrubs, and ornamental trees.

WHEN TO PLANT
Plant lilyturf in the spring and early fall.

WHERE TO PLANT
Lilyturf does well in rich, fertile, organic, well-drained soil in almost any sun exposure. If planting under a tree, multiply the trunk's diameter by three and do not plant any closer than this distance to the trunk.

HOW TO PLANT
Keep plants well watered prior to installation. Delineate the bed, removing undesirable plants by digging or with an herbicide. Rototill or spade the soil to a depth of 6 to 8 inches, using caution under trees, and mix 6 inches of amendments with the existing soil before raking the bed smooth. If planting in a sloped area, use erosion netting. Dig a hole three times the diameter of the root ball. Pinch back the flowers and one-quarter of the stem. Remove the plant from the pot and loosen the roots if pot bound. Place the plant at a depth slightly higher than previously grown, backfill the hole,

firm the soil, and water thoroughly. Place 1 inch of mulch around the plants.

CARE AND MAINTENANCE
This plant benefits from monthly fertilizing with a balanced food during the growing season, with none applied after August. Water if the growing season is dry, that is, if there is less than 1 inch of water in a 10-day period. If possible, water in the winter also. In late fall, mow to remove any leaf debris that may have collected and to encourage fuller plantings. Dig up and remove in the spring or fall to control growth. Weeds will be a problem for up to 5 years in a new planting area; careful use of herbicides or hand digging are the only real solutions. Divide every 5 years to maintain vigor. Pests and diseases are not a problem.

ADDITIONAL INFORMATION
Lilyturf is available in pots ranging from 2¼-inch cell packs to 1-gallon containers. The only advantage to larger plants is that they require less care and take a shorter time to infill. The rough formula for determining how long it will take 2¼-inch plants to cover an area of ground is: 2 or more years if planted 6 inches apart, 3 or more years if planted 9 inches apart, and 5 years or more if planted 12 inches apart. Check plants for consistent leaf color and size.

ADDITIONAL SPECIES, CULTIVARS, OR VARIETIES
Liriope muscari has a wider blade and is a clump-growing variety, and *Liriope muscari* 'Variegata' has a white stripe running the length of the leaf.

Did You Know?
Lilyturf belongs to the lily family which is native to Japan, China, and Vietnam. Another common name is "monkey grass," which seems to imply that this plant belongs to an entirely different kind of family. The species name, spicata, means "spike," and refers to the flowering habit.

Myrtle

Vinca minor

Flower Color: Blue
Bloom Period: Spring
Type: Broadleaf Evergreen
Zones: 4 through 8
Color photograph on page 247.

Light Requirements:

The lustrous, dark green foliage of myrtle and its pastel blue spring flower make it a favorite among ground covers. Even though the leaves grow thickly close to the ground, the thin stems are still visible. This growth habit creates a look that incorporates both fine and coarse textures. You can take advantage of all of its fine attributes by simply allowing myrtle to spread and naturalize. Companion plantings to consider include any spring flowering bulb or the Norway spruce.

WHEN TO PLANT

Plant myrtle in the spring or early fall.

WHERE TO PLANT

Myrtle does well in average to rich, fertile, organic, well-drained soil, from the full sun to deep shade. If planting under a tree, measure the trunk's diameter, multiply by three, and do not install any closer than this distance to the trunk.

HOW TO PLANT

Keep plants well watered prior to installation. Delineate the bed, removing undesirable plants by digging or with an herbicide. Rototill or spade the soil to a depth of 6 to 8 inches, using caution under trees, and mix 6 inches of amendments with the existing soil before raking the bed smooth. If planting in a sloped area, use erosion netting. Dig a hole three times the diameter of the root ball. Pinch back the flowers and one-quarter of the stem. Remove the plant from the pot and loosen the roots if pot bound. Place the plant at a depth slightly higher than previously grown, backfill the hole, firm the soil, and water thoroughly. Place 1 inch of mulch around the plants.

CARE AND MAINTENANCE

This plant benefits from monthly fertilizing with a balanced food during the growing season, with none applied after August. Water if the growing season is dry, that is, if there is less than 1 inch of water in a 10-day period. If possible, water in the winter also. In late fall, mow to remove any leaf debris that may have collected, reducing potential disease problems. Trim, prune, or cut back in the spring or fall to control growth. Weeds will be a problem for up to 5 years in a new planting area; careful use of herbicides or hand digging are the only real solutions. Geotextile weed barriers can be used, but they slow establishment times. Pests are not a problem, and with proper drainage, neither are diseases.

ADDITIONAL INFORMATION

Myrtle is available in pots ranging from 2¹/₄-inch cell packs to 1-gallon containers. The only advantage to larger plants is that they require less care and take a shorter time to infill. The rough formula for determining how long it will take 2¹/₄-inch plants to cover an area of ground is: 2 or more years if planted 6 inches apart, 3 or more years if planted 9 inches apart, and 5 years or more if planted 12 inches apart. Check plants for consistent leaf color and size.

ADDITIONAL SPECIES, CULTIVARS, OR VARIETIES

Vinca minor 'Alba' is a white-flowering variety, and *Vinca minor* 'Bowlesii' has a darker blue flower that is produced in greater numbers.

Did You Know?

Myrtle belongs to the dogbane family, most members of which are found in the tropics. Its relatives provide edible fruits, parts used in the manufacture of medicines, and types of sap for rubber production. This ground cover is native to various regions of Europe. The species name, minor, *refers to the smaller leaf.*

Stone Crop

Sedum spurium 'Dragon's Blood'

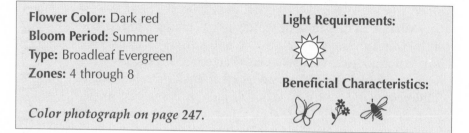

Flower Color: Dark red
Bloom Period: Summer
Type: Broadleaf Evergreen
Zones: 4 through 8

Color photograph on page 247.

Light Requirements:

Beneficial Characteristics:

The reddish bronze foliage of stone crop gives this ground cover a unique, and nearly "unreal" look. It thrives on a dry, hot, sunny slope, colorfully filling in gaps between boulders. When the summer days are at their hottest, stone crop produces red, star-shaped flowers that set the ground on fire. Once the flowers die, the ever-red foliage returns to view, shrinking as days grow colder until the plant resembles a red moss. Companion plantings to consider are yellow false cypress and Saint Johnswort.

WHEN TO PLANT

Plant stone crop in the spring and into early summer.

WHERE TO PLANT

Stone crop requires a well-drained site, and will thrive in a poor, average, or rich organic soil, with varying nutrient levels.

HOW TO PLANT

Keep plants well watered prior to installation. Delineate the bed, removing undesirable plants by digging or with an herbicide. Rototill or spade the soil to a depth of 6 to 8 inches, using caution under trees, and mix 6 inches of amendments with the existing soil before raking the bed smooth. If planting in a sloped area, use erosion netting. Dig a hole three times the diameter of the root ball. Remove the plant from the pot and loosen the roots if pot bound. Place the plant at a depth slightly higher than previously grown, backfill the hole, firm the soil, and water thoroughly. Place 1/2 inch of mulch around the plants.

CARE AND MAINTENANCE

This plant benefits from one fertilizing with a balanced food during the growing season, with none applied after mid-August. Water only if there is an extended drought period, that is, if there is less than 1 inch of rain in more than 14 days. Trim or cut back in the spring or fall to control growth. Divide plants every 4 to 5 years in a new planting area. Weeds are a problem for up to 5 years in a new planting area; the careful use of herbicides or hand digging are the only real solutions. Geotextile weed barriers can be used, but they slow establishment times. Pests and diseases and not problematic.

ADDITIONAL INFORMATION

Stone crop is available in pots ranging from 2¹/₄-inch cell packs to 1-gallon containers. The only advantage to larger plants is that they require less care and take a shorter time to infill. The rough formula for determining how long it will take 2¹/₄-inch plants to cover an area of ground is: 2 or more years if planted 6 inches apart, 3 or more years if planted 9 inches apart, and 5 years or more if planted 12 inches apart. Check plants for consistent leaf color and size.

ADDITIONAL SPECIES, CULTIVARS, OR VARIETIES

Sedum spurium 'Tricolor' has a variegated, multi-colored leaf, and *Sedum spurium* 'Weihenstephaner Gold' is yellow flowered.

🌿 Did You Know?

Stone crop is a member of a nonthorny cactus group which includes the kalanchoe. This ground cover is native to the Caucasus mountains and is found growing in spots with very little soil. The species name, spurium, *means "false," and possibly refers to a false cactus.*

Sweet Woodruff

Galium ordoratum

Flower Color: White
Bloom Period: Late spring
Type: Herbaceous
Zones: 4 through 8

Color photograph on page 247.

Light Requirements:

Beneficial Characteristic:

A sea of perfectly tailored sweet woodruff plants is perfect for the wide shaded space. The plant's single whirled, darker green leaf overlaps with the leaves of neighboring plants, making a dense, finely textured carpet. This density of foliage helps sweet woodruff magnify the aesthetic qualities of any adjacent plant, which seems to pop out and seem even more astounding. In mid-summer, when the garden is beginning to quiet down a little from the explosion of late spring, this ground cover produces a cluster of small, fragrant, star-shaped flowers that, depending on the weather, float above the leaf for a considerable period of time. The blossoms can give the impression that a frost has occurred. Companion plantings to consider are hostas, witch hazels, and amur maple.

WHEN TO PLANT
Plant sweet woodruff in the early spring and early fall.

WHERE TO PLANT
Sweet woodruff requires a rich, organic, well-drained soil. If planting under a tree, measure the diameter of the trunk, multiply by three, and do not install the plants any closer to the trunk than this distance.

HOW TO PLANT
Keep plants well watered prior to installation. Delineate the bed, removing undesirable plants by digging or with an herbicide. Rototill or spade the soil to a depth of 6 to 8 inches, using caution under trees, and mix 6 inches of amendments with the existing soil before raking the bed smooth. If planting in a sloped area, use erosion netting. Dig a hole three times the diameter of the root ball. Remove the plant from the pot and loosen the roots if pot bound. Place the plant at a depth slightly higher than previously grown,

backfill the hole, firm the soil, and water thoroughly. Place 1 inch of mulch around the plants.

Care and Maintenance
This plant benefits from twice-monthly fertilizing with a balanced food during the growing season, with none applied after mid-August. Water if the growing season is dry, that is, if there is less than 1 inch of water in a 10-day period. In late fall, mow to remove any leaf debris that may have collected and to encourage fuller plantings. Trim, prune, or cut back in the spring or fall to control growth. Weeds will be a problem for up to 5 years in a new planting area; careful use of herbicides or hand digging are the only real solutions. Geotextile weed barriers can be used, but they slow establishment times. Pest and disease problems are minimal.

Additional Information
Sweet woodruff is available in pots ranging from 1-pint to 1-gallon containers. The only advantage to larger plants is that they require less care and take a shorter time to infill. Quantity needed is related to area's square footage and pot size. General rules on spacing and coverage time frame for 1 pint plants are 6 inches apart one to two years, 9 inches spacing three to four years plus 12 inches means five years plus. Inspect plants for consistent leaf color and size. The rough formula for determining how long it will take 1-pint plants to cover an area of ground is: 1 to 2 years if planted 6 inches apart, 3 to 4 years if planted 9 inches apart, and 5 or more years if planted 12 inches apart.

Additional Species, Cultivars, or Varieties
There are none available.

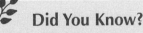

Did You Know?
Odoratum, *the species name of sweet woodruff, refers to the fragrant quality of the crushed leaf, which is used for flavoring May wine.*

135

Winter Creeper

Euonymus fortunei 'Colorata'

Flower Color: Pinkish
Bloom Period: Summer
Type: Broadleaf Evergreen
Zones: 4 through 8
Color photograph on page 247.

Light Requirements:

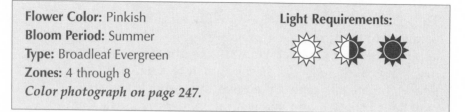

The 2-inch-long, elliptical, dark-green leaves of winter creeper grow so thickly that their supporting stems are completely obscured. Lighter markings on the leaves and a paler underside, when exposed, work to highlight this ground cover, especially in shady plantings. Winter creeper does not flower for several years after it is first planted, but with maturity produces a pale pink blossom. When pollinated, the flower develops into a capsule holding a red fruit that attracts birds. The cold of winter stimulates a change in the color of the foliage, which contributes to this ground cover's multiple seasonal appeal. Plant winter creeper in larger spaces and allow it to naturalize to take full advantage of its superior qualities. Companion plantings to consider are lilac and Japanese maples.

WHEN TO PLANT

Plant winter creeper in the spring or early fall.

WHERE TO PLANT

Winter creeper does well in average to rich, fertile, organic, well-drained soil, and thrives in sites that range from full sun to deep shade. If planting under a tree, multiply the trunk's diameter by three and do not install plants any closer than this distance to the trunk.

HOW TO PLANT

Keep plants well watered prior to installation. Delineate the bed, removing undesirable plants by digging or with an herbicide. Rototill or spade the soil to a depth of 6 to 8 inches, using caution under trees, and mix 6 inches of amendments with the existing soil before raking the bed smooth. If planting in a sloped area, use erosion netting. Dig a hole three times the diameter of the root ball. Remove the plant from the pot and loosen the roots if pot bound.

Place the plant at a depth slightly higher than previously grown, backfill the hole, firm the soil, and water thoroughly. Place 1 inch of mulch around the plants.

CARE AND MAINTENANCE

This plant benefits from twice-monthly fertilizing with a balanced food during the growing season, with none applied after mid-August. Water if the growing season is dry, that is, if there is less than 1 inch of water in a 10-day period. In late fall, mow to remove any leaf debris that may have collected and to encourage fuller plantings. Trim, prune, or cut back in the spring or fall to control growth. Weeds will be a problem for up to 5 years in a new planting area; careful use of herbicides or hand digging are the only real solutions. Geotextile weed barriers can be used, but they slow establishment times. Clinging roots along stem enable this ground cover to climb nearly any obstacle; prune as needed. Diseases are not problematic. If white scale appears, control as needed.

ADDITIONAL INFORMATION

Winter creeper is available in pots ranging from 2¹/₄-inch cell packs to 1-gallon containers. The only advantage to larger plants is that they require less care and take a shorter time to infill. The rough formula for determining how long it will take 2¹/₄-inch plants to cover an area of ground is: 2 or more years if planted 6 inches apart, 3 or more years if planted 9 inches apart, and 5 years or more if planted 12 inches apart. Check plants for consistent leaf color and size.

ADDITIONAL SPECIES, CULTIVARS, OR VARIETIES

Euonymus fortunei 'Minima' and *Euonymus fortunei* 'Kewensis' are varieties that have smaller leaves.

Did You Know?

Winter creeper is related to the bittersweet vine, which is native to Missouri, and the burning bush, which is found naturally from Central Japan to Southern Korea.

CHAPTER FIVE

Lawns

A LL LANDSCAPING DECISIONS and plant choices for residential yards, whether urban, suburban, or rural, rest (so to speak) upon the lawn. Its health and beauty directly affect the overall impression of the yard, and the contrasts it provides in height, color, and texture to all the other plantings add unity and depth to every view.

We demand much of lawn grass. It must be beautiful but also able to take a beating, durable to weather and foot traffic. We want it to perform both as a backyard athletic field and as a setting for mani-cured flower beds. Today's lawn grass meets these performance standards, while also stabilizing the soil from erosion and buffering temperatures by absorbing heat, making it the single most important element of a yard.

Prior to the late 1940s, only royalty and wealthy people enjoyed the tasteful qualities of lawns as we know them today. Until then, green spaces around most homes were largely random mixtures of whatever was growing, and they were mowed primarily to keep out snakes or mosquitoes or to make a pathway to the clothesline. During the 1950s, Americans' leisure time greatly increased, and much of that extra time went into work on their homes and lawns. At the same time, agricultural chemical companies began offering new formulas for weed control and fertilizers for residential use, and seed companies began marketing basically pure, weed-free grass seeds for lawns—the first available type being the 'Merion' Kentucky bluegrass. Affordable, sophisticated, and easier-to-use equipment for mowing and watering also became available. All of these new prod-ucts, as well as tougher turfgrasses, pesticides, and herbicides, made attractive, tasteful, aesthetically pleasing lawns available to middle-class homeowners. Lawns became a hot topic of discussion and a source of usually friendly competition among neighbors.

Chapter Five

Today, there are two very different types of lawn grasses available, warm-season grasses and cool-season grasses. The Missouri River valley offers a generally useful dividing line between the growing zones for these grasses. North of the river, warm-season grasses will struggle to survive and often die. South of the river, either type will survive.

Building a healthy, beautiful, and lasting lawn requires careful and thorough planning. Begin by evaluating the existing lawn, its health and particular makeup. Then determine the scope of the improvement project, whether a total or partial renovation is anticipated, and the nature of the proposed changes in the landscape. Consider how the lawn will be used, the quantity of shade, and how the lawn changes depending on the time of year. Next, complete a site evaluation, detailing the topography, the amount of sunlight the yard has at different times of day, and whether nearby plantings will be affected by any proposed changes. Consider where building downspouts, overhangs, and shadows are necessary concerns. All of this information will help determine the best type of lawn grass for a particular yard.

The basic ways of establishing turfgrasses in a landscape are seeding, sodding, plugging, and sprigging. Each method has pluses and minuses. They differ in expense, planting time and physical effort required to plant, degree of difficulty in maintaining, and fertilizing requirements. Though the endeavor to establish a beautiful lawn may seem a demanding leisure-time activity, the returns are incomparable. Healthy lawn grasses not only look good to your neighbors and passersby, their soft springy texture feels good on your feet and they revive your spirits with their green message of life, growth, and beauty.

Creeping Red Fescue

Festuca rubra ssp. *rubra*

Color: Pale green
Texture: Very fine
Type: Cool season

Light Requirements:

The creeping red fescue offers smooth transitions in a landscape shaped by shadows from overhead branching. The fine-textured blades, which are reddish purple at the base, spread easily across patches of shadow, rolling up around tree trunks, shrubs, and the foundations of buildings, gazebos, and stone benches. It pools around stepping stones in cooler corners of the yard and carpets quiet seating sanctuaries. Soft to the touch, but able to stand up to competition from tree roots, mosses, and lichens, creeping red fescue offers a vibrant alternative to traditional shade-tolerant groundcovers.

WHEN TO PLANT

The best time of year for seeding is from September through early October when the warm ground speeds germination. The second best time is later in the spring. Overseed as needed, at least every fall, to get the best coverage.

WHERE TO PLANT

The brighter the light and more distinctive the shadows cast in a location, the better conditions are for the stand of turf. Although creeping red fescue is shade tolerant, be aware that the spacing between individual grass plants may have to be considerable in areas of deep shade, which will have an impact on the lawn's visual performance.

HOW TO PLANT

Delineate the area to be planted. Dig up undesired plants or remove them with an herbicide. Have a sample of soil tested, and add the nutrients that the soil test indicates are needed and also 1 to 2 inches of organic amendments. Rototill, using caution under trees, or hand spade to blend the existing soil with new amendments. Rake the area smooth and ensure proper drainage. Spread weed-free seed and starter fertilizer and rake lightly. Use erosion netting if the site is sloped. Keep the surface moist until seed germinates; then water for longer periods of time but do not allow puddles to form.

CARE AND MAINTENANCE

During the first growing season, fertilize the grass monthly, using the seed-starter formula. After the first season, fertilize monthly from September through early December. Apply liquid iron in the summer to improve the grass color. From April through mid-June, and mid- September to the last mowing, allow grass to grow to $2^1/2$ to 3 inches. During the summer, allow grass to grow to 3 to $3^1/2$ inches. Never cut off more than 2 inches, and continue mowing until growth stops. Water the lawn in the morning, ensuring that it receives 1 inch of water every 10 days. Core aerate if the soil is compacted and if thatch is becoming a problem. Minimize herbicide applications, controlling weeds instead by digging.

ADDITIONAL INFORMATION

Sod is generally not available for the creeping red fescues, but if you obtain sod, see the entry on bluegrass for sod installation. For the best performance in a shaded area, purchase high-quality seed and mix several varieties together. Disperse seed with a calibrated spreader, 5 to 7 pounds per 1000 square feet. To maximize coverage, make two passes over the lawn, the second one perpendicular to the first. Sharpen mower blades two or more times a year, but it is not necessary to bag lawn clippings. Do not allow fallen leaves to accumulate on the lawn, and try to minimize foot traffic. Relatives of creeping red fescue are found in meadows throughout North America, from Canada to Mexico, and also in Northern Africa and Europe. This group, sometimes called the chewing fescues, was originally cultivated as a pasture or forage grass.

ADDITIONAL SPECIES, CULTIVARS, OR VARIETIES

Festuca rubra ssp. *trichophylla* 'Dawson', *Festuca rubra rubra* 'Flyer', and *F. r.* ssp. *rubra* 'Pennlawn' are three additional varieties. All can be combined to get the best coverage.

Kentucky Bluegrass

Poa pratensis

Color: Blue-green

Texture: Fine

Type: Cool season

Light Requirements:

Kentucky bluegrass is the standard bearer by which all other lawn grasses are evaluated, with virtually none matching its classic qualities. Smooth and evenly graceful, a lawn of pure bluegrass is breathtaking to all beholders. Its fine texture, when considered en masse, has a giant coarseness that sets off all plantings, and its cooling blue-green color offers a striking contrast to trees, shrubs, and colorful flower beds. Sometimes the exceptional beauty of a Kentucky bluegrass lawn reverses the roles between lawn and plantings, allowing the lawn to become the focal point and the plantings its ornaments. Bluegrass is a cool-season grass, becoming semi-dormant in the heat of summer and returning to grandeur in the fall.

WHEN TO PLANT

Seeding is best from September to early October, and also possible in mid-spring. Sodding can occur any time of year, except when the ground is frozen, with spring or fall being the best times.

WHERE TO PLANT

Plant in well-drained soil, in full sun or very light shade.

HOW TO PLANT

Delineate the area to be planted. Dig up undesired plants or remove them with an herbicide. Have a sample of soil tested, and add the nutrients that the soil test indicates are needed and also 1 to 2 inches of organic amendments. Rototill, using caution under trees, or hand spade to blend the existing soil with new amendments. Rake area smooth and ensure proper drainage. If laying sod, place sod pieces edge to edge with no gaps and water immediately, staking upper corners on a slope. If seeding, disperse seed with a calibrated spreader, 2 to 3 pounds per 1000 square feet, making two passes to maximize coverage. Apply seed-starter fertilizer and rake lightly. Use erosion netting if the site is sloped. Keep the ground moist until seed germinates, then water for longer periods of time but do not allow puddles to form.

Care and Maintenance

During the first growing season, fertilize the grass monthly, whether sodded or seeded, using the seed-starter formula. After the first season, fertilize monthly with winterizer from September through early December, depending on the weather. Do not apply any herbicides or pesticides during the first two months on either sod or seed, and then apply only with proper diagnosis. From April through mid-June, and mid-September to the last mowing, allow grass to grow to $2^1/2$ to 3 inches. During the summer, allow grass to grow to 3 to $3^1/2$ inches. Never cut off more than 2 inches, and continue mowing until growth stops. Water the lawn in the morning, ensuring that it receives 1 inch of water every week. Core aerate in mid-spring and power rake in the fall if the development of thatch makes it necessary.

Additional Information

Bluegrass goes into various levels of dormancy in the summer and should not be fertilized at this time. Sod should have soil that is $1/2$ inch thick, with white roots throughout and no dead patches. Sod is perishable, so purchase only as much as can be laid in the dedicated time and keep it moist prior to installation. Sod is considered established once it resists when tugged on. Purchase weed-free seed and overseed each September for 5 years. Sharpen mower blades twice a year. Bagging lawn clippings is not necessary, but do not allow leaves to accumulate on lawn. Bluegrass is native to Northern Africa and Europe and has become naturalized in various areas in the cool temperate regions. It was first planted and harvested as a cash crop in Kentucky. An easily digested and nutritious forage plant, bluegrass is invaluable for pasture plantings.

Additional Species, Cultivars, or Varieties

Overseeding even established bluegrass lawns can be beneficial. Consider using *Poa pratensis* 'Adelphi', 'Ram 1', or 'Midnight', among others.

Perennial Rye

Lolium perenne

Color: Blue-green
Texture: Medium
Type: Cool season

Light Requirements:

Perennial rye is simply a tough and durable plant. It may not win awards, but its glossy foliage and reddish base provide this variety with some aesthetic overtones. Rather than standing alone, perennial rye is best used as part of a mix, and has proven itself almost essential to lawns grown on Missouri soil and exposed to Missouri weather. Though not as blue-green as bluegrass, perennial rye still functions nicely when mixed with bluegrass or turf-type fescues and never appears out of place.

WHEN TO PLANT

The best time of year for seeding is from September through early October when the warm ground speeds germination. The second best time is later in the spring. Overseed every fall to ensure consistent coverage since this variety is somewhat short-lived.

WHERE TO PLANT

Plant in a well-drained site in full sun.

HOW TO PLANT

Delineate the area to be planted. Dig up undesired plants or remove them with an herbicide. Have a sample of soil tested, and add the nutrients that the soil test indicates are needed and also 1 to 2 inches of organic amendments. Rototill, using caution under trees, or hand spade to blend the existing soil with new amendments. Rake the area smooth and ensure proper drainage. If laying sod, place sod pieces edge to edge with no gaps and water immediately, staking upper corners on a slope. If seeding, disperse seed with a calibrated spreader, 6 to 7 pounds in the fall or 9 to 10 pounds in the spring per 1000 square feet, making two passes to maximize coverage. Apply seed-starter fertilizer and rake lightly. Use erosion netting if the site is sloped. Keep the ground moist by watering up to four times daily until seed germinates. Then water for longer periods of time, but less often, and do not allow puddles to form.

CARE AND MAINTENANCE

Use a seed-starter formula to fertilize the grass during establishment. After the first season, fertilize monthly with winterizer from September through early December, depending on the weather. Apply liquid iron in summer to improve color. From April through mid-June, and mid-September to the last mowing, allow grass to grow to $2^1/2$ to 3 inches. During the summer, allow grass to grow to 3 to $3^1/2$ inches. Never cut off more than 2 inches, and continue mowing until growth stops. Water the lawn in the morning, ensuring that it receives 1 inch of water every 10 days. Core aerate yearly in mid-spring, and power rake in the fall. Apply herbicides on an as-needed basis. Pest problems are minimal.

ADDITIONAL INFORMATION

Sod is generally not available for the perennial ryes, but if it is obtained see the bluegrass entry for installation instructions. You will get the best performance with a mixture of several varieties of perennial rye. Purchase high-quality seed and disperse it with a calibrated spreader, making two passes to maximize coverage. Sharpen mower blades two or more times a year. Bagging lawn clippings is not necessary, but do not allow leaves to accumulate on the lawn.

ADDITIONAL SPECIES, CULTIVARS, OR VARIETIES

Improved selections include *Lolium perenne* 'Pennant', 'Manhattan II' , and 'Citation II'.

🌿 Did You Know?

Though called rye, this particular native of Eurasia is used in pastures only. It is a very distant relative of the grass family plant that produces the rye used in food production for humans. The species name, perenne, *refers to the fact that this type of rye grass is perennial.*

Tall Turf-Type Fescue

Festuca arundinacea

Color: Medium green
Texture: Medium
Type: Cool season

Light Requirements:

This newer group of turfgrasses, released approximately 20 years ago, offer more tolerance to the extremes of weather and variable climate that Missouri experiences every year. These fescues have a narrower blade and are less clump-forming that the K-31 grasses, and although they are somewhat less dynamic than the bluegrass, they are also tougher and more durable. This cool-season grass maintains its vigor and beauty through most of the hot and humid summer. Adaptable to a number of lawn situations, it works well as a complement overseeded into established lawns or can stand alone as a turfgrass.

When to Plant
Seeding is best from September to early October, or also possible in mid-spring. Sodding can occur any time of year, except when the ground is frozen, with spring or fall being the best times.

Where to Plant
Plant in well-drained soil in full sun or very light shade.

How to Plant
Delineate the area to be planted. Dig up undesired plants or remove them with an herbicide. Have a sample of soil tested, and add the nutrients that the soil test indicates are needed and also 1 to 2 inches of organic amendments. Rototill, using caution under trees, or hand spade to blend the existing soil with new amendments. Rake the area smooth and ensure proper drainage. If laying sod, place sod pieces edge to edge with no gaps and water immediately, staking upper corners on a slope. If seeding, disperse seed with a calibrated spreader, 7 pounds in the fall or 10 pounds in the spring per 1000 square feet, making two passes to maximize coverage. Apply seed-starter fertilizer and rake lightly. Use erosion netting if the site is sloped. Keep the ground moist by watering up to four times daily

until seed germinates. Then water for longer periods of time, but less often, and do not allow puddles to form.

Care and Maintenance

During the first growing season, fertilize the grass monthly, whether sodded or seeded, using the seed-starter formula. After the first season, fertilize monthly with winterizer from September through early December, depending on the weather. Do not apply any herbicides or pesticides during the first two months on either sod or seed, and after time, apply only with proper diagnosis. From April through mid-June, and mid-September to the last mowing, allow grass to grow to 2^1/$_2$ to 3 inches. During the summer, allow grass to grow to 3 to 3^1/$_2$ inches. Never cut off more than 2 inches, and continue mowing until growth stops. Water the lawn in the morning, ensuring that it receives 1 inch of water every 10 days. Core aerate in mid-spring if needed; power rake in the fall if necessary.

Additional Information

Do not fertilize in the summer. Sod will have about 20 percent bluegrass to hold this clump-forming grass together. Sod should have soil that is ^{1}/$_2$ inch thick, with white roots throughout and no dead patches. Sod is perishable, so purchase only as much as can be laid in the dedicated time and keep it moist prior to installation. Sod is considered established once it resists when tugged on. Purchase weed-free seed, mix several types together, and overseed each September for 5 years. Sharpen mower blades two or more times a year. Bagging lawn clippings is not necessary, but do not allow leaves to accumulate on lawn. This diverse group of plants included in the genus Festuca range in color from silver blue to pure green. Some grow as tall as 7 feet, while and others reach only 6 inches.

Additional Species, Cultivars, or Varieties

New varieties become available almost every year. Consider using *Festuca arundinacea* 'Houndog', 'Finelawn', or 'Jaguar'.

Zoysia

Zoysia japonica

Color: Dark green
Texture: Medium
Type: Warm season

Light Requirements:

Zoysia is an aggressively growing and spreading lawn grass that is brilliant green for 5 months out of the year and then alters dramatically when fall frosts begin. Its green quickly changes to a pale straw color, which remains until the following spring. A hint of green appears overnight in mid-spring. Then a new sea of green rolls in, signaling another summer of barefoot magic.

WHEN TO PLANT

Sodding, plugging, or sprigging can occur from mid-May through mid-August.

WHERE TO PLANT

Plant in well-drained soil in full sun or very light shade.

HOW TO PLANT

Delineate the area to be planted. Dig up undesired plants or remove them with an herbicide. Have a sample of soil tested, and add the nutrients that the soil test indicates are needed and also 1 to 2 inches of organic amendments. Rototill, using caution under trees, or hand spade to blend the existing soil with new amendments. Rake the area smooth and ensure proper drainage. If laying sod, place sod pieces edge to edge with no gaps and water immediately, staking upper corners on a slope. Apply a seed-starter fertilizer to help roots establish. Water to keep the ground moist under the sod or around plugs and springs, all of which are considered established once they resist a tug. After established, water less frequently but for longer periods of time and do not allow puddles to form.

CARE AND MAINTENANCE

Fertilize monthly from May through September, using a type of fertilizer labeled with a first number that is twice the other two numbers shown on the bag. Do not apply any herbicides or pesticides during the first two months after installation, and then apply only with proper diagnosis. Allow grass to grow to 1 to 2 inches and continue cutting until growth stops. Water in the morning, ensuring that it receives 1 inch per week of moisture. Power rake in mid-spring just before greening up occurs, and core aerate in the fall. Pests and disease problems are minimal with proper care.

ADDITIONAL INFORMATION

Although zoysia seed is available, seeding is not the recommended planting approach. Sod should have soil that is $1/2$ inch thick, with white roots throughout and no dead patches. It can be laid as whole pieces, or cut and plugged in smaller divisions. Plugs can be purchased growing in flats; sprigs are bareroot plants. All are perishable, so purchase only as much as can be laid in the dedicated time and keep the sod moist prior to installation. Sod is considered established when it resists tug. Sharpen mower blades two or more times a year. Bagging lawn clippings is not necessary, but do not allow leaves to accumulate on lawn.

ADDITIONAL SPECIES, CULTIVARS, OR VARIETIES

There are none available.

Did You Know?

The species name, japonica, *refers to this plant's native habitat in Japan, although the original plants were brought to North America from Korea in the early 1900s. The zoysia's hardiness was improved in the 1950s when the Meyer variety expanded the regions where zoysia would survive.*

CHAPTER SIX

Ornamental Grasses

THE HIGHLY DIVERSE, REMARKABLY HARDY, and handsome
group of plants classed as ornamental grasses can be used to
superb effect in any garden or landscape, regardless of its style or
size. A tall-growing variety, for example, may stand at the end of a
hedgerow in a formal garden, lending its statuesque dignity and
subtle shades of color. Or an informal garden may be spruced up
with several types of grasses attractively arranged with shrubbery or
perennials or placed beside a favorite bench.

Most individual grass cultivars can be traced to native roots
in many cooler and cold-temperature climates around the world.
They have been used as landscaping elements since the mid-1800s,
but maintained the status of a sporadic garden novelty until the last
40 years. At that time, people began to observe that these grasses
had an impressive ability to grow in very inhospitable places. Not
only did they thrive as well in dry sand dunes as in seasonal
drainage ditches, in both swampy and very dry soils, but their
colonies were ever-increasing. Production nurseries very soon real-
ized the new landscaping solutions provided by this group of
low-care, aesthetically appealing plants. Now each year, specialists
bring forth new varieties of grasses, each with its own splendid
characteristics.

Ornamental grasses offer multi-season appeal, from early May
until mid-February. Each type has distinctive blades and flowers,
and a specific variety can go through several seasonal color changes
in foliage and flower color each year. Their fine-textured, highly animated leaves are a delight to the eye up close, and at a distance
maintain an extremely airy feeling. When placed among perennials,
shrubs, annuals, or other grasses, tall-growing varieties add dynamic

Chapter Six

uplift and vertical relief to the view. Smaller-growing clump forms provide textural and color excitement, and the low, ground-covering types can work to unify many landscape settings. Colonization occurs either through wind-pollinated seedlings or via offshoots of the root system, which sometimes migrate away from the original spot and leave the old center barren. Each variety, owing to its natural growing situation, has its best uses, but that fact hardly limits what landscaping problems can be solved and artistic effects can be achieved with this magnificent group of plants.

Blue Lyme Grass

Leymis arenarius

Height: 2 to 3 feet
Bloom Period: Summer
Blade Color: Blue-green
Zones: 4 through 8

Color photograph on page 246.

Light Requirements:

Beneficial Characteristics:

The qualities of fine texture, a spreading habit, and a semi- to truly evergreen nature, depending on the weather, characterize this grass. The blades and the flowers are a striking bluish, gray-green color. It must be given space to roam as it does have invasive tendencies. The aggressive top growth is the result of the continually moving and advancing root system. This trait makes blue lyme grass an excellent choice for erosion control, while at the same time the plant provides unique aesthetic benefits. This flexible plant can also be attractively grown in clumps in larger containers.

WHEN TO PLANT

Plant blue lyme grass in late spring through early summer to give it ample time to establish and create a show the first year.

WHERE TO PLANT

Blue lyme grass does well in a hot, sunny location with average to poor soil, which is well drained. If planting in a container, use a 20-inch diameter pot or larger.

HOW TO PLANT

Dig a hole that is twice the width and equal to or slightly less than the depth of the root ball. Do not plant in any sort of depression because the plant will suffer a major setback if water is allowed to collect and stand. Pulverize the existing soil; do not add amendments or fertilizer. Remove the plant from the container and loosen the roots if pot bound. The practice of carefully removing any dead reeds from the clump is optional. Be aware that some reeds which appear dead may not actually be so, and make sure not to damage any actively growing sections. Set the plant into the hole and back-

fill, creating a shallow well. Add 1 inch of mulch to conserve moisture, during first growing season only. Check
the plant regularly for 2 weeks after installation, and water
if the soil is dry.

CARE AND MAINTENANCE

This plant's semi- to evergreen nature means that there is
no cause for concern when its blades flop or are knocked
over during fall and winter rains and snows. Do nothing
until the late spring after new growth has begun; then
selectively remove the dead blades. If growing the plant in
a container, follow the same procedure. There are no pest
and disease problems. Do not use fertilizer, which will only
cause floppy, messy growth.

ADDITIONAL INFORMATION

When selecting a plant, choose one that shows obvious
new growth. Because this plant has evergreen qualities,
last season's foliage should still have fairly good color and
should not have been cut back. Select a 1 or 2 gallon pot,
both of which can be divided into smaller sections. Do
not worry if the number of blades looks sparse in the
container, but check to make sure the root system is full.
Remember if blue lyme grass is not planted in the full
sun where the soil is well drained, all its best qualities will
be lost. Companion plantings to consider are burning bush,
pfitzer, bayberry, and St. Johnswort.

ADDITIONAL SPECIES, CULTIVARS, OR VARIETIES

There are none available.

🌿 Did You Know?

*Blue lyme grass is native to or naturalized in a widespread
area that stretches from Europe into Asia, in drier, thinner,
and/or rocky soils. The species name,* areniarus, *means "of
sandy places." One common name, wild rye, derives from the
fact that the seed and foliage are used as forage for grazing
animals.*

Feather Reed Grass

Calamagrostis × acutiflora 'Karl Foerster'

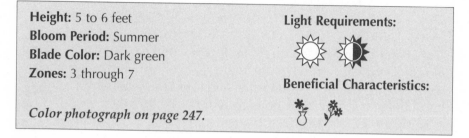

Height: 5 to 6 feet
Bloom Period: Summer
Blade Color: Dark green
Zones: 3 through 7

Color photograph on page 247.

Light Requirements:

Beneficial Characteristics:

The extremely rigid, upright stature of feather reed grass makes it useful as a living architectural element in the landscape. Plant it in sunny locations that require framing or as a symbolic gatepost between adjoining landscape areas. It provides a good screen for roads or undesired views, an eye-catching reflection in a pond or water feature, and works well mingled with perennials or annuals, or standing alone in the distance. Feather reed grass is happy in wet or drier soil, and offers dazzling fall color.

WHEN TO PLANT

It is best to plant feather reed grass during its dormant period in the fall or early spring. Installing it before new growth begins allows for better root establishment and a better show during the first year.

WHERE TO PLANT

Feather reed grass does well in a hot sunny location with average to poor, wet or dry, heavy soil.

HOW TO PLANT

Dig a hole that is twice the width and equal to or slightly less than the depth of the root ball. Do not plant in a depression even though this plant is wet-soil tolerant. Pulverize the existing soil; do not add amendments or fertilizer. Remove the plant from the container and loosen the roots if pot bound. The practice of carefully removing any dead reeds from the clump is optional. Be aware that some reeds which appear dead may not actually be so, and make sure not to damage any actively growing sections. Set the plant into the hole and backfill, creating a shallow well. Add 1 inch of mulch to conserve moisture, during first growing season only. Check the plant

154

regularly for 2 weeks after installation. Soil should be kept moist during establishment.

CARE AND MAINTENANCE
Do not allow drought stress during the first growing season. In the late fall, add 1 to 2 inches of mulch around the perimeter, but not over the top. The blades are attractive in winter and provide protection for the crown, so allow them to remain until mid-February. Then cut them back to 8 inches, a length that will minimize damage to sprouting new growth. Divide the plants every 4 to 5 years. There are no pest and disease problems. Fertilizer will only cause floppy, messy growth.

ADDITIONAL INFORMATION
When selecting a plant, choose one with obvious new growth. Do not remove the brown stumps from last year's growth because they can sprout again. Select a 1- or 2-gallon pot. The flowers can be cut and hung upside-down before fully mature for using in seasonal arrangements. Plant feather reed grass in the full sun or all the best qualities will be lost. Companion plantings to consider are deciduous holly, pussy willow, and red twig dogwood.

ADDITIONAL SPECIES, CULTIVARS, OR VARIETIES
A shorter vase-shaped variety with variegated foliage is *Calamagrostis acutiflora* × 'Overdam', which requires protection from mid to late-afternoon sun.

🌿 Did You Know?
Feather reed grass is a relatively new introduction from Germany. It is one of the few cultivars of grasses that will grow at a rate and to a height which is considered normal in very heavy clay soils. The species name, acutiflora, *indicates that the flower has a pointed shape.*

Fountain Grass

Pennisetum setaceum

Height: 2 to 3 feet
Bloom Period: Mid-summer early fall
Blade Color: Medium-green
Zones: 4 through 8

Color photograph on page 247.

Light Requirements:

Beneficial Characteristics:

Fountain grass is named for its low-mounding growth habit which resembles a living fountain overflowing to the ground. The fountain-like impact is most enhanced when the wind blows through a mass of fountain grass plants. The numerous pinkish purple flower clusters shoot above the foliage, and when they bounce and weave in the wind they accentuate the plant's rounded fountain silhouette. Fountain grass is tough, durable, able to flourish in dry soil, and heat tolerant, all qualities which make it an excellent choice for plantings adjacent to roads, driveways, walks, and patios. Its rounded shape works to soften shrub plantings and adds a new flowing dimension to beds of annuals or perennials. Plant this effervescent plant in sunny locations.

WHEN TO PLANT

Plant fountain grass in the late spring through early summer to give it ample time to establish and create a show the first year.

WHERE TO PLANT

Fountain grass does well in a hot sunny location with average to poor soil, which is well drained and has no sitting water.

HOW TO PLANT

Dig a hole that is twice the width and equal to or slightly less than the depth of the root ball. Do not plant in a depression because fountain grass is not wet soil tolerant beyond establishment time. Pulverize the existing soil; do not add amendments or fertilizer. Remove the plant from the container and loosen the roots if pot bound. Set the plant into the hole and backfill, creating a shallow well. Add 1 to 2 inches of mulch to conserve moisture. During the first month, check the plant regularly; if the soil is dry, water the plant.

CARE AND MAINTENANCE
In the late fall, add 1 to 2 inches of mulch around the perimeter of the plant, but not over the top. The blades are attractive in winter and provide protection for the crown, so allow them to remain until mid-February. Then cut them back to no shorter than 6 inches, a length that will minimize damage to sprouting new growth. Divide the plants every 4 to 5 years. There are no pest or disease problems. Fertilizer will only cause floppy, messy growth.

ADDITIONAL INFORMATION
When selecting a plant, choose one with obvious new growth. Do not remove the brown stumps from last year's growth because they can sprout again. Select a 1 or 2-gallon pot. Cut flowers can be hung upside-down before fully mature to use in seasonal arrangements. Plant fountain grass in the full sun or all the best qualities will be lost. Companion plantings to consider are globe arborvitae, barberry, and lilac.

ADDITIONAL SPECIES, CULTIVARS, OR VARIETIES
Two dwarf varieties are *Pennisetum alopecuroides* 'Hameln' which is 24 inches tall, or one that grows to a height less than 1 foot is *Pennisetum alopecuroides* 'Little Bunny'.

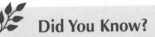

Did You Know?
This species is native to the northern temperate regions of Africa. The name setaceum *means "bristle-like," and refers to the plant's inflorescence. Close relatives can be found throughout the world. Some are used for food crops and forage by animals, while others have escaped cultivation and are considered noxious.*

Giant Reed Grass

Arundo donax

Height: 6 feet or more
Bloom Period: Summer
Blade Color: Pale blue-green
Zones: 4 through 9
Color photograph on page 247.

Light Requirements:

The growth in one season of the giant reed grass is awe-inspiring to behold. Slowly emerging from the ground in spring, the plant gains momentum each day as the soil warms and can reach a summer height of up to 10 feet. Its 3-inch-wide, blue-green blades are attached to very stout stalks, giving this grass the appearance of rogue corn escaped from the farm. The coarse texture of the individual plant is obvious when viewed up close or in the distance, but the inflorescence is quite the opposite. This giant's flower is a soft, fine-textured plume that gracefully rises above the sturdy foliage. Giant reed grass is quite useful as a freestanding focal point, a seasonal screen, a soil stabilizer on the banks of ponds and streams, and even as a dramatic conversation piece when established in a large planter on the deck or patio.

WHEN TO PLANT

Plant giant reed grass in the late spring through early summer to give it ample time to establish and create a show the first year.

WHERE TO PLANT

Giant reed grass does well in a hot sunny location with average soil, which can be either wet or dry. The healthiest plant occurs when planted in a wetter situation. If planting in a container, choose one that is larger than 20 inches in diameter.

HOW TO PLANT

Dig a hole that is twice the width and equal to or slightly less than the depth of the root ball. Do not plant in a depression even though this plant is wet soil tolerant. Pulverize the existing soil; do not add amendments or fertilizer. Remove the plant from the container and loosen the roots if pot bound. The practice of removing dead reeds from the plant is optional. Be sure not to damage actively growing sections. Set the plant into the hole and backfill, creating a shallow well. Add 1 to 2 inches of mulch to conserve moisture. During the first month, check the plant regularly; if the soil is dry, water the plant.

CARE AND MAINTENANCE

Do not allow drought stress to occur during the first growing season. In the late fall, add 1 to 2 inches of mulch around the perimeter, but not over the top. Because of the structural quality of the stems, cut them back in December to prevent damage to the crown of the plant. There are no pest or disease problems. Fertilizer will only cause floppy, messy growth.

ADDITIONAL INFORMATION

Select a plant that shows obvious new growth. Brown stumps from previous season's growth are not a problem and will not resprout the next year. Select a 1- or 2-gallon pot. Plant giant reed grass in the full sun or all the best qualities of this plant will be lost. Companion plantings to consider are inkberry and summersweet.

ADDITIONAL SPECIES, CULTIVARS, OR VARIETIES

Arundo donax 'Versicolor' is an equally tall type with a striped, green and whitish leaf.

Did You Know?

Giant reed grass is native to the Mediterranean regions of the world. It has escaped cultivation and can be found naturalizing sunny streambeds and banks in Missouri. This grass is a true reed, which means that the stem is hollow between the joints similar to a cornstalk. Its habit and root system make it a candidate for controlling erosion.

Japanese Blood Grass

Imperata cylindrica 'Red Baron'

Height: 1 to 2 feet
Bloom Period: Summer
Blade Color: Red and green
Zones: 4 through 7
Color photograph on page 247.

Light Requirements:

Japanese blood grass takes its name from the crimson color of its blades. When the stem first emerges from the ground in spring, the leaves are green. As the warm days lengthen, the red coloration appears at mid-leaf and slowly flows toward the pointed tip. The colorful blades are well spaced, very upright, and radiate visual heat. A little planning will allow you to get the most from this plant's unique traits. Single plants are less eye-catching than a massed group of blood grass. Place them in front of a sunny shrub or perennial border, or use them to create a festive atmosphere in the herb or vegetable garden. They are best sited where they can be viewed every day with little effort, so that their crimson transformation can be fully enjoyed.

WHEN TO PLANT

Plant Japanese blood grass in late spring through early summer to give it ample time to establish and create a show the first year.

WHERE TO PLANT

Japanese blood grass does well in a sunny location with average or better soil, which should be well drained and basically dry.

HOW TO PLANT

Dig a hole that is twice the width and equal to or slightly less than the depth of the root ball. Do not plant in a depression even though this plant is wet soil tolerant. Pulverize the existing soil; do not add amendments or fertilizer. Remove the plant from the container and loosen the roots if pot bound. The practice of removing dead reeds from the plant is optional. Be sure not to damage actively growing sections. Set the plant into the hole and backfill, creating a shallow well. Add 1 to 2 inches of mulch to conserve moisture. During the first month, check the plant regularly; if the soil is dry, water the plant.

Care and Maintenance

Do not allow drought stress to occur during first growing season. In late fall add 1 to 2 inches of mulch around the perimeter, but not over the top. Allow the blades to remain until early spring, and then remove as needed, being careful not to damage the sprouting new growth. This new growth emerges from an underground root system, so it is also advisable not to cultivate nearby soil. Divide the plants every 4 to 5 years. There are no pest or disease problems. Fertilizer will only cause floppy, messy growth.

Additional Information

When selecting a plant, choose one that shows obvious new growth. The number of leaves in the pot may be sparse; the massiveness of the root system is more important. Also, some or full coloration should be obvious. Brown stumps from the previous season's growth are not a problem and will not resprout the next year. Select a 1- or 2-gallon pot. Plant Japanese blood grass in the full sun or the color's best qualities will be diminished. Companion plantings to consider are yews or yellow false cypress.

Additional Species, Cultivars, or Varieties

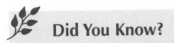

There are none available.

ORNAMENTAL GRASSES

🌿 Did You Know?

The green-bladed relatives of Japanese blood grass are very aggressive and extremely difficult to remove once established. The species name, Cylindrica, refers to the circular pattern created as the blades emerge from the ground.

Lemon Grass

Cymbopogon citratus

Height: Up to 3 feet
Habit: Mounded
Type: Annual Grass

Light Requirements:

Beneficial Characteristic:

Color photograph on page 247.

Although this plant is considered an herb, that label should not disqualify it from use as a purely aesthetic element of the landscape. Smooth and elegant in appearance, easily animated by breezes, and providing a wealth of fine texture whether viewed from a distance or up close, lemon grass is prized in many landscape settings. The grass releases a remarkable lemony fragrance when the foliage is cut and used for summer arrangements. Although this plant may be more difficult to find than other, supposedly more glamorous spring annuals, it is well worth the search. Lemon grass is not only beautiful to look at, it also feels good when you brush against the leaves on walks through the garden. Keep lemon grass in a pot by the back door all summer, and you'll have a ready supply to flavor ice tea.

WHEN TO PLANT

Plant lemon grass in spring as soon as available. The comparative shortness of Missouri's growing season may prevent any flower stalks from forming.

WHERE TO PLANT

Lemon grass requires full sun and an average or better soil which is well drained.

HOW TO PLANT

Delineate the bed. Remove any weeds or undesirable plants by digging or using an herbicide. Spade or rototill the planting area, using caution under trees, mix 6 inches of soil amendments with the existing soil, and rake the surface smooth. Dig a hole three times the width and slightly less than the height of the root ball. Remove the plant from the container, loosening the roots if they are pot bound, place in the hole, backfill, and water thoroughly. Remove flowers and pinch back ¹/₄ of the stem for a bushier plant. Add 1 to 2 inches of mulch. If planting in a pot, first fill the pot one-quarter full with gravel, then add well-drained potting soil, and follow the preceding planting instructions.

CARE AND MAINTENANCE

Fertilize once a month using a water-soluble fertilizer. Weed on an as-needed basis. Check the soil regularly, daily in the hottest weather, and water if dry.

ADDITIONAL SPECIES, CULTIVARS, OR VARIETIES

There are none available.

Did You Know?

A member of the grass family, lemon grass is native to Southern India and Ceylon. The species name, citratus, refers to the citric aroma of the foliage, which produces lemon oil. Lemon grass is used as an ingredient in many types of herbal teas and drinks.

Maiden Grass

Miscanthus sinensis 'Gracillimus'

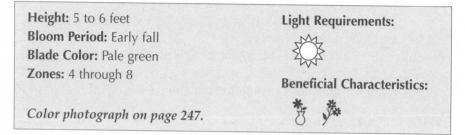

Height: 5 to 6 feet
Bloom Period: Early fall
Blade Color: Pale green
Zones: 4 through 8

Color photograph on page 247.

Light Requirements:

Beneficial Characteristics:

Since being introduced from the Orient, maiden grass has risen to a royal stature while it is also seen as something of workhorse. This twin status and its popularity reflect the plant's winning aesthetic qualities and its adaptability, versatility, and low care requirements. Maiden grass enjoys a wide spectrum of landscape uses, ranging from poolside or water's-edge plantings, to foundation and sidewalk trim, patio screens, and as a source for cut flowers. The fine-textured, vase-shaped foliage persists from late May through January and protects any plants positioned at the base of the grass from midday sun. The pinkish red inflorescence rises above the summer foliage. Both the leaves and flowers slowly change to tones of tan as the days grow shorter and temperatures cooler, providing new textural relief to the fall and winter landscape.

WHEN TO PLANT

Plant maiden grass in the late spring through early summer to give it ample time to establish and create a show the first year.

WHERE TO PLANT

Maiden grass prefers a hot sunny location with average or better soil, which can be either wet or dry. If planting in a container, use a pot that is 20 inches or larger in diameter.

HOW TO PLANT

Dig a hole that is twice the width and equal to or slightly less than the depth of the root ball. Do not plant in a depression even though this plant is wet soil tolerant. Pulverize the existing soil; do not add amendments or fertilizer. Remove the plant from the container and loosen the roots if pot bound. The practice of removing dead reeds from the plant is optional. Be sure not to damage actively growing sections. Set the plant into the hole and backfill, creating a shallow well. Add 1 to 2 inches of mulch to conserve moisture. During the first month, check the plant regularly; if the soil is dry, water the plant.

CARE AND MAINTENANCE

Minimize drought stress. In the late fall add 1 to 2 inches of mulch around the perimeter, not over the top. The foliage offers winter appeal and protection for the crown of the plant, so allow the blades to remain until mid-February. Then before new growth appears, cut the blades back to 8 inches. Divide the plants every 4 to 5 years. There are no pest or disease problems. Fertilizer will only cause floppy, messy growth.

ADDITIONAL INFORMATION

When selecting a plant, choose one that shows obvious new growth. Brown stumps from the previous season's growth are not a problem and will not resprout the next year. Select a 1- or 2-gallon pot. Cut flowers can be hung upside-down before fully mature for use in seasonal arrangements. Plant maiden grass in the full sun or the plant's best qualities will be lost. Companion plantings to consider in wetter soils are chameleon plant and astilbe; in dry soil, try canna, creeping phlox, and liveforever.

ADDITIONAL SPECIES, CULTIVARS OR VARIETIES

The purple leaves of the eulalia *M. sinensis* var. *purpurascens* will turn reddish purple in late summer. Zebra grass *M. sinensis* 'Zebrinus' has exciting horizontal yellow banding on the leaf.

Did You Know?

The sight of wind blowing through maiden grass is extremely appealing. There is entertainment value in allowing some of the long leaves to remain in the spring when birds will try to carry them off for their nests. The species name, sinensis, *means "of China," the native home of this grass.*

Prairie Dropseed Grass N

Sporobolus heterolepsis

Height: 3 feet
Bloom Period: Summer
Blade Color: Bright green
Zones: 4 through 8
Color photograph on page 247.

Light Requirements:

This highly attractive native prairie grass is at home in meadow or wildflower plantings, but has proven its beauty and usefulness in many other landscape settings. This fine-bladed, emerald green grass has a mounded silhouette that works remarkably well in many situations. When placed at the base of a fence, or light post, or mailbox, its soft shape offers a perfect transition from the vertical structure to the surrounding horizontal landscape. It provides a bright green anchor to slow the eye as it moves across the backyard or property line, or gracefully smoothes the space between a boulder and a garden bed. The buff, tannish flower that emerges midsummer and the gradual fading of this grass to tan tones in the fall add to its year-round appeal.

WHEN TO PLANT

Plant prairie dropseed grass in the spring through early summer to give it ample time to establish and create a show the first year.

WHERE TO PLANT

Prairie dropseed grass does well in a hot sunny location with average to poor soil, which is very well drained.

HOW TO PLANT

Dig a hole that is twice the width and equal to or slightly less than the depth of the root ball. Do not plant in a depression or low spot. Pulverize the existing soil; do not add amendments or fertilizer. Remove the plant from the container and loosen the roots if pot bound. The practice of removing dead reeds from the plant is optional. Be sure not to damage actively growing sections. Set the plant into the hole and backfill, creating a shallow well. Add 1 to 2 inches of mulch to conserve moisture. During the first month, check the plant regularly; if the soil is dry, water the plant.

CARE AND MAINTENANCE
In the late fall add 1 to 2 inches of mulch around the perimeter, not over the top. The foliage offers winter appeal and protection for the crown of the plant, so allow the blades to remain until mid-February. Then before new growth appears, cut the blades back to 6 inches. There are no pest or disease problems. Fertilizer will only cause floppy, messy growth.

ADDITIONAL INFORMATION
When selecting a plant, choose one that shows obvious new growth. Brown stumps from the previous season's growth are not a problem and will not resprout the next year. Select a 1- or 2-gallon pot. Plant prairie dropseed grass in the full sun or the plant's best qualities will be lost. Companion plantings to consider in wetter soils are barberry and purple leaf sand cherry.

ADDITIONAL SPECIES, CULTIVARS, OR VARIETIES
There are none available.

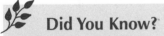

ORNAMENTAL GRASSES

Did You Know?

Relatives of prairie dropseed grass can be found throughout the world. Each flower may be branched or forked in a unique way, and they emit a pleasant subtle fragrance in the summer.

Red Fountain Grass

Pennisetum setaceum 'Rubrum'

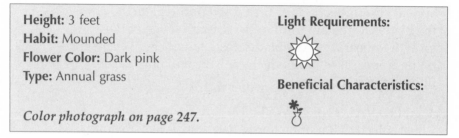

Height: 3 feet
Habit: Mounded
Flower Color: Dark pink
Type: Annual grass

Color photograph on page 247.

Light Requirements:

Beneficial Characteristics:

Red fountain grass is relatively new to the market, and since its introduction has received nothing but rave reviews from seasoned gardeners as well as beginners. The rich deep maroon color of the leaves combined with the lighter red, fuzzy airiness of the inflorescence that hovers above the foliage grant a air of rustic elegance to any view. What a great addition to any planting! It can be planted in large beds all to itself, in individual decorative containers or pots, or mixed with other annuals or perennials. Both the flower and leaf can be cut and used in fresh arrangements, and the inflorescence can be dried for future use. The possibility of successfully wintering over the entire plant in a sunny window in the basement is certainly worth a try. Red fountain grass requires very low maintenance and contributes to a uniquely stylish look, whether massed in large beds, mixed with other annuals and perennials, or planted in decorative containers.

WHEN TO PLANT

Plant red fountain grass in spring, as soon as available.

WHERE TO PLANT

Red fountain grass requires full sun and does well in an average or better soil which is well drained.

HOW TO PLANT

Delineate the bed. Remove any weeds or undesirable plants by digging or using an herbicide. Spade or rototill the planting area, using caution under trees, mix 6 inches of soil amendments with the existing soil, and rake the surface smooth. Dig a hole three times the width and slightly less than the height of the rootball. Remove the plant from the container, loosening the roots if they are pot bound, place in the hole, backfill, and water thoroughly. Add 1 to 2 inches of mulch. If planting in a pot, first fill the pot one-quarter full with gravel, then add well-drained potting soil, and follow the preceding planting instructions.

CARE AND MAINTENANCE
Fertilize once a month using a water-soluble fertilizer. Weed on an as-needed basis. Check the soil regularly, daily in the hottest weather, and water if dry.

ADDITIONAL INFORMATION
Purchase the plants in pots of various sizes. A quick formula for determining the proper quantity of plants is to divide the square footage of the bed by one-half the height of the plant and by one-half the width of the plant (as noted on its tag); whichever result is larger is the number of plants you should plant per square foot. To determine the spacing between plants, divide the height and the width of the plant by 2. The lower number which results determines the spacing between plants. For example, for a plant that is 6 inches tall and 8 inches wide and a bed that is 12 feet square, you should plant 4 plants per square foot (12/4 = 3), and the plants should be spaced 3 inches apart (6/2 = 3).

ADDITIONAL SPECIES, CULTIVARS, OR VARIETIES
There are none available.

🌿 Did You Know?

Native to Africa, this plant is one of the few readily available annual species of Pennisetum. *The species name,* setaceum, *refers to the bristle-like quality of the flowers. The variety name,* 'rubrum', *means "reddish."*

Ribbon Grass

Phalaris arundinacea 'Picta'

Height: 1 foot

Bloom Period: Summer

Blade Color: White and green

Zones: 4 through 8

Color photograph on page 247.

Light Requirements:

If you are looking for a plant that will provide an unusual show throughout the growing season, consider ribbon grass. This plant is named for the alternating green and white stripes that run the entire length of its blades. In shaded settings it provides daytime landscape lighting, and at night it will reflect moonlight. This grass is a highly aggressive grower so be sure to allow it ample room to spread or be prepared to remove sections of it on a regular basis. Its blanketing ability makes ribbon grass a good candidate for erosion control. It can help stabilize the sides of a pond, works as good ground cover between the house and a walk, and can be used to soften the hard edges of a reflective water feature. The whitish pink inflorescence is almost invisible above the dynamic foliage. Ribbon grass makes stunning landscape statement when well understood and properly managed.

WHEN TO PLANT

Plant ribbon grass in the spring through early summer or in the early fall.

WHERE TO PLANT

Ribbon grass prefers a hot sunny location or a partly shaded setting with average to heavy clay soil which should be moist or wetter. Heavier clay soils will reduce this plant's invasiveness.

HOW TO PLANT

Dig a hole that is twice the width and equal to or slightly less than the depth of the root ball. Do not plant in a depression even though this plant is wet soil tolerant. Pulverize the existing soil; do not add amendments or fertilizer. Remove the plant from the container and loosen the roots if pot bound. The practice of removing dead reeds from the plant is optional. Be sure not to damage actively growing sections. Set the plant into the hole and backfill, creating a shallow well. Add 1 to 2 inches of mulch to conserve moisture. During the first month, check the plant regularly; if the soil is dry, water the plant.

CARE AND MAINTENANCE

For the best performance, do not allow drought stress to occur at any time. Ribbon grass that is planted in the full sun, and sometimes in part shade, will probably sunburn in sections. If this occurs, set the mower height on high and mow over the sunburned area. This plant will mat down during heavy rain falls. Mowing prior to matting will help encourage a neater appearance, or simply let it go if the matting does not bother you. There are no pest or disease problems. Fertilizer will only cause floppy, messy, and really wild growth.

ADDITIONAL INFORMATION

Select a plant, in a 1- or 2-gallon pot, in the early spring before new growth begins or after the pots are overflowing with blades. If the plant is still dormant, the brown stumps from previous year's growth are not a problem and will not resprout the next year. Check the plant for a well-developed root system. Companion plantings to consider are bridal wreath and witch hazel.

ADDITIONAL SPECIES, CULTIVARS, OR VARIETIES

There are none available.

Did You Know?

Relatives of ribbon grass are found in the northern temperate regions of North America, Europe, and Northern Africa. The seeds of one species are harvested for canary or birdseed. The species name, arundinacea, *means "bamboolike" and refers to the invasiveness of ribbon grass. The variety, 'Picta', means "painted" or "variegated."*

Switch Grass

Panicum virgatum

Height: 4 feet or more	**Light Requirements:**
Bloom Period: Summer	
Blade Color: Medium-green	
Zones: 2 through 9	
	Beneficial Characteristic:
Color photograph on page 247.	

The robust vitality and adaptability of this native grass are evidenced in the fact that it can be found growing from Nova Scotia all the way to Central Mexico. Switch grass grows in large clumps with huge numbers of individual fine-textured blades that have a fountainlike growing habit. In mid-summer the inflorescence pushes through the foliage and sits about a foot above the mounded blades. The opened maroon flower has an unusually wispy configuration and works well in seasonal arrangements. When the wind-pollinated seeds drift with breezes, the landscape almost sparkles. The foliage and flower stalks persist through much of the winter, adding tans and browns to the landscape. The size of switch grass clumps makes this plant especially suitable for large landscape spaces. Mass plantings can ease and screen undesirable views, act as a backdrop for other plantings, and help create landscape barriers. If planted on a slope or hillside to help prevent erosion, switch grass requires a minimum of maintenance. Planted alone or among sunny wildflowers, perennials, and/or shrubs, this impressive ornamental grass is sure to be the focal point.

WHEN TO PLANT
Plant switch grass in late spring through early summer to give it ample time to establish and create a show the first year.

WHERE TO PLANT
Switch grass does well in a hot sunny location with average to poor soil, which can either be dry or quite wet.

HOW TO PLANT
Dig a hole that is twice the width and equal to or slightly less than the depth of the root ball. Do not plant in a depression even though this plant is wet soil tolerant. Pulverize the existing soil; do not add

amendments or fertilizer. Remove the plant from the container and loosen the roots if pot bound. The practice of removing dead reeds from the plant is optional. Be sure not to damage actively growing sections. Set the plant into the hole and backfill, creating a shallow well. Add 1 to 2 inches of mulch to conserve moisture. During the first month, check the plant regularly; if the soil is dry, water the plant.

CARE AND MAINTENANCE

Do not allow drought stress to occur during the first growing season. In the late fall add 1 to 2 inches of mulch around the perimeter, not over the top. The foliage offers winter appeal and protection for the crown of the plant, so allow the blades to remain until mid-February. Then before new growth appears, cut the blades back to 6 inches. There are no pest or disease problems. Fertilizer will only cause floppy, messy growth.

ADDITIONAL INFORMATION

Select a plant, in a 1- or 2-gallon pot, which shows obvious new growth. The brown stumps from the previous year's growth are not a problem and will not resprout the next year. Check the plant for a well-developed root system. Plant switch grass in the full sun or all its best qualities will be lost.

ADDITIONAL SPECIES, CULTIVARS, OR VARIETIES

The foliage of *Panicum virgatum* 'Hänse Herms' will turn a shade of red in the fall.

Did You Know?

Many members of the genus Panicum *are food for wild and domesticated animals. The blades provide forage for grazing animals, while the seeds range in use from millet for birds to a seed additive in hog food. Animals often seek protection during winter's harshest weather in clumps of switch grass.*

Variegated Cord Grass

Spartina pectinata 'Aureomarginata'

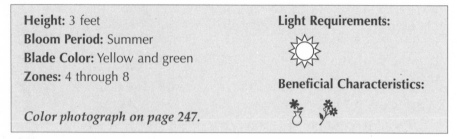

Height: 3 feet
Bloom Period: Summer
Blade Color: Yellow and green
Zones: 4 through 8

Color photograph on page 247.

Light Requirements:

Beneficial Characteristics:

The wonderful weeping quality and overall yellow color of variegated cord grass work to create an instant impact wherever it is planted. This is a fine-textured grass whose blade margins are accentuated with linear highlights. The darker tan inflorescence shoots 2 feet or more above the clump of cascading blades, making it appear to float unattached. Variegated cord grass is the master of wet soil and does very well positioned in lower wet spots or on the top of retaining walls where water collects. Whether planted alone, or intermingled with other sunny, wet soil tolerant shrubs or groundcovers, or massed at the edge of a water feature, this unique ornamental grass is a source of year-round pleasure.

WHEN TO PLANT

Plant variegated cord grass in the late spring through early summer to give it ample time to establish and create a show the first year.

WHERE TO PLANT

Variegated cord grass does well in a hot sunny location with average or better soil, which can be either wet or dry. The best aesthetic qualities will occur if it is sited in a wetter soil situation. If plating in a container, use a pot that is 20 or more inches in diameter.

HOW TO PLANT

Dig a hole that is twice the width and equal to or slightly less than the depth of the root ball. Do not plant in a depression even though this plant is wet soil tolerant. Pulverize the existing soil; do not add amendments or fertilizer. Remove the plant from the container and loosen the roots if pot bound. The practice of removing dead reeds from the plant is optional. Be sure not to damage actively growing sections. Set the plant into the hole and backfill, creating a shallow well. Add 1 to 2 inches of mulch to conserve moisture. During the first month, check the plant regularly; if the soil is dry, water the plant.

CARE AND MAINTENANCE

Do not allow drought stress to occur during the first growing season. In the late fall add 1 to 2 inches of mulch around the perimeter, not over the top. The foliage offers winter appeal and protection for the crown of the plant, so allow the blades to remain until mid-February. Then cut the blades back to 8 inches, minimizing the damage to sprouting new growth. There are no pest or disease problems. Fertilizer will only cause floppy, messy growth.

ADDITIONAL INFORMATION

When selecting a plant, choose one that shows obvious new growth. Brown stumps from the previous season's growth are not a problem and will not resprout the next year. Select a 1- or 2-gallon pot. Cut flowers can be hung upside-down before fully mature for use in seasonal arrangements. Plant variegated cord grass in the full sun or its best qualities will be lost. Companion plantings to consider in wetter soils are red twig dogwood and inkberry.

ADDITIONAL SPECIES, CULTIVARS, OR VARIETIES

There are none available.

Did You Know?

Variegated cord grass is native to the marshy prairies of the midwestern United States, with other relatives found in many locations throughout the world. The species name, pectinata, *means "comblike" and refers to the shape of the inflorescence. If the seeds are gathered and germinated, they will not have the variegated quality, but will revert back to the unimproved variety.*

CHAPTER SEVEN

Perennials

EVEN PEOPLE WHO ARE NOT GARDENERS are likely to be acquainted with at least a few members of the very large group of durable and adaptable plants known as perennials. They come in all sizes, shapes, textures, and colors, and are found in the furthermost reaches of the world. Perennials store energy in their root systems all through the cold season and every year emerge from a safe winter hideaway when the soil temperature is just right for each variety. One after another, their familiar faces reappear, bringing gardens and yards to life just as we remember them.

Even though perennials are highly versatile as a group, successful planting requires more than simply liking a plant and placing it on impulse. Careful site evaluation is always the first step, whether siting a single plant or developing a garden or collection. Here are some important preliminary steps to choosing perennials for your yard or garden.

1. Determine whether a potential location changes during the year, how much sun it receives and at what times of day. Investigate the site's existing plantings and nearby plants, their health, habits, and aggressiveness. Examine the site's topography and how it is affected by winds and rain. Think also about how much time you have to give to the plant, and the site's ease of access for the equipment needed to prepare it properly for planting and for maintaining it. Site analysis will considerably reduce the number of suitable perennial candidates, but it is more than likely that several varieties will work well together in nearly any site.

2. Now to narrow the list of candidates even further, look closely at every plant. Consider their textures, forms, colors, sizes, and bloom periods. Studying these attributes and the contrasts they offer is necessary to making the most of any perennial planting.

Chapter Seven

The most obvious way that plants create an impact is through the color of their flower and foliage. White, for example, makes objects appear larger. Yellow, which is vibrant and warm, can be an energizing or relieving element, depending on the surroundings. Shades of blue range from cool to exciting in effect and create depth, but are lost in shade. Pink is chameleon-like and best when used as a supporting color. Red is very strong and advancing, which foreshortens views. Be cautious with purple and violets, which if overused can be depressing. Oranges provide warmth up close but from a distance sometimes can appear blurred.

A second way plants create impact is through their texture, an attribute that changes during the growing season depending on whether the plant is in flower or not, and on the relative size of the plant parts in relation to the surroundings. Consideration of texture and what impression it will create directly affects decisions about spacing between plants. And gardeners should keep in mind that the qualities of fine texture that they may struggle to achieve are nearly always lost when the garden is viewed from a distance. The third element in a plant's impact is its form: for example, outline or silhouette, vertical or horizontal profile, vaselike or mounded. Various forms create different reactions in the spectator. Vertical and vaselike forms equal action and movement, while horizontal and mounded forms are passive in effect. The shapes of single and massed plants characterize the overall feel of a garden section or the entire view.

Setting realistic goals and making careful choices about color, texture, form, size, and growing period are necessary when choosing and installing perennials. But thoughtful planning of this kind will provide you with years of pleasure in all your beautiful perennial choices.

Asparagus

Asparagus officinalis

Height: 4 feet plus
Growth Habit: Upright
Bloom Period: Summer
Flower Color: Yellowish green
Zones: 4 through 8
Color photograph on page 247.

Light Requirements:

Beneficial Characteristic:

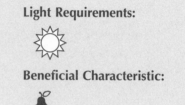

An excellent plant for the sunny garden, this perennial provides an additional bonus at the dinner table. Asparagus is one of the first plants to emerge in the spring, when its straight spear habit adds interest and vertical excitement to the garden. As the stalks mature, they explode into airy fernlike foliage whose quality is not duplicated by any other perennial plant. The plants are separate sexes, so if seed formation from the red fruits which are only on the females is desired, some males are needed as pollinators. As quirky as it sounds, asparagus plants dotted in the yard offer unrivaled aesthetic rewards.

WHEN TO PLANT
Plant in late March in southern Missouri, early April in midstate, and late April in the northern part of the state.

WHERE TO PLANT
Asparagus does well in full sun in a rich, highly organic soil which is moist and well drained.

HOW TO PLANT
Soak the roots prior to planting. Delineate a bed, digging up undesirable plants or removing them with an herbicide. Rototill or spade the soil to a depth of 6 to 8 inches, blend a total of 6 inches of organic matter with the existing soil, and rake smooth, creating a raised bed. Dig a hole or trench twice the width of the spread of the root system, remove a single root from the bundle, and place it in the hole with the eye 4 to 6 inches below the surface. Backfill, firm soil, water the plant thoroughly, and place 1 inch of mulch over planting.

CARE AND MAINTENANCE
Fertilize asparagus with a balanced food, after harvest. Water an

equivalent to 1 inch each week if the growing season is dry. Do not harvest any plants during the first year, and take only a few spears during the second. After that time, cut asparagus until late June, stopping the harvest when the spears are pencil size or smaller. Overcutting can weaken the entire plant colony. Pest and disease problems can be minimized by a fall removal of the garden debris in which insects overwinter. Weeds can be trouble for several years in a new garden, and careful use of herbicides or hand digging are the only real solutions. Add 1 inch of mulch as needed to conserve moisture and help with weed control.

ADDITIONAL INFORMATION

At garden centers and through mail-order nurseries, select disease-free, one-year-old crowns which look like pips or eyes with stringy roots dangling down. The garden centers have plants which are dormant and sold as bundles of bareroot plants. The stems should be flexible and consistent in color. Mail-order perennial plants arrive bareroot wrapped in moss. Two of the better varieties of males are Jersey Giant and Jersey Knight, and Mary Washington is a good female variety.

ADDITIONAL SPECIES, CULTIVARS, OR VARIETIES

There are none available.

Did You Know?

Asparagus and rhubarb are the only two vegetables that are perennial and have great aesthetic qualities. A surprising member of the lily family, asparagus has an underground root system growth habit that is invasive. This perennial is native to Europe, Asia, and Northern Africa, and has naturalized in various locations in North America.

Aster

Aster hybridus

Height: 1 to 2 feet
Growth Habit: Mounded
Bloom Period: Late summer and fall
Flower Color: Various
Zones: 4 through 8
Color photograph on page 248.

Light Requirements:

Beneficial Characteristics:

The forgotten fall-blooming flower, the aster's finely textured foliage and huge number of colorful blossoms make it a star performer in the sunny garden. When plants are massed together, their foliage creates an exaggerated mounded habit that resembles miniature rolling hills. The flower colors are as vibrant as those generally found in the summer garden, and their contrast with classic fall tones, hues, and tints provides a final bolt of intense color near the end of the gardening season.

WHEN TO PLANT

Plant in early spring through early summer and again in the fall.

WHERE TO PLANT

Asters do well in rich organic soil in full sun, and in a spot where water does not sit.

HOW TO PLANT

Regardless of the size of the pot purchased, keep the plant watered prior to planting. Delineate a bed, digging up undesirable plants or removing them with an herbicide. Rototill or spade the soil to a depth of 6 to 8 inches, blend a total of 6 inches of organic matter with the existing soil, and rake smooth, creating a raised bed. Use erosion netting if the site is sloped. Dig a hole twice the width of the pot or a minimum of 12 inches, carefully remove the plant from the pot, loosening the roots if they are pot bound. Place the plant in the hole so that base of plant is slightly higher than surrounding ground,

backfill, firm soil, water the plant thoroughly, and place
1 inch of mulch around the plant.

CARE AND MAINTENANCE

During the growing season, fertilize twice monthly with a
balanced food. Water as needed to prevent any drought
stress, equivalent to 1 inch each week. Cut back the leaves
every 2 weeks from early May through early July, pinch
back the flower buds as needed until end of August to
delay flowering. Pest and disease problems are minimal.
Weeds can be trouble for several years in a new garden,
and careful use of herbicides or hand digging are the only
real solutions. Divide every 3 to 5 years for health, vigor,
and to control size.

ADDITIONAL INFORMATION

Select the best plants at garden centers and through mail-
order nurseries. Garden centers have plants in containers
from 4-inch to 1-gallon pots. The only advantage to the
larger size is that they will bloom sooner. Look for consistent color of foliage. Plants should be actively growing
when purchased. Mail-order plants arrive bareroot
wrapped in moss or in smaller pots.

ADDITIONAL SPECIES, CULTIVARS, OR VARIETIES

A. novi-belgii 'Alert' is a red flowering dwarf variety; a
taller growing, extended blooming variety is *Aster × frikar-
tii*. 'Monch' has pale blue flowers.

Did You Know?

*The aster is a member of the sunflower family, whose close
relatives can be found in the cooler temperate regions across the
world. Other common names include starwort, which means
star-shaped flower, and frost flower, so named because of its
late season blooming. Seeds that form will not come true to the
mother plant.*

Astilbe

Astilbe × arendsii

Height: 1 foot or more
Growth Habit: Spreading
Bloom Period: Summer
Flower Color: Various
Zones: 4 through 8
Color photograph on page 248.

Light Requirements:

Beneficial Characteristics:

The astilbe fulfills the same role for the shade garden as daylilies do for sunny areas, by providing color which is unequaled by any other plant. Its finely textured, numerously segmented collection of leaves grow into a soft mound. As the heat of late spring begins to climb, spikes of a large number of flowers appear in the shape of a feathery plume. If carefully orchestrated, astilbe plants provide a color series that highlights the shady areas of the landscape and makes a striking contrast with neighboring shade garden plants. Their effect is compounded dramatically if the plants are massed in close proximity.

WHEN TO PLANT

Plant in spring through early summer or in early fall.

WHERE TO PLANT

Astilbe require consistently moist, rich, organic soil in a location that is protected from any sun other than very early or late in the day sunlight. If planting under a tree, measure the trunk diameter, multiply by five, and do not install the plants any closer than this distance to the trunk.

HOW TO PLANT

Regardless of the size of the pot purchased, keep the plant watered prior to planting. Delineate a bed, digging up undesirable plants or removing them with an herbicide. Rototill or spade the soil to a depth of 6 to 8 inches, using extreme caution when working under trees because of possible root damage. Blend a total of 6 inches of organic matter with the existing soil and rake smooth, creating a raised bed. During establishment, use erosion netting if the site is sloped. Dig a hole 3 times the width of the root system, carefully remove the plant from the pot, and loosen the roots if they are pot bound. Place the plant in the hole, so that the base is slightly higher than the surrounding ground. Backfill the hole, firm the soil, water the plant thoroughly, and place 1 inch of mulch around the plant.

CARE AND MAINTENANCE

Astilbe benefit from twice-monthly fertilizing during the growing season with a balanced food for the first 2 to 3 years. Water the plant if the growing season is dry, an equivalent of 1 inch each week. It's important to keep the soil damp. Astilbe cannot be allowed drought stress at any time while growing. Cut back the plant as the foliage turns brown. Weeds can be trouble for up to 6 years in a new garden, and careful use of herbicides or hand digging are the only real solutions.

ADDITIONAL INFORMATION

Select the best plants at garden centers and through mail-order nurseries. Garden centers have plants in containers from 4-inch to 1-gallon pots. The only advantage to the larger size is that they will bloom sooner. If the plant is dormant, check for the amount of roots. If it is leafed out, look for consistent size and color of foliage (some have red-toned foliage, some green). Mail-order plants arrive bareroot wrapped in moss or in smaller pots.

ADDITIONAL SPECIES, CULTIVARS, OR VARIETIES

Astilbe simplicifolia 'Sprite', which has pink flowers and a darker green foliage, was named the 1994 Perennial Plant of the Year.

🌿 Did You Know?

Astilbe belongs to the same family as currants and gooseberries, and is native to both North America and Asia. It can be cut for fresh flower arrangements or dried after cutting, or simply left in the garden since it does such a good job of maintaining its color.

Balloonflower

Platycodon grandiflorus

Height: 1 to 2 feet
Growth Habit: Upright
Bloom Period: Summer
Flower Color: Various
Zones: 4 through 8
Color photograph on page 248.

Light Requirements:

Beneficial Characteristics:

The balloonflower requires a patient variety of gardener. For the first couple of years after it is planted, it is often one of the last plants to emerge from winter's dormancy, and once awake its stems may be weak and sluggishly creep along the ground. But patience is well rewarded once the plant's glossy medium-green foliage rises up and small, round flower buds begin to form. As the buds mature, they swell like small inflated balloons until they are almost an inch in diameter. Then the balloon pops and star-shaped flower petals peel backwards, delighting children and adults alike.

WHEN TO PLANT

Plant balloonflowers in the early spring through early summer and again in the fall. June and July are the best months for seeding.

WHERE TO PLANT

Balloonflowers require full sun and rich, organic, and very well-drained soil. Consider placing the plants adjacent to a structure for support.

HOW TO PLANT

Regardless of the size of the pot purchased, keep the plant watered prior to planting. Delineate a bed, digging up undesirable plants or removing them with an herbicide. Rototill or spade the soil to a depth of 6 to 8 inches, blend a total of 6 inches of organic matter with the existing soil, and rake smooth, creating a raised bed. Use erosion netting if the site is sloped. Dig a hole twice the width of the pot or a minimum of 12 inches, carefully remove the plant from the pot, and loosen the roots if they are pot bound. Place the plant in the hole, so that the base is slightly higher than the surrounding ground.

Backfill the hole, firm the soil, water the plant thoroughly, and place 1 inch of mulch around the plant.

CARE AND MAINTENANCE

Fertilize balloonflowers with a balanced food monthly during the growing season. Water as needed to prevent any drought stress, an equivalent of 1 inch each week. Cut back the foliage only after the seeds have formed and fallen or been gathered. Depending on the specific plant, a support system may be necessary to prevent flopping. Pest and disease problems are minimal. Weeds can be trouble for several years in a new garden, and careful use of herbicides or hand digging are the only real solutions.

ADDITIONAL INFORMATION

Select the best plants at garden centers and through mail-order nurseries. Garden centers have plants in containers from 4-inch to 1-gallon pots. The only advantage to the larger size is that they will bloom sooner. Plants should be actively growing when purchased. Look for consistent size and color of foliage. Mail-order plants arrive bareroot wrapped in moss or in smaller pots.

ADDITIONAL SPECIES, CULTIVARS, OR VARIETIES

Platycodon grandiflorus 'Sentimental Blue' is a compact dwarf-growing variety.

 Did You Know?

Native to eastern Asia, the balloonflower is a member of the campanula family, most of which have bell-shaped flowers. The species name, grandiflorus, *means large flowered. The balloonflower is an excellent cutting flower and gives any fresh arrangement a unique look.*

PERENNIALS

Barrenwort

Epimedium × rubrum

Height: Up to 1 foot
Growth Habit: Spreading
Bloom Period: Spring
Flower Color: Red and yellow
Zones: 4 through 8
Color photograph on page 248.

Light Requirements:

Barrenwort is a versatile, high-performing woodland plant. It functions well as a ground cover, its somewhat evergreen qualities stabilizing the ground while giving greenery during the winter. In early spring, cut back the oval leaves that are attached to wirelike stems. This will help rejuvenate the plant and also allow for a better view of the flower whose stem is shorter than the foliage. New leaves will soon emerge. Barrenwort's unusual growing habit allows it to be used as a single specimen plant in a shady rock garden, or with a little work as the living edge along a winding pathway.

WHEN TO PLANT

Plant barrenwort in spring through early summer or in early fall.

WHERE TO PLANT

Barrenwort does well in moist, well-drained, rich organic soil in a location that is protected from any midday sun. If planting under a tree, measure the trunk diameter, multiply by three, and do not install plants any closer than this distance to trunk.

HOW TO PLANT

Regardless of the size of the pot purchased, keep the plant watered prior to planting. Delineate a bed, digging up undesirable plants or removing them with an herbicide. Rototill or spade the soil to a depth of 6 to 8 inches, using extreme caution when working the soil under trees because of possible damage to their roots. Blend a total of 6 inches of organic matter with the existing soil and rake smooth, creating a raised bed. During establishment, use erosion netting if the site is sloped. Dig a hole three times the width of the root system, carefully remove the plant from the pot, and loosen the roots if they are pot bound. Place the plant in the hole, so that the base is slightly higher than the surrounding ground. Backfill the hole, firm the soil, water the plant thoroughly, and place 1 inch of mulch around the plant.

CARE AND MAINTENANCE

Barrenwort benefits from twice-monthly fertilizing during the growing season with a balanced food for the first 2 to 3 years. Water if the growing season is dry, an equivalent to 1 inch each week. Keep the soil damp but do not allow standing water. Cut back the plants after the foliage is at least 50 percent brown and remove any leaf debris to help reduce pests and disease, which are minimal anyway. Weeds can be trouble for several years in a new garden, and careful use of herbicides or hand digging are the only real solutions. Divide the plants every 4 to 5 years.

ADDITIONAL INFORMATION

Select the best plants at garden centers and through mail-order nurseries. Garden centers have plants in containers from 4-inch to 1-gallon pots. The only advantage to the larger size is that they will bloom sooner. If plants are dormant, check for the amount of roots. If they are leafed out, look for consistent size and color of foliage. Mail-order plants arrive bareroot wrapped in moss or in smaller pots.

ADDITIONAL SPECIES, CULTIVARS, OR VARIETIES

Epimedium versicolor 'Sulphureum' is yellow flowered and the most aggressively growing variety of barrenwort.

Did You Know?

Barrenwort belongs to the same family as the thorny barberry bush. The species name, rubrum, *refers to the red color of the flower, which also has some yellow or white highlights. Another common name, bishop's hat, refers to the shape of the individual inflorescence.*

Bleeding Heart

Dicentra spectabilis 'Luxuriant'

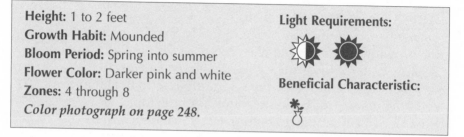

Height: 1 to 2 feet
Growth Habit: Mounded
Bloom Period: Spring into summer
Flower Color: Darker pink and white
Zones: 4 through 8
Color photograph on page 248.

Light Requirements:

Beneficial Characteristic:

The bleeding heart's very finely textured leaf has an airy, surreal look, like that of a mutated fern. Its heavily dissected leaves are a pale blue-green color that is unmatched in woodland gardens. The stem emerges from the center of the plant and rises with an arching habit above the foliage. Very small buds then open, revealing the inflorescence. The two-toned, heart-shaped flower dangles from the stem like a Valentine pendant on a necklace. This improved variety is more heat and sun tolerant and under ideal conditions can continue to bloom in the early fall.

WHEN TO PLANT

Bleeding heart is best planted in early fall, but can also be planted in spring through early summer.

WHERE TO PLANT

Bleeding heart does best in moist, well-drained, rich organic soil in a location that is protected from any midday sun. If planting under a tree, measure trunk's diameter, multiply by three, and do not install the plants any closer than this distance to trunk.

HOW TO PLANT

Regardless of the size of the pot purchased, keep the plant watered prior to planting. Delineate a bed, digging up undesirable plants or removing them with an herbicide. Rototill or spade the soil to a depth of 6 to 8 inches, using extreme caution when working the soil under trees because of possible damage to their roots. Blend a total of 6 inches of organic matter with the existing soil and rake smooth, creating a raised bed. Use erosion netting if the site is sloped. Dig a hole three times the width of the root system, carefully remove the plant from the pot, and loosen the roots if they are pot bound. Place the plant in the hole, so that the base is slightly higher than the surrounding ground. Backfill the hole, firm the soil, water the plant thoroughly, and place 1 inch of mulch around the plant.

CARE AND MAINTENANCE

Bleeding heart benefits from twice-monthly fertilizing during the growing season with a balanced food for the first 2 to 3 years. Water if the growing season is dry, an equivalent to 1 inch each week. Keep the soil damp, but do not allow standing water. Do not cut back the plants, but remove older or damaged leaves that have died. This reduces pest and disease problems, which are minimal anyway. Weeds can be trouble for several years in a new garden, and careful use of herbicides or hand digging are the only real solutions. Dividing the plants is not necessary.

ADDITIONAL INFORMATION

Select the best plants at garden centers and through mail-order nurseries. Garden centers have plants in containers from 4-inch to 1-gallon pots. The only advantage to the larger size is that they will bloom sooner. If plants are dormant, check for the amount of roots. If they are leafed out, look for consistent size and color of foliage. Mail-order plants arrive bareroot wrapped in moss or in smaller pots.

ADDITIONAL SPECIES, CULTIVARS, OR VARIETIES

A close relative is *Dicentra cucullaria*, which is found in the woodland stream beds of Missouri. The unimproved variety *Dicentra spectabilis* goes dormant by early summer.

PERENNIALS

Did You Know?

Bleeding heart is member of a very small family which sometimes is included in the poppy family. It is native to Japan, where it can be found growing in sunny locations as well as in the shade. Spectabilis *means "showy" and refers to eye-catching shape and color of the flowering.*

Chinese Peony

Paeonia lactiflora

Height: 3 feet
Growth Habit: Mounded
Bloom Period: Late spring
Flower Color: White
Zones: 3 through 8
Color photograph on page 248.

Light Requirements:

Beneficial Characteristics:

The peony requires some patience to cultivate, but it has remained one of the most popular perennial plants for generations. Sometimes a plant takes several years to reach full bush size and true flower color. In early spring, the peony's red foliage thrusts upward like a small hand reaching for the sky. The red leaves change to dark green as flower buds spread over the center of the plant. While the leaves unfurl, the alternating flower buds are lifted higher on their stem and continue to swell into nearly perfect spheres. The bud's overlapping protective sheathes peel back, allowing the large peony flower to pop out, an elaborately frilled and fragrant blossom. All varieties finish flowering within a week, so mix early-, mid-, and late-season bloomers to create a lasting and splendid supply of peonies.

WHEN TO PLANT

Plant peonies in early spring through early summer and again in the fall.

WHERE TO PLANT

Peonies do well in full sun in a spot where consistent moisture is available. Do not plant near woody plants to minimize competition between roots for moisture.

HOW TO PLANT

Regardless of the size of the pot purchased, keep the plant watered prior to planting. Delineate a bed, digging up undesirable plants or removing them with an herbicide. Rototill or spade the soil to a depth of 6 to 8 inches, blending in a total of 6 inches of organic matter, and rake smooth, creating a raised bed. Use erosion netting if the site is sloped. Dig a hole twice the width of the pot or a minimum of 12 inches. Carefully remove the plant from the pot and loosen the roots if they are pot bound. Place the plant in the hole, so that the base is slightly higher than the surrounding ground. Backfill the hole, firm the soil, water the plant thoroughly, and place 1 inch of mulch around the plant.

CARE AND MAINTENANCE

Peonies benefit from feeding with a low-analysis fertilizer every few years; apply fertilizer after flowering. Water as needed to prevent any drought stress, an equivalent of 1 inch each week. Peonies typically attract ants, who are gathering nectar from the buds and cause no trouble to the plant. Several leaf and bud diseases are possible and can be minimized by cutting back and removing the foliage in late August. Weeds can be trouble for several years in a new garden, and careful use of herbicides or hand digging are the only real solutions. Do not divide unless absolutely necessary.

ADDITIONAL INFORMATION

Select the best plants, and best size for your garden space, at garden centers and through mail-order nurseries. Garden centers have plants in containers from 6-inch to 2-gallon pots. The only advantage to the larger size is that they will bloom sooner. Plants should be actively growing when purchased. Check for consistent color of foliage. Mail-order plants arrive bareroot wrapped in moss or in smaller pots.

ADDITIONAL SPECIES, CULTIVARS, OR VARIETIES

Paeonia suffruticosa is a woody shrub type with very unique flowers that blooms earlier in the spring. *Paeonia tenuifolia* is a variety with highly dissected, fernlike leaves.

Did You Know?

The peony is native to China and a pillar of traditional Chinese gardens. The species name, lactiflora, *means "milky white," the traditional color of peony flowers. Some plants were hybridized to grow longer stems for use in tall vases and will flop over in the garden setting.*

Common Mallow

Hibiscus moscheutos

Height: 2 to 4 feet
Growth Habit: Upright
Bloom Period: Summer
Flower Color: Red, white, or pink
Zones: 4 through 8
Color photograph on page 248.

Light Requirements:

Beneficial Characteristic:

To the unknowing eye, the shrublike common mallow may at first look like an overgrown weed. In spring its large green leaves with pale undersides are arranged so thickly they nearly obscure the upright stem entirely. Their coarseness creates a dramatic background for early-blooming perennials and annuals, and this plant also is an asset to a mixed sunny shrub border. Once the summer heats up, common mallow steps out of the background to center stage. Its perfectly circular flowers pop open and unfold to widths of up to 10 inches, each a brilliant circle of pure color. Children who are not much bigger than common mallow are especially bewitched by its fantastic flowers.

WHEN TO PLANT

Plant common mallow in early spring through early summer and again in the fall.

WHERE TO PLANT

Common mallow requires full sun. It should be sited where consistent moisture is available and can also tolerate standing water. Place the plant in background to create best impact for foliage.

HOW TO PLANT

Regardless of the size of the pot purchased, keep the plant watered prior to planting. Delineate a bed, digging up undesirable plants or removing them with an herbicide. Rototill or spade the soil to a depth of 6 to 8 inches, blending in a total of 6 inches of organic matter, and rake smooth, creating a raised bed. Use erosion netting if the site is sloped. Dig a hole twice the width of the pot or a minimum of 12 inches. Carefully remove the plant from the pot and loosen the roots if they are pot bound. Place the plant in the hole, so that the

base is slightly higher than the surrounding ground. Backfill the hole, firm the soil, water the plant thoroughly, and place 1 inch of mulch around the plant.

CARE AND MAINTENANCE

For the first 2 or 3 years, fertilize common mallow with a balanced fertilizer in spring. Water to prevent any drought stress, an equivalent of 1 inch each week. Cut back dead stems in the fall as they will not regenerate. Common mallow has the ability to self seed and spread. Pest and disease problems are minimal. Weeds can be trouble for several years in a new garden, and careful use of herbicides or hand digging are the only real solutions. Do not divide frequently or you may cause problems for the plant. Common mallow may self-seed and colonize an area. Divide the plants every 3 years for health, vigor, and to control size.

ADDITIONAL INFORMATION

Select the best plants, and best size for your garden space, at garden centers and through mail-order nurseries. Garden centers have plants in containers from 6-inch to 2-gallon pots. The only advantage to the larger size is that they will bloom sooner. Plants should be actively growing when purchased. Check for consistent color of foliage. Mail-order plants arrive bareroot wrapped in moss or in smaller pots.

ADDITIONAL SPECIES, CULTIVARS, OR VARIETIES

Hibiscus coccineus 'Lord Baltimore' has 10-inch flowers. The flowers of the *Hibiscus moscheutos* 'Turn of the Century' are two-toned, red and pink.

Common Yarrow

Achillea millifolium

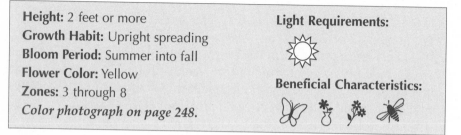

Height: 2 feet or more
Growth Habit: Upright spreading
Bloom Period: Summer into fall
Flower Color: Yellow
Zones: 3 through 8
Color photograph on page 248.

Light Requirements:

Beneficial Characteristics:

Yarrow possesses a number of top-notch qualities, even though it tends to topple in areas where night temperatures are warmer than 70 degrees Fahrenheit. It's easy to grow, has a long blooming period, a unique foliage and flower arrangement, and provides excellent cut flowers. The finely textured leaves spread and wind through the planting space via an underground root system. Shooting up through these paler green leaves are flower stalks which act as pedestals for flat platelike disks of tiny tightly clustered yellow flowers. New foliage growth that begins at ground level while the plant is still in flower indicates all is well for next year. The leaf is aromatic, and the flowers can be cut at various stages of maturity for differing colors in arrangements. Yarrow is very attractive to many different pollinating insects. All of these qualities make it a perfect choice for a new gardener, great for children's gardens, and a favorite of seasoned gardeners.

WHEN TO PLANT
Tough and durable, yarrow can be planted any time of the year when the ground is not frozen, but it will do best if planted in spring or early fall.

WHERE TO PLANT
Plant yarrow in full sun in average or better soil that is well drained.

HOW TO PLANT
Regardless of the size of the pot purchased, keep the plant watered prior to planting. Delineate a bed, digging up undesirable plants or removing them with an herbicide. Rototill or spade the soil to a depth of 6 to 8 inches, blending in a total of 6 inches of organic matter, and rake smooth, creating a raised bed. Use erosion netting if the

site is sloped. Dig a hole twice the width of the pot or a minimum of 12 inches. Carefully remove the plant from the pot and loosen the roots if they are pot bound. Place the plant in the hole, so that the base is slightly higher than the surrounding ground. Backfill the hole, firm the soil, water the plant thoroughly, and place 1 inch of mulch around the plant.

CARE AND MAINTENANCE

For the first 2 or 3 years, fertilize yarrow with a balanced food twice monthly throughout the growing season. Water if the growing season is extremely dry, an equivalent of 1 inch each week. Cut back plants through the growing season after the foliage is at least 50 percent brown and remove any leaf debris. This will help reduce pest and disease problems, which a should be minimal anyway. Weeds can be trouble for several years in a new garden, and careful use of herbicides or hand digging are the only real solutions. Divide plants to control size.

ADDITIONAL INFORMATION

Select the best plants, and best size for your garden space, at garden centers and through mail-order nurseries. Garden centers have plants in containers from 4-inch to 2-gallon pots. The only advantage to the larger size is that they will bloom sooner. Plants should be actively growing when purchased. Check for consistent color of foliage. Mail-order plants arrive bareroot wrapped in moss or in smaller pots.

ADDITIONAL SPECIES, CULTIVARS, OR VARIETIES

Achillea 'Summer Pastels' provide softer hues and *Achillea millefolium* 'Paprika' adds reddish orange flowers to the summer garden.

Daylily

Hemerocallis ssp.

Height: 2 to 3 feet
Growth Habit: Arching
Bloom Period: Summer
Flower Color: Various
Zones: 4 through 8
Color photograph on page 248.

Light Requirements:

Beneficial Characteristics:

Probably no plant is more widely known nor has won the interest and dedication more fully than this group of lilies. They can be found growing almost anywhere, from along abandoned fencerows and roadways, to spacious suburban yards, and tidy urban flower beds. Their allure results from many factors: their great variety, the relatively easy work it takes to grow them, the fact that their medium-green grasslike leaves transition very smoothly from one designated landscape area to another, and, of course, their exciting star-shaped flowers that float above the foliage on sticklike stems. Daylilies include early, mid-season, and late-season bloomers and can be relied on to carry the summer with brilliant style. There are also deciduous and evergreen types. The American Hemerocallis Society classifies them into three categories: evergreen, semi-evergreen, and dormant. Several varieties offer a bonus of welcome fragrance when in bloom.

WHEN TO PLANT

Daylilies are tough and durable and can be planted at any time of year when the ground is not frozen. They do best when planted in spring or early fall.

WHERE TO PLANT

Plant daylilies in full sun, and in average or better soil where there is no standing water.

HOW TO PLANT

Regardless of the size of the pot purchased, keep the plant watered prior to planting. Delineate a bed, digging up undesirable plants or removing them with an herbicide. Rototill or spade the soil to a depth of 6 to 8 inches, blend a total of 6 inches of organic matter with the existing soil, and rake smooth, creating a raised bed. Use erosion netting if the site is sloped. Dig a hole twice the width of the pot or a minimum of 12 inches. Carefully remove the plant from the pot and loosen the roots if they are pot bound. Place the plant in the hole, so that the base is slightly higher than the surrounding ground. Backfill the hole, firm the soil, water the plant thoroughly, and place 1 inch of mulch around the plant.

CARE AND MAINTENANCE

Daylilies benefit from a spring application of balanced fertilizer for the first 2 to 3 years. Water if the growing season is extremely dry, an equivalent of 1 inch each week. Cut back the plants through the growing season after the foliage is at least 50 percent brown and remove any leaf debris. This will reduce pest and disease problems, which should be minimal. Weeds can be trouble for several years in a new garden, and careful use of herbicides or hand digging are the only real solutions. Divide the plants every 3 to 5 years to control size, vigor, and flowering quantity.

ADDITIONAL INFORMATION

Select the best plants at garden centers and through mail-order nurseries. Garden centers have plants in containers from 4-inch to 1-gallon pots. The only advantage to the larger size is that they will bloom sooner. Plants should actively growing when purchased. Check for consistent size and color of foliage. Mail-order plants arrive bareroot wrapped in moss or in smaller pots.

ADDITIONAL SPECIES, CULTIVARS, OR VARIETIES

There are over 20,000 registered cultivars. Two repeat bloomers are *Hemerocallis* 'Eenie Weenie' and *Hemerocallis* 'Stella d'Oro'; both are yellow flowered.

Fall Windflower

Anemone × hybrida

Height: 1 to 4 feet
Growth Habit: Upright
Bloom Period: Late summer into fall
Flower Color: Various
Zones: 4 through 8
Color photograph on page 248.

Light Requirements:

Beneficial Characteristics:

The mystery about the fall windflower is that this beautiful perennial is virtually unknown. Its darker green, dissected or segmented leaves form a mound from the time they emerge in the spring through the entire growing season. The color and bulkiness of its foliage habit make it a great backdrop for early-blooming, fine-textured plants. When the heat of summer has passed and nights are enjoyably cool, the fall windflower steps forth to give late-season pollinators a source of food. The fine stem rises above the foliage, carrying a blossom that even from up close looks to be merely suspended in mid-air. Its blooms spark the late-season garden with color and are a delight, especially when planted in masses, to watch floating on autumn breezes.

WHEN TO PLANT

Plant fall windflowers in the early spring through early summer and again in the fall.

WHERE TO PLANT

Fall windflowers do well in rich, organic, moist soil that is well drained and in part shade to fuller sun.

HOW TO PLANT

Regardless of the size of the pot purchased, keep the plant watered prior to planting. Delineate a bed, digging up undesirable plants or removing them with an herbicide. Rototill or spade the soil to a depth of 6 to 8 inches, blend a total of 6 inches of organic matter with the existing soil, and rake smooth, creating a raised bed. Use erosion netting if the site is sloped. Dig a hole twice the width of the pot or a minimum of 12 inches. Carefully remove the plant from the pot and loosen the roots if they are pot bound. Place the plant in the hole, so that the base is slightly higher than the surrounding ground. Backfill the hole, firm the soil, water the plant thoroughly, and place 1 inch of mulch around the plant.

CARE AND MAINTENANCE

Fall windflowers benefit from a spring application of a balanced fertilizer for the first 2 to 3 years. Water if needed to prevent any drought stress, an equivalent of 1 inch each week. Cut back the flowers when bloom is finished, as the seed will set. Weeds can be trouble for several years in a new garden, and careful use of herbicides or hand digging are the only real solutions. Divide the plants every 3 or more years for health, vigor, and to increase the number of plants.

ADDITIONAL INFORMATION

Select the best plants at garden centers and through mail-order nurseries. Garden centers have plants in containers from 4-inch to 1-gallon pots. The only advantage to the larger size is that they will bloom sooner. Plants should actively growing when purchased. Check for consistent size and color of foliage. Mail-order plants arrive bareroot wrapped in moss or in smaller pots.

ADDITIONAL SPECIES, CULTIVARS, OR VARIETIES

Anemone tomentosa 'Robustissima' (grapeleaf anemone) has darker green foliage and is an excellent cutting flower.

Did You Know?

The fall windflower belongs to the buttercup family, which includes two plants that are native to Missouri, columbine and meadow anemone. This hybrid is the result of crossing several different natural species, such as the one found in Japan and a variety that has a leaf similar to the grapevine.

Fortune's Hosta

Hosta fortunei

Height: 2 feet or more
Growth Habit: Mounded
Bloom Period: Early summer
Flower Color: Pale bluish lavender
Zones: 3 through 9
Color photograph on page 248.

Light Requirements:

Beneficial Characteristics:

The smoothed domed silhouette and wonderful textural variety of hosta plants make them an attractive addition to any shade garden, whether planted in single clumps or artfully arranged in masses. Hosta serve as a graceful transitions between woody plants and lower growing perennials. Their foliage ranges in color from cool to lime greens, yellows, whites, and bluish gray-green tones. Their tall, delicate stems support pale lavender flowers that lighten even the deepest shade. Introduced only 25 years ago to American landscapes, this plant has soared to the top of popularity polls.

WHEN TO PLANT

Plant hosta in spring through early summer or in the early fall.

WHERE TO PLANT

Hosta do well in moist, well-drained, rich organic soil that is protected from any midday sun. If planting under a tree, measure the trunk diameter, multiply by three, and do not install plants any closer than this distance to the trunk.

HOW TO PLANT

Regardless of the size of the pot purchased, keep the plant watered prior to planting. Delineate a bed, digging up undesirable plants or removing them with an herbicide. Rototill or spade the soil to a depth of 6 to 8 inches, using extreme caution under trees to avoid possibly damaging their roots. Blend a total of 6 inches of organic matter with the existing soil and rake smooth, creating a raised bed. Use erosion netting if the site is sloped. Dig a hole three times the width of the root system. Carefully remove the plant from the pot and loosen the roots if they are pot bound. Place the plant in the hole, so that the base is slightly higher than the surrounding ground.

Backfill the hole, firm the soil, water the plant thoroughly, and place 1 inch of mulch around the plant.

CARE AND MAINTENANCE

Hostas benefit from twice monthly fertilizing during the growing season with a balanced food for the first 2 to 3 years. Water if the growing season is dry, an equivalent of 1 inch each week, keeping the soil damp but not allowing any standing water. When flowering is finished, remove stalks. Cut back plants after foliage is at least 50 percent brown and remove any leaf debris. This will reduce pest and disease problems, which are minimal anyway. Weeds can be trouble for several years in a new garden, and careful use of herbicides or hand digging are the only real solutions. It is not necessary for their health, but the plants can be divided every 4 to 5 years to expand the collection.

ADDITIONAL INFORMATION

Select the best plants at garden centers and through mail-order nurseries. Garden centers have plants in containers from 4-inch to 1-gallon pots. The only advantage to the larger size is that they will bloom sooner. If plants are dormant, check for the amount of roots. If leafed out, check for consistent size and color of foliage. Mail-order plants arrive bareroot wrapped in moss or in smaller pots.

ADDITIONAL SPECIES, CULTIVARS, OR VARIETIES

Hosta plantaginea has a very large, fragrant white flower. *Hosta ventricosa* has a pale lavender flower whose bud opens immediately.

Did You Know?

Hostas belong to the lily family native to many areas in Japan and have been in cultivation for many centuries. One common name, plantain lily, refers to the similarities to a common lawn weed in leaf shape. The species name, fortunei, *is a derivative of the last name of the person who discovered the species.*

Hardy Sage

Salvia × superba

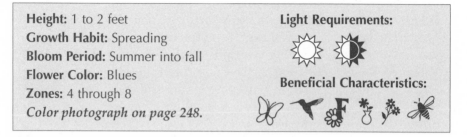

Height: 1 to 2 feet
Growth Habit: Spreading
Bloom Period: Summer into fall
Flower Color: Blues
Zones: 4 through 8
Color photograph on page 248.

Light Requirements:

Beneficial Characteristics:

The hardy sage flowers in cool shades of blue that offer a breath of relief during the heat of summer. This plant has spreading growth habit, its darker green foliage blanketing the ground and the vertical flowering stalks powerfully punctuating the landscape. The crowning touch, the blue blooms, flower from early to mid-summer after many other flowers have disappeared. Hardy sage is very easy to grow, and its extraordinary aesthetic attributes makes it a bonus to any garden no matter the style.

WHEN TO PLANT

Plant hardy sage in early spring through early summer and again in fall.

WHERE TO PLANT

Hardy sage does well in rich, organic, moist soil that is well drained and in full sun.

HOW TO PLANT

Regardless of the size of the pot purchased, keep the plant watered prior to planting. Delineate a bed, digging up undesirable plants or removing them with an herbicide. Rototill or spade the soil to a depth of 6 to 8 inches, blend a total of 6 inches of organic matter with the existing soil, and rake smooth, creating a raised bed. Use erosion netting if the site is sloped. Dig a hole twice the width of the pot or a minimum of 12 inches. Carefully remove the plant from the pot and loosen the roots if they are pot bound. Place the plant in the hole, so that the base is slightly higher than the surrounding ground.

Backfill the hole, firm the soil, water the plant thoroughly, and place 1 inch of mulch around the plant.

CARE AND MAINTENANCE

Hardy sage benefits from monthly fertilizing throughout the growing season with a balanced food for the first 2 to 3 years. Water if needed to prevent any drought stress, an equivalent of 1 inch each week. Periodically cut back the flowers to encourage a rebloom later in the growing season. Weeds can be trouble for several years in a new garden, and careful use of herbicides or hand digging are the only real solutions. Divide the plants every 3 or more years for health, vigor, and to increase the number of plants.

ADDITIONAL INFORMATION

Select the best plants at garden centers and through mail-order nurseries. Garden centers have plants in containers from 4-inch to 1-gallon pots. The only advantage to the larger size is that they will bloom sooner. Plants should actively growing when purchased. Check for consistent size and color of foliage. Mail-order plants arrive bareroot wrapped in moss or in smaller pots.

ADDITIONAL SPECIES, CULTIVARS, OR VARIETIES

Salvia × *sylvestris* ' May Night', which has deep purple flowers and is a compact grower, was named the Perennial Plant of the Year in 1997.

Did You Know?

A member of the mint family, the sages are a diverse group of plants that include annuals, perennials, herbs, and woodies. Some with fragrant leaves are used for perfumes; others with woolly leaves and still others traditionally have been used for medicinal purposes. The species, Superba, *means "showy or proud."*

Hollyhock

Alcea rosea

Height: 4 feet or more	**Light Requirements:**
Growth Habit: Upright	
Bloom Period: Summer	
Flower Color: Mixed	
Zones: 4 through 8	**Beneficial Characteristics:**
Color photograph on page 249.	

An old-time favorite, the hollyhock is no snob about where it makes its home. Growing equally well in pastures or in formal perennial borders, the hollyhock spells summer with a flair. Its straight-up growth habit creates dramatic vertical relief in the sun garden. A basal rosette of circular and coarsely textured leaves first appears. Then a tall skewer of a stem erupts from the center of the plant. The flowers are so numerous they almost obscure the stem. Very few plants have such a fantastic flower arrangement or give more lasting pleasure.

WHEN TO PLANT

Plant hollyhocks in early spring through early summer and again in the fall. June and July are the best time if planting from seed.

WHERE TO PLANT

Plant hollyhocks in full sun where the soil is rich, organic, and very well drained. Consider placing the plants adjacent to a structure for support.

HOW TO PLANT

Regardless of the size of the pot purchased, keep the plant watered prior to planting. Delineate a bed, digging up undesirable plants or removing them with an herbicide. Rototill or spade the soil to a depth of 6 to 8 inches, blend a total of 6 inches of organic matter with the existing soil, and rake smooth, creating a raised bed. Use erosion netting if the site is sloped. Dig a hole twice the width of the pot or a minimum of 12 inches. Carefully remove the plant from the pot and loosen the roots if they are pot bound. Place the plant in the hole, so that the base is slightly higher than the surrounding ground. Backfill the hole, firm the soil, water the plant thoroughly, and place 1 inch of mulch around the plant.

CARE AND MAINTENANCE

Hollyhocks benefit from monthly fertilizing throughout the growing season with a balanced food. Water if needed to prevent any drought stress, an equivalent of 1 inch each week. Cut back foliage only after seeds have formed and fallen or been gathered. Depending on the specific plant, a support system may be necessary to prevent flopping. Weeds can be trouble for several years in a new garden, and careful use of herbicides or hand digging are the only real solutions. Pest and disease problems are minimal.

ADDITIONAL INFORMATION

This plant is a biennial; during the first year, it produces only the foliage, and during the second, it produces both the leaf and flower. The pattern repeats year after year. Select the best plants at garden centers and through mail-order nurseries. Garden centers have plants in containers from 4-inch to 1-gallon pots. The only advantage to the larger size is that they will bloom sooner. Plants should actively growing when purchased. Check for consistent size and color of foliage. Mail-order plants arrive bareroot wrapped in moss or in smaller pots.

ADDITIONAL SPECIES, CULTIVARS, OR VARIETIES

Alcea rosea 'Nigra' is a 5-foot variety with almost black (deepest purple) flowers; *Alcea officinalis* 'Romney Marsh' has foliage that is narrower and very different in appearance from the traditional leaf.

Did You Know?

The hollyhock is native to Asia Minor, but because of ease of growth and propagation it has spread throughout the world's cooler temperate regions. It belongs to the hibiscus family, which also includes cotton and okra. To ensure flowers every year, purchase plants in leaf only for 2 or 3 years in a row.

Iris

Iris spp. 'Bearded hybrids'

Height: 1 to 2 feet	**Light Requirements:**
Growth Habit: Upright	
Bloom Period: Spring	
Flower Color: Mixed	**Beneficial Characteristic:**
Zones: 4 through 8	
Color photograph on page 249.	

The bearded iris, fleur-de-lis, and flags are just three of the common names associated with this traditional variety of iris. Very much at home along the hog wire fencing of the countryside or standing in pristine formal garden, irises first begin to put on a show in early spring. Coarse, pale green foliage appears and elongates in a fan configuration. Just as the foliage reaches maximum height, a strange looking spear emerges at the center. The bud unfurls and finally opens to reveal an extraordinary blossom which combines almost all of the colors and shades of nature in a single flower, depending on the variety. Cool weather allows the inflorescence to persist for a longer period of time. When the bloom finishes, the flower folds up, leaving no sign of the remarkable beauty so recently exposed. Irises are a must in every garden, yard, and landscape.

WHEN TO PLANT

Irises are tough and durable and can be planted any time of year when the ground is not frozen, but do best if planted in July or August.

WHERE TO PLANT

Plant irises in the full sun in just about any kind of well-drained soil.

HOW TO PLANT

Regardless of the size of the pot purchased, keep the plant watered prior to planting. Delineate a bed, digging up undesirable plants or removing them with an herbicide. Rototill or spade the soil to a depth of 6 to 8 inches. It is not necessary to add any organic matter, but up to 6 inches of organic matter can be blended with the existing soil before it is raked smooth. Place rhizome right on top of the ground and push down slightly. If using container-grown plant, divide into root sections before planting. Firm the soil, water the plant thoroughly, and place 1 inch of mulch around the plant, but not over root.

CARE AND MAINTENANCE

Feed irises monthly from mid May until late July with a lower analysis fertilizer. Weeds can be trouble for several years in a new garden, and careful use of herbicides or hand digging are the only real solutions. Divide every three years and discard nonleafing sections.

ADDITIONAL INFORMATION

Select the best plants at garden centers and through mail-order nurseries. Garden centers have plants in containers from 4-inch to 1-gallon pots. The only advantage to the larger size is that they will bloom sooner. Check for consistent color of foliage. Mail-order plants arrive bareroot wrapped in moss or in smaller pots.

ADDITIONAL SPECIES, CULTIVARS, OR VARIETIES

Iris cristata is a low-growing species which blooms earlier in the spring and has the same type of groundcover growth habit.

Did You Know?

A very diverse group of plants, irises can be found in just about every type of environment in the northern temperate regions. The bearded flower is divided in various parts, the standards point upward, and the beard is a marking that entices insects in for a feast of pollen.

Lady's Mantle

Alchemilla mollis

Height: 1 to 2 feet
Growth Habit: Mounded
Bloom Period: Late spring
Flower Color: Greenish
Zones: 4 through 8
Color photograph on page 249.

Light Requirements:

A semi-evergreen, low-growing, coarsely textured plant, lady's mantle when viewed from a distance nearly resembles a boulder overgrown with lichens and moss. Closer inspection reveals a perfectly marvelous plant which has a subtle beauty that is hard to pinpoint. The foliage which sprays out parallel to the ground is an unusual shade of green, and the saucer-shaped leaf bears markings on the edge that look and feel as if it were embossed by a machine. After watering, a rainfall, or the heavy morning dew, a bead of water sits in the leaf-saucer, sparkling like a diamond. Lady's mantle is a true jewel for any garden.

WHEN TO PLANT

Plant lady's mantle in Spring through early summer or in early fall.

WHERE TO PLANT

Plant lady's mantle in moist, well-drained, rich organic soil in a location that is protected from any midday sun. If planting under a tree, measure the trunk's diameter, multiply by three, and do not install plants any closer than this distance to the trunk.

HOW TO PLANT

Regardless of the size of the pot purchased, keep the plant watered prior to planting. Delineate a bed, digging up undesirable plants or removing them with an herbicide. Rototill or spade the soil to a depth of 6 to 8 inches, using extreme caution under trees to avoid possibly damaging their roots. Blend a total of 6 inches of organic matter with the existing soil and rake smooth, creating a raised bed. Use erosion netting if the site is sloped. Dig a hole three times the width of the root system. Carefully remove the plant from the pot and loosen the roots if they are pot bound. Place the plant in the hole, so that the base is slightly higher than the surrounding ground. Backfill the hole, firm the soil, water the plant thoroughly, and place 1 inch of mulch around the plant.

CARE AND MAINTENANCE

Lady's mantle benefit from twice-monthly fertilizing during growing season with a balanced food for the first 2 to 3 years. Water if the growing season is dry, an equivalent of 1 inch each week. Keep the soil damp but allow no standing water. Do not cut back plants, but remove older or damaged leaves that have died. Doing so helps reduce pest and disease problems, which are minimal anyway. Weeds can be trouble for several years in a new garden, and careful use of herbicides or hand digging are the only real solutions. Dividing plants is not necessary.

ADDITIONAL INFORMATION

Select the best plants at garden centers and through mail-order nurseries. Garden centers have plants in containers from 4-inch to 1-gallon pots. The only advantage to the larger size is that they will bloom sooner. If dormant, check for the amount of roots; if leafed out, check for consistent size and color of foliage. Mail-order plants arrive bareroot wrapped in moss or in smaller pots.

ADDITIONAL SPECIES, CULTIVARS, OR VARIETIES

A more true-green, smaller-leafed species with a chartreuse flower is *Alchemilla erythropoda* (red-stemmed lady's mantle).

Did You Know?

Lady's mantle, a member of the rose family, is native to Europe where the dried and ground roots traditionally have been used for medicinal purposes. Mollis, the species name, means "soft and hairy," an accurate description of the look and feel of the foliage.

Lily-of-the-Valley

Convallaria majalis

Height: Up to 1 foot
Growth Habit: Spreading
Bloom Period: Spring
Flower Color: White
Zones: 4 through 8
Color photograph on page 249.

Light Requirements:

Beneficial Characteristics:

Lily of the valley combines delicately beautiful and sweetly fragrant flowers with a dense, coarse-textured foliage that carpets the shade garden. Its dark green, elliptical leaves emerge in early spring, sprouting at equal intervals from a root system that spreads at a very shallow depth. While the foliage is at its peak color, spikes arise from the center of the plants and out shoots a series of neatly spaced, white, bell-shaped, fragrant flowers. Easy to care for and aesthetically rewarding, this member of the lily family is delightful wherever planted and exceptionally well suited for plantings around seating areas, where its lovely fragrance can be enjoyed, or aligning pathways. The flowers can also be cut and used in smaller vases.

When to Plant

Plant lily of the valley in spring time through early summer or in early fall; set plants no further than 8 inches apart.

Where to Plant

Lily of the valley requires moist, well-drained, rich organic soil in a location that is protected from any midday sun. If planting under a tree, measure the trunk diameter, multiply by three, and do not install plants any closer than this distance to the trunk.

How to Plant

Regardless of the size of the pot purchased, keep the plant watered prior to planting. Delineate a bed, digging up undesirable plants or removing them with an herbicide. Rototill or spade the soil to a depth of 6 to 8 inches, using extreme caution under trees to avoid possibly damaging their roots. Blend a total of 6 inches of organic matter with the existing soil and rake smooth, creating a raised bed.

Use erosion netting if the site is sloped. Dig a hole three times the width of the root system. Carefully remove the plant from the pot and loosen the roots if they are pot bound. Place the plant in the hole, so that the base is slightly higher than the surrounding ground. Backfill the hole, firm the soil, water the plant thoroughly, and place 1 inch of mulch around the plant.

CARE AND MAINTENANCE

Lily of the valley benefits from twice monthly fertilizing during the growing season with a balanced food for the first 2 to 3 years. Water if the growing season is dry, an equivalent of 1 inch each week, keeping the soil damp but not allowing any standing water. Cut back plants after foliage is at least 50 percent brown and remove any leaf debris. This will reduce pest and disease problems, which are minimal anyway. Weeds can be trouble for several years in a new garden, and careful use of herbicides or hand digging are the only real solutions. Divide plants every 4 to 5 years.

ADDITIONAL INFORMATION

Select the best plants at garden centers and through mail-order nurseries. Garden centers have plants in containers from 4-inch to 1-gallon pots. The only advantage to the larger size is that they will bloom sooner. If dormant, check for the amount of roots; if leafed out, check for consistent size and color of foliage. Mail-order plants arrive bareroot as pips, single eyes, wrapped in moss or in smaller pots.

ADDITIONAL SPECIES, CULTIVARS, OR VARIETIES

Convallaria majalis 'Rosea' is a pink flowering cultivar. The cultivar *Convallaria majalis* 'Aurea-variegata' has yellow and green variegated leaves.

Liveforever

Hylotelephium spectabile

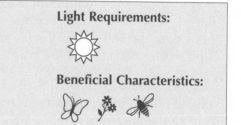

Height: 1 to 2 feet
Growth Habit: Mounded
Bloom Period: Late summer
Flower Color: Lavender pink
Zones: 4 through 8
Color photograph on page 249.

Light Requirements:

Beneficial Characteristics:

Liveforever is truly a four-season perennial. During the winter, its low clump of miniature, pale gray-green foliage thrives when most other greenery has vanished. The cluster of leaves enlarges with warmer days, looking something like the helmet of a spring soldier pushing up from underground. As the days lengthen with summer, a large rosette of flowers, like a stalk of pale green broccoli, rises above the leaves. The stem lengthens, bending under its heavy flower, and when the pink blossoms open late in the season they attract butterflies and other pollen gatherers. Check the flowering plant carefully and you'll see next year's leaves already growing at its base.

WHEN TO PLANT

Tough and durable liveforever can be planted any time of year when the ground is not frozen, but does best if planted in spring or early fall.

WHERE TO PLANT

Plant liveforever in full sun in average to poor soil that is well drained.

HOW TO PLANT

Regardless of the size of the pot purchased, keep the plant watered prior to planting. Delineate a bed, digging up undesirable plants or removing them with an herbicide. Rototill or spade the soil to a depth of 6 to 8 inches and rake smooth, creating a raised bed. It is not necessary to add any organic matter to the soil. Dig a hole twice the width of the pot or a minimum of 12 inches. Carefully remove the plant from the pot and loosen the roots if they are pot bound. Place the plant in the hole, so that the base is slightly higher than the surrounding ground. Backfill the hole, firm the soil, water the plant thoroughly, and place 1 inch of mulch around the plant.

CARE AND MAINTENANCE

Liveforever can be forgotten once it is planted. It needs no care or maintenance. The stems elongate during the growing season and will flop over just prior to flowering. This will happen regardless of planting technique or soil quality or fertility. It will be more pronounced if the plant is fertilized or first planted in rich soil. Weeds can be trouble for several years in a new garden, and careful use of herbicides or hand digging are the only real solutions. Divide liveforever frequently to increase the number of plants.

ADDITIONAL INFORMATION

Select the best plants at garden centers and through mail-order nurseries. Garden centers have plants in containers from 4-inch to 2-gallon pots. The only advantage to the larger size is that they will bloom sooner. Plants should be actively growing when purchased. Mail-order plants arrive bareroot as pips, single eyes, wrapped in moss or in smaller pots.

ADDITIONAL SPECIES, CULTIVARS, OR VARIETIES

Sedum spectabile 'Variegatum' has a pale green and yellow leaf. The flower of *Sedum spectabile* 'Brilliant' is a deeper color.

Did You Know?

Members of this family can be found throughout the northern temperate regions of the world. The species name, spectabile, *means "showy" and refers to the large broccoli like flower head. Liveforever is one of the easiest plants to propagate. Simply break off a section of the stem and stick it into well-drained soil.*

Mums

Chrysanthemum morifolium

Height: 1 to 3 feet
Growth Habit: Mounded
Bloom Period: Fall
Flower Color: Mixed
Zones: 4 through 8
Color photograph on page 249.

Light Requirements:

Beneficial Characteristics:

No fall picture is complete without mums. They invigorate the fading fall garden with a rich harvest of colors. The highly dissected, medium-to-dark-green foliage makes a perfectly stout, fine-textured plant in a sunny garden. If this variety is allowed to grow, it will flower during the summer, so the gardener who wants a fall bloom must cut back foliage and work to keep blooms pinched back. Such careful attention is well rewarded when cooler fall days bring bright mum blossoms and altering hues of color as the flowers age.

WHEN TO PLANT
Plant mums in early spring through early summer and again in the fall.

WHERE TO PLANT
Plant in full sun in a spot where water does not sit, but also in a place that can be easily watered if necessary. Drought stress should never occur.

HOW TO PLANT
Regardless of the size of the pot purchased, keep the plant watered prior to planting. Delineate a bed, digging up undesirable plants or removing them with an herbicide. Rototill or spade the soil to a depth of 6 to 8 inches, blending in a total of 6 inches of organic matter, and rake smooth, creating a raised bed. Use erosion netting if the site is sloped. Dig a hole twice the width of the pot or a minimum of 12 inches. Carefully remove the plant from the pot and loosen the roots if they are pot bound. Place the plant in the hole, so that the base is slightly higher than the surrounding ground. Backfill the

hole, firm the soil, water the plant thoroughly, and place 1 inch of mulch around the plant.

CARE AND MAINTENANCE

Fertilize mums with a balanced food twice monthly throughout the growing season. Water as needed to prevent any drought stress, an equivalent of 1 inch each week. Cut back the leaves back every two weeks from early May through early July, and pinch back flower buds as needed until mid-August to ensure fall flowering. Pest and disease problems are minimal. Weeds can be trouble for several years in a new garden, and careful use of herbicides or hand digging are the only real solutions. Divide mums every 3 to 5 years for health, vigor, and to control size.

ADDITIONAL INFORMATION

Select the best plants, and best size for your garden space, at garden centers and through mail-order nurseries. Garden centers have plants in containers from 4-inch to 2-gallon pots. The only advantage to the larger size is that they will bloom sooner. Plants should be actively growing when purchased. Check for consistent color of foliage. Mail-order plants arrive bareroot wrapped in moss or in smaller pots.

ADDITIONAL SPECIES, CULTIVARS, OR VARIETIES

Numerous types of mums are available, many with differing growth habits and flowering sizes and structures.

Did You Know?

This member of the sunflower family is native to China where it is commonly planted in traditional garden settings. Several close members of the ornamental mum are used for a variety of purposes, including as an insecticide, in medicine, and one is eaten as a green leafy vegetable in the Orient.

Obedient Plant

Physostegia virginiana

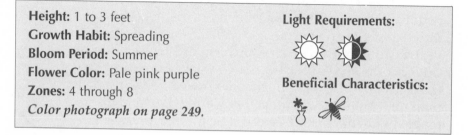

Height: 1 to 3 feet
Growth Habit: Spreading
Bloom Period: Summer
Flower Color: Pale pink purple
Zones: 4 through 8
Color photograph on page 249.

Light Requirements:

Beneficial Characteristics:

Aptly named, the obedient plant does just about anything you want it to. It is remarkably easy to grow and fills many different roles in a multitude of garden settings. The plant's rapidly growing, spreading root system allows for quick coverage and almost instant impact in a location. The density of the foliage is more pronounced near the ground; further up the stem, the size and shape of the leaves change. The flower stalks emerge above the dense foliage, producing tubular flowers up to 1½ inches long. Obedient plants are especially dramatic when used to outline a garden space or placed along a walk or patio.

WHEN TO PLANT

Plant in early spring through early summer and again in the fall.

WHERE TO PLANT

Plant in full sun in a spot where water does not sit, but not in a place that will be difficult to water if necessary. Drought stress should never occur.

HOW TO PLANT

Regardless of the size of the pot purchased, keep the plant watered prior to planting. Delineate a bed, digging up undesirable plants or removing them with an herbicide. Rototill or spade the soil to a depth of 6 to 8 inches, blending in a total of 6 inches of organic matter, and rake smooth, creating a raised bed. Use erosion netting if the site is sloped. Dig a hole twice the width of the pot or a minimum of 12 inches. Carefully remove the plant from the pot and loosen the roots if they are pot bound. Place the plant in the hole, so that the base is slightly higher than the surrounding ground. Backfill the

hole, firm the soil, water the plant thoroughly, and place
1 inch of mulch around the plant.

CARE AND MAINTENANCE
For the first 2 or 3 years, fertilize obedient plants with a
balanced fertilizer in spring. Water as needed to prevent
any drought stress, an equivalent of 1 inch each week. Cut
back flowers periodically through the growing season to
encourage a bloom later in the season. Pest and disease
problems are minimal. Weeds can be trouble for several
years in a new garden, and careful use of herbicides or
hand digging are the only real solutions. Divide obedient
plants every 3 years for health, vigor, and to control size.

ADDITIONAL INFORMATION
Select the best plants, and best size for your garden
space, at garden centers and through mail-order nurseries.
Garden centers have plants in containers from 4-inch to
2-gallon pots. The only advantage to the larger size is that
they will bloom sooner. Plants should be actively growing
when purchased. Check for consistent color of foliage.
Mail-order plants arrive bareroot wrapped in moss or in
smaller pots.

ADDITIONAL SPECIES, CULTIVARS, OR VARIETIES
Physostegia virginiana 'Summer Snow' is a taller variety
with pure white flowers.

Did You Know?

*Called "viriginia" because it was first discovered in Virginia,
this plant been in cultivated since the mid-1600s. It was named
"obedient" not because it is easy to raise, but because if the
plant is gently turned it will remain pointed in that direction.
This plant is especially well suited for a children's garden.*

Purple Coneflower

Echinacea purpurea

Height: 2 to 3 feet
Growth Habit: Upright
Bloom Period: Summer
Flower Color: Purple
Zones: 4 through 8
Color photograph on page 249.

Light Requirements:

Beneficial Characteristics:

The coneflower is cousin to the sunflower and a good representative of the wide diversity in that family. Its strong stalk emerges in the spring from an overwinter clump of foliage. The coarse, sandpaper-like leaves are alternately arranged on the stem. Large and closely placed near the ground, the leaves are smaller and more widely placed as they climb upward toward the flower head. The vivid pink-purple petals and brownish-green disk of the flower stand out in the sunny garden. Because purple is a receding color, be sure to place coneflowers at the front or in the middle of the garden.

WHEN TO PLANT

Tough and durable, coneflowers can be planted at any time when the ground is not frozen, although they do best when planted in spring or early fall.

WHERE TO PLANT

Plant coneflowers in full sun in average or better soil that is well drained.

HOW TO PLANT

Regardless of the size of the pot purchased, keep the plant watered prior to planting. Delineate a bed, digging up undesirable plants or removing them with an herbicide. Rototill or spade the soil to a depth of 6 to 8 inches, blending in a total of 6 inches of organic matter, and rake smooth, creating a raised bed. Use erosion netting if the site is sloped. Dig a hole twice the width of the pot or a minimum of 12 inches. Carefully remove the plant from the pot and loosen the roots if they are pot bound. Place the plant in the hole, so that the base is slightly higher than the surrounding ground. Backfill the

hole, firm the soil, water the plant thoroughly, and place 1 inch of mulch around the plant.

CARE AND MAINTENANCE

For the first 2 or 3 years, fertilize coneflowers with a balanced food twice monthly throughout the growing season. Water if season is extremely dry, an equivalent of 1 inch each week. Cut back flowers periodically through the growing season to encourage a bloom later in the season. Pest and disease problems are minimal. Weeds can be trouble for several years in a new garden, and careful use of herbicides or hand digging are the only real solutions. Do not divide frequently or you may cause problems for the plant. Coneflowers may self seed and colonize an area. Divide plants every 3 years for health and vigor, and to control size.

ADDITIONAL INFORMATION

Select the best plants, and best size for your garden space, at garden centers and through mail-order nurseries. Garden centers have plants in containers from 4-inch to 2-gallon pots. The only advantage to the larger size is that they will bloom sooner. Plants should be actively growing when purchased. Check for consistent color of foliage. Mail-order plants arrive bareroot wrapped in moss or in smaller pots.

ADDITIONAL SPECIES, CULTIVARS, OR VARIETIES

Echinacea purpurea 'Magnus', which has a rose pink flower, was voted the best plant of 1998 by the Perennial Plant Association. A white-flowering variety is *Echinacea purpurea* 'White Swan'.

Did You Know?

The toughness and durability of the coneflower was bred in its native home, the prairie regions of the American Midwest. The purple ray flowers attract butterflies and other pollen gatherers. The species name, purpurea, *refers to the purple color of the flower.*

Shasta Daisy

Chrysanthemum × superbum

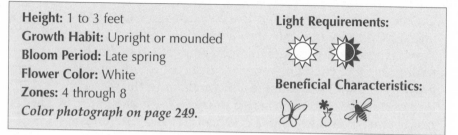

Height: 1 to 3 feet
Growth Habit: Upright or mounded
Bloom Period: Late spring
Flower Color: White
Zones: 4 through 8
Color photograph on page 249.

Light Requirements:

Beneficial Characteristics:

Imagine a spring snowfall on greening lawns, and you capture the impact of masses of shasta daisies. The plant's dark green basal rosette of leaves is formed during the preceding growing season and offers some color in the winter garden. Come summer, the flower stalks shoot up out of the thicket of foliage, supporting buds that soon mature into the shasta's classic white-petalled flower with its egg-yolk-yellow center. The blooms attract bees and other pollen gatherers. Their activity sets seeds which are moved through the garden by rain fall. The shasta daisy is a classic plant which has undergone many changes in recent years, including a complete name change (formerly called chrysanthemum) and an explosion of new varieties.

WHEN TO PLANT

Plant shasta daisies in early spring through early summer and again in the fall.

WHERE TO PLANT

Plant shasta daisies in full sun in a spot where water does not sit, but also in a place that can be easily watered if necessary. Drought stress should never occur.

HOW TO PLANT

Regardless of the size of the pot purchased, keep the plant watered prior to planting. Delineate a bed, digging up undesirable plants or removing them with an herbicide. Rototill or spade the soil to a depth of 6 to 8 inches, blending in a total of 6 inches of organic matter, and rake smooth, creating a raised bed. Use erosion netting if the site is sloped. Dig a hole twice the width of the pot or a minimum of 12 inches. Carefully remove the plant from the pot and loosen the roots if they are pot bound. Place the plant in the hole, so that the

base is slightly higher than the surrounding ground. Backfill the hole, firm the soil, water the plant thoroughly, and place 1 inch of mulch around the plant.

CARE AND MAINTENANCE

For the first 2 or 3 years, fertilize shasta daisies with a balanced food twice monthly throughout the growing season. Water to prevent any drought stress, an equivalent of 1 inch each week. Cut back flowers periodically through the growing season to encourage rebloom later in the season. Shasta daisies have the ability to self seed and spread. Pest and disease problems are minimal. Weeds can be trouble for several years in a new garden, and careful use of herbicides or hand digging are the only real solutions. Divide plants every 3 years for health, vigor, and to control size.

ADDITIONAL INFORMATION

Select the best plants, and best size for your garden space, at garden centers and through mail-order nurseries. Garden centers have plants in containers from 4-inch to 2-gallon pots. The only advantage to the larger size is that they will bloom sooner. Plants should be actively growing when purchased. Check for consistent color of foliage. Mail-order plants arrive bareroot wrapped in moss or in smaller pots.

ADDITIONAL SPECIES, CULTIVARS, OR VARIETIES

Two extended blooming varieties are the taller 'Alaska' and the shorter 'Silver Princess'.

Did You Know?

Shasta daisies belong to the sunflower family which is native to the Pyrenees Mountains of the French and Spanish border. The species name, superbum, refers to the number and size of showy flowers each plant produces. An excellent cutting flower, shastas can be beautifully arranged with for arrangement with flowering bulbs.

Spiked Speedwell

Veronica spicata

Height: 1 to 2 feet
Growth Habit: Upright
Bloom Period: Summer
Flower Color: Blue
Zones: 4 through 8
Color photograph on page 249.

Light Requirements:

Beneficial Characteristics:

It may be difficult to believe that a plant as elegant as speedwell is one of the easier perennials to raise. Its glossy, dark green, pointed foliage alternates and whorls around the upright spearlike stems, providing a dramatic foil for early-spring-flowering bulbs, annuals, and perennials. Its flowers, elongated spikes of iridescent blue, are without equal. The flowers bloom from the bottom up, the spent blossoms a brownish red color that enhances the new blossoms. Speedwell may bloom for as long as 6 weeks, depending on the weather. A classy plant to the end, even after flowering speedwell maintains an attractive foliage as the garden heads into the fall.

WHEN TO PLANT

Plant speedwell in early spring through early summer and again in the fall.

WHERE TO PLANT

Plant speedwell in full sun in a spot where water does not sit, but also in a place that can be easily watered if necessary. Drought stress should never occur.

HOW TO PLANT

Regardless of the size of the pot purchased, keep the plant watered prior to planting. Delineate a bed, digging up undesirable plants or removing them with an herbicide. Rototill or spade the soil to a depth of 6 to 8 inches, blending in a total of 6 inches of organic matter, and rake smooth, creating a raised bed. Use erosion netting if the site is sloped. Dig a hole twice the width of the pot or a minimum of 12 inches. Carefully remove the plant from the pot and loosen the roots if they are pot bound. Place the plant in the hole, so that the

base is slightly higher than the surrounding ground. Backfill the hole, firm the soil, water the plant thoroughly, and place 1 inch of mulch around the plant.

CARE AND MAINTENANCE

For the first 2 or 3 years, fertilize speedwell with a balanced food twice monthly throughout the growing season. Water to prevent any drought stress, an equivalent of 1 inch each week. Cut back flowers periodically through the growing season to encourage rebloom later in the season. Shasta daisies have the ability to self seed and spread. Pest and disease problems are minimal. Weeds can be trouble for several years in a new garden, and careful use of herbicides or hand digging are the only real solutions. Divide plants every 3 to 4 years for health, vigor, and to control size.

ADDITIONAL INFORMATION

Select the best plants, and best size for your garden space, at garden centers and through mail-order nurseries. Garden centers have plants in containers from 4-inch to 2-gallon pots. The only advantage to the larger size is that they will bloom sooner. Plants should be actively growing when purchased. Check for consistent color of foliage. Mail-order plants arrive bareroot wrapped in moss or in smaller pots.

ADDITIONAL SPECIES, CULTIVARS, OR VARIETIES

A lower growing variety is *Veronica* × 'Goodness Grows'. An extended white blooming one is *Veronica spicata* 'Icicle'.

Did You Know?

Relatives can be found as far away as New Zealand, but this particular plant is native to Northern Europe and Asia. The species name, spicata, *refers to the spike habit of the inflorescence. Speedwell's cool blue blossoms make it an excellent flower for fresh arrangements.*

Tall Phlox

Phlox paniculata

Height: 2 feet or more
Growth Habit: Upright
Bloom Period: Summer
Flower Color: Pinkish purple
Zones: 4 through 8
Color photograph on page 249.

Light Requirements:

Beneficial Characteristics:

An old-time perennial, tall phlox has welcomed many generations of gardeners to summer. Its stout growing stem reaches almost unnoticed above many surrounding plants and just when it reaches its peak height, the flowers appear. The cone-shaped flower clusters contain more blossoms than can be counted, and give off just a hint of fragrance. Tall phlox is very much at home with other plantings, but does best if not too crowded, so that it has room to stretch. Give phlox some room, and you'll be rewarded with excellent cutting flowers for summer bouquets.

WHEN TO PLANT

Tough and durable, tall phlox can be planted any time of the year when the ground is not frozen, but it will do best if planted in spring or early fall.

WHERE TO PLANT

Plant tall phlox in full sun in average or better soil that is well drained.

HOW TO PLANT

Regardless of the size of the pot purchased, keep the plant watered prior to planting. Delineate a bed, digging up undesirable plants or removing them with an herbicide. Rototill or spade the soil to a depth of 6 to 8 inches, blending in a total of 6 inches of organic matter, and rake smooth, creating a raised bed. Use erosion netting if the site is sloped. Dig a hole twice the width of the pot or a minimum of 12 inches. Carefully remove the plant from the pot and loosen the roots if they are pot bound. Place the plant in the hole, so that the base is slightly higher than the surrounding ground. Backfill the

hole, firm the soil, water the plant thoroughly, and place 1 inch of mulch around the plant.

CARE AND MAINTENANCE

For the first 2 or 3 years, fertilize speedwell with a balanced food twice monthly throughout the growing season. Water if the growing season is extremely dry, an equivalent of 1 inch each week. Cut back flowers periodically through the growing season to encourage rebloom later in the season. Pest and disease problems are minimal. A powdery mildew may occur on the leaf, but this is a cosmetic problem only. Weeds can be trouble for several years in a new garden, and careful use of herbicides or hand digging are the only real solutions. Divide plants to control size.

ADDITIONAL INFORMATION

Select the best plants, and best size for your garden space, at garden centers and through mail-order nurseries. Garden centers have plants in containers from 4-inch to 2-gallon pots. The only advantage to the larger size is that they will bloom sooner. Plants should be actively growing when purchased. Check for consistent color of foliage. Mail-order plants arrive bareroot wrapped in moss or in smaller pots.

ADDITIONAL SPECIES, CULTIVARS, OR VARIETIES

Phlox paniculata 'David' is a fragrant white-blooming variety that is very attractive to butterflies and mildew resistant as well.

Did You Know?

Phlox are native to and found in North America and Siberia only. The species name, paniculata, *refers to the compound or multiple flowering clusters. Seed produced by plants generally will not come back true to the variety.*

Threadleaf Coreopsis

Coreopsis verticillata 'Zagreb'

Height: 1 to 2 feet
Growth Habit: Mounding
Bloom Period: Summer
Flower Color: Yellow
Zones: 3 through 8
Color photograph on page 249.

Light Requirements:

Beneficial Characteristics:

In the past 20 years, no plant has been more popular than this variety of coreopsis and its very close relatives. The needlelike foliage is so delicate it is difficult to see even at close quarters. Positioned in front of other sun-loving plants, threadleaf Coreopsis hides their unattractive lower foliage while softening their fall. Threadleaf Coreopsis also works well when randomly dotted in an among other plants or massed to create an airy section of foliage that floats and bounces on summer breezes. Its airiness is maximized when threadleaf Coreopsis's almost artificially perfect yellow-petaled flowers appear, floating as if unattached to any stem.

WHEN TO PLANT

Tough and durable, threadleaf Coreopsis can be planted any time of the year when the ground is not frozen, but it will do best if planted in spring or early fall.

WHERE TO PLANT

Threadleaf Coreopsis does well in full sun in average or better soil that is well drained.

HOW TO PLANT

Regardless of the size of the pot purchased, keep the plant watered prior to planting. Delineate a bed, digging up undesirable plants or removing them with an herbicide. Rototill or spade the soil to a depth of 6 to 8 inches, blending in a total of 6 inches of organic matter, and rake smooth, creating a raised bed. Use erosion netting if the site is sloped. Dig a hole twice the width of the pot or a minimum of 12 inches. Carefully remove the plant from the pot and loosen the roots if they are pot bound. Place the plant in the hole, so that the

base is slightly higher than the surrounding ground. Backfill the hole, firm the soil, water the plant thoroughly, and place 1 inch of mulch around the plant.

CARE AND MAINTENANCE

For the first 2 or 3 years, fertilize threadleaf coreopsis with a balanced food twice monthly throughout the growing season. Water if the growing season is extremely dry, an equivalent of 1 inch each week. Cut back flowers periodically through the growing season to encourage continuous rebloom. Pest and disease problems are minimal. Weeds can be trouble for several years in a new garden, and careful use of herbicides or hand digging are the only real solutions. Divide plants to control size.

ADDITIONAL INFORMATION

Select the best plants, and best size for your garden space, at garden centers and through mail-order nurseries. Garden centers have plants in containers from 4-inch to 2-gallon pots. The only advantage to the larger size is that they will bloom sooner. Plants should be actively growing when purchased. Check for consistent color of foliage. Mail-order plants arrive bareroot wrapped in moss or in smaller pots.

ADDITIONAL SPECIES, CULTIVARS, OR VARIETIES

The *Coreopsis rosea* 'American Dream' (pink coreopsis), which has foliage very similar to 'Zagreb' and pink flowers with yellow centers, is more tolerant of wetter soils.

Did You Know?

Unimproved relatives of threadleaf Coreopsis are native and can be found growing from Maryland to Florida and west to Arkansas. Threadleaf Coreopsis refers to the small insect-appearing seeds produced by the flowers. The species name, verticillata, means "in circles around the stem," and refers to the plant's arrangement of leaves.

Roses

THE QUALITIES OF BLOOMING ROSES have been put to good use in love and language: a bouquet of a dozen roses or even a single stem means romance the world over; "taking time to smell the roses" means appreciating the very best that life has to offer; and when you "come out smelling like a rose," you are looking very good indeed. For the past two centuries, professionals and amateurs alike have spent much time producing newer, better, brighter, and bigger rose varieties for everyone to enjoy. So beloved are these flowers that over ten thousand types have been hybridized at one time or another. Roses have always been and will undoubtedly continue to be the most revered single group of plants. The number of roses produced worldwide each year is staggering: 40 million plants for garden use and 20 million stems for the greenhouse cut-flower industry.

Roses are divided in groups according to their arrangement of flowers, their size, and their typical growth habits. The groups most commonly found in gardens and used in floral arrangements are the hybrid teas, grandiflora, floribunda, polyantha, climbing, miniature, pillar, and shrub, but many other members of the rose family are equally beautiful and prized by rose growers.

The key to an attractive, productive, and long-lived rose planting is careful planning and preparation. Although one occasionally spots a garland of wild roses clinging to a weathered old fence along the highway, or a bright stand of roses at the edge of a vacant lot, roses that bloom without the benefits of careful cultivation are the exception rather than the rule. Usually such "untended" roses are examples of older varieties that produce single flushes of flowers and thus do not compare to today's more fruitful varieties.

Chapter Eight

The following two steps are essential when establishing a rose bed, adding a single plant to an existing bed, or evaluating an existing planting:

First, check the site for the amount of sun exposure. Roses love the sun, the more the better. Morning sunlight is especially good for drying foliage and reducing leaf diseases, but be cautious of intense afternoon sun which will fade rose flower petals. A rose bed should receive a daily minimum of at least six hours of direct sunlight.

Next, check the soil profile. Determine how well the soil drains (water cannot sit around plantings) and the proximity of plantings allowed by their root systems (which should not compete).

If the proposed site measures up, it's best to prepare the bed at least a full season prior to installing the roses. This allows for a settling of all the soil components (see below) prior to planting. If an existing rose planting does not meet these criteria, scout out a new location and relocate the roses in early spring.

Whether you plant a single rose that spreads its blooms lavishly upon a trellis or create an intricately varied rose bed, you'll be rewarded year after year by a brilliant display of color and intoxicating fragrance. Each rose has its own spectacular attributes, and some varieties are less demanding to raise but equally magnificent to behold. Five members of the rose family are featured in this chapter.

Climbing 'Zephirine Drouhin'

Rosa 'Zephirine Drouhin'

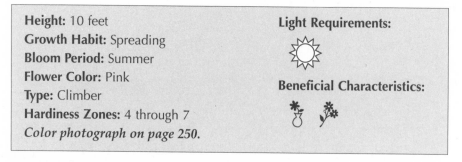

Height: 10 feet
Growth Habit: Spreading
Bloom Period: Summer
Flower Color: Pink
Type: Climber
Hardiness Zones: 4 through 7
Color photograph on page 250.

Light Requirements:

Beneficial Characteristics:

Climbing 'Zephirine Drouhin' is often used to create a living structure within a landscape. Its long and flexible willowy canes are easily trained to conform to almost any shape: an archway, a garlanded window, a spiraling fence. The thornless shafts make 'Zephirine Drouhin' especially easy to manipulate. The initial flush of flowers occurs on the ends of the stems, followed by lateral sprouts along the main stems. A gorgeous burst of semi-double pink flowers occurs every six weeks from June until mid-September, providing spectacular color all summer long.

WHEN TO PLANT

Purchase and plant climbing 'Zephirine Drouhin' in spring through early summer.

WHERE TO PLANT

Plant at the base of an arbor, trellis, or fence, and weave or attach rose branches to the supporting structure as the plant grows. If you wish to create a pattern on a fence, space climbing plants 7 to 10 feet apart.

HOW TO PLANT

Soak bareroot roses 12 to 24 hours prior to planting, or use water-containerized plants. Dig a hole for the plant approximately 2 feet x 2 feet x 2 feet, making a cone-shaped pile of soil in the center of the hole that allows the graft to sit 2 inches below the surface if you live in a northern part of the state. (In southeast Missouri, the graft should sit 1/2 inch below the surface—it will not require as much protection as it would if planted farther north). Place the rose plant in the hole over the mound, backfill, firm the soil, water to soak the area, and prune flowers or any damaged canes. Add 2 inches of loose organic bark mulch placed away from the rose stems.

CARE AND MAINTENANCE

Beginning in mid-May, fertilize monthly with rose food, making a last application in mid-August. Never allow drought stress to occur. Water deeply in the morning, keeping foliage as dry as possible. Mulch 2 inches deep around the perimeter of the plant but not adjacent to the canes. Prune to control unruly growth, removing dead stems, spent flowers, and any debris. Gently bend climbing stems and weave them or otherwise attach them to a trellis or other framework. To protect plants during winter, place 4 to 6 inches of loose organic bark mulch over the crown, then cover with 4 inches of dense compost. Place several small tree branches over the mound to eliminate erosion of mulch and compost. Gradually remove the mulch after the last frost. 'Zephirine Drouhin' has fewer pest and disease problems than do most rose varieties. Should a problem appear, identify it and apply correct control as needed. Do not spray in the heat of the day under any circumstances.

ADDITIONAL INFORMATION

'Zephirine Drouhin' can be purchased bareroot, dormant, or actively growing in containers. Purchase only Grade Number 1 roses, the largest and healthiest available. Plants should have three green stems, each larger than your index finger and all pointing in different and upward directions. Potted roses should be in a 2-gallon pot. Flowers may be present on potted roses; try to find some with full-size, dark green, unspotted leaves. Climbing roses are mutations of the hybrid tea rose. They cannot truly climb, but they easily conform to a supporting shape or structure if woven or attached to it. The first climbers flowered only once a year, but persistent hybridizers kept the climber's desirable habits while gradually adding more flowering cycles.

ADDITIONAL SPECIES, CULTIVARS, OR VARIETIES

There are none available.

Europeana Rose

Rosa 'Europeana'

Height: Over 4 feet
Growth Habit: Upright
Bloom Period: Summer through fall
Flower Color: Reddish pink
Type: Pillar or floribunda
Hardiness Zones: 4 through 7
Color photograph on page 250.

Light Requirements:

Beneficial Characteristics:

The direct and upward growth of the pillar Europeana makes it especially suitable for narrow garden spaces, where it may mimic a doorway, hide or decorate a post, or simply stand in the spotlight. The Europeana's tall stems create vertical relief in a garden. Its iridescent green leaves, reddish brown thorns, and crown of glowing dark pink flowers make it an instant center of attention.

WHEN TO PLANT

Purchase and plant Europeana roses spring through early summer.

WHERE TO PLANT

Site in full sun in very well-drained soil. Locate in front of a structure, or plant it freestanding in the landscape. If creating a hedge of Europeana roses, allow 2 feet between plants.

HOW TO PLANT

Delineate the rose bed. Dig up any undesired plants or remove them with an herbicide. Spade or rototill the area, then blend a minimum of 6 inches of organic matter into the existing spaded soil. Soak bare-root roses 12 to 24 hours prior to installing or use water-containerized plants. Dig a hole for the plant approximately 2 feet x 2 feet x 1 foot, making a cone-shaped pile of soil in the center of the hole that will allow the crown to sit $1/2$ inch below the surface. Place the rose plant in the hole over the mound, backfill, firm the soil, water to soak the area, and prune flowers or any damaged canes. Add 2 inches of loose organic bark mulch placed away from rose stems.

CARE AND MAINTENANCE

Beginning in mid-May, fertilize monthly with rose food, making a last application in mid-August. Never allow drought stress to occur. Water deeply in the morning, keeping foliage as dry as possible. Mulch 2 inches deep around the perimeter of the plant but not adjacent to canes. Prune to control unruly growth, removing dead stems, spent flowers, and any debris. To protect plants during winter, place 4 to 6 inches of loose organic bark mulch over crown, then cover with 4 inches of dense compost. Place several small tree branches over the mound to eliminate erosion of mulch and compost. Gradually remove mulch after last frost. Europeana has fewer pest and disease problems than most rose varieties. Should a problem appear, properly identify and apply correct control as needed. Do not spray in the heat of day under any circumstances.

ADDITIONAL INFORMATION

Europeana roses can be purchased bareroot dormant, or actively growing in containers. Purchase only Grade Number 1 roses, the largest and healthiest available. Plants should have three green stems, each larger than your index finger and all pointing in different and upward directions. Potted roses should be in a 2-gallon pot. Flowers may be present; look for full-size, dark green, unspotted leaves.

ADDITIONAL SPECIES, CULTIVARS, OR VARIETIES

There are none available.

Did You Know?

Pillar floribundas include roses that are neither true climbers nor shrub types. They are tall, strong, erect plants whose canes are too rigid to bend.

'The Fairy' Rose

Rosa 'The Fairy'

Height: Over 2 feet
Growth Habit: Loosely upright
Bloom Period: Summer through fall
Flower Color: Pink
Type: Polyantha
Hardiness Zones: 4 through 7
Color photograph on page 250.

Light Requirements:

Beneficial Characteristics:

'The Fairy' has qualities attractive to both beginner and veteran rose growers. It is relatively easy to grow, and its large cluster of smaller, delicately pink flowers, enhanced by medium-green foliage, create miniature bouquets to ornament the garden. The weight of the numerous blooms may create a weeping affect, offering a charming and unexpected texture to many settings.

WHEN TO PLANT
Purchase and plant 'The Fairy' in spring through early summer.

WHERE TO PLANT
Site in full sun in very well-drained soil.

HOW TO PLANT
Delineate the rose bed. Dig up any undesired plants or remove them with an herbicide. Spade or rototill the area, then blend a minimum of 6 inches of organic matter into the existing spaded soil. If planting bareroot roses, soak 12 to 24 hours prior to installing or use water-containerized plants. Dig a hole for the plant approximately 2 feet x 2 feet x 1 foot, making a cone-shaped pile of soil in the center of the hole that allows the crown to sit 1/2 inch below the surface. Place the rose plant in the hole over the mound, backfill, firm the soil, water to soak the area, and prune flowers or any damaged canes. Add 2 inches of loose organic bark mulch placed away from rose stems.

CARE AND MAINTENANCE
Beginning in mid-May, fertilize monthly with rose food, making a last application in mid-August. Never allow drought stress to occur. Water deeply in the morning, keeping foliage as dry as possible.

Mulch 2 inches deep around perimeter of plant but not adjacent to canes. Prune to control unruly growth, removing dead stems, spent flowers, and any debris. To protect plants during winter, place 4 to 6 inches of loose organic bark mulch over the crown, then cover with 4 inches of dense compost. Place several small tree branches over the mound to eliminate erosion of mulch and compost. Gradually remove mulch after the last frost and cut back the plant to 12 to 15 inches. 'The Fairy' has fewer pest and disease problems than most rose varieties. Should a problem appear, properly identify and apply correct control as needed. Do not spray in the heat of day under any circumstances.

ADDITIONAL INFORMATION

Roses can be purchased bareroot dormant or actively growing in containers. Purchase only Grade Number 1 roses, the largest and healthiest available. Plants should have three green stems, each larger than your index finger and all pointing in different and upward directions. Potted roses should be in a 2-gallon pot. Flowers may be present; look for full-size, dark green, unspotted leaves.

ADDITIONAL SPECIES, CULTIVARS, OR VARIETIES

There are none available.

Did You Know?

'The Fairy' is a polyantha rose, a smaller version of the floribunda type, whose diminutive size makes this rose more adaptable and versatile in the general landscape. Polyantha roses are able to maintain good aesthetic qualities whether planted in masses, mingled with sunny perennials or shrubs, or dotted in the yard for emphasis.

'Frau Dagmar Hastrup' Rose

Rosa Rugosa 'Frau Dagmar Hastrup'

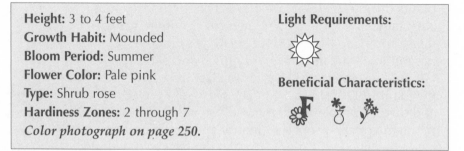

Height: 3 to 4 feet
Growth Habit: Mounded
Bloom Period: Summer
Flower Color: Pale pink
Type: Shrub rose
Hardiness Zones: 2 through 7
Color photograph on page 250.

Light Requirements:

Beneficial Characteristics:

The toughest members of the rose family, not only durable and able to perform varied tasks but also quite beautiful, are the shrub roses. The lovely 'Frau Dagmar Hastrup' offers a lasting and sophisticated solution to any number of landscape problems, from hiding unsightly structures to gracefully linking separate beds to demarcating boundaries in a large garden. Its old-fashioned, single-petaled, fragrant pink flowers bloom off and on throughout the growing season, creating a reliable color focus. Bright red rose hips forming from prior blooms introduce a uniquely beautiful element to the landscape. Given adequate room to spread, 'Frau Dagmar Hastrup' offers years of serviceable beauty.

WHEN TO PLANT

Purchase and plant 'Frau Dagmar Hastrup' in spring through early summer.

WHERE TO PLANT

Site in full sun in very well-drained soil. Locate in front of a structure or plant it free-standing in the landscape. If creating a hedge of 'Frau Dagmar Hastrup' roses, allow 3 or more feet between plants.

HOW TO PLANT

Delineate the rose bed. Dig up any undesired plants or remove them with an herbicide. Spade or rototill the area, then blend a minimum of 6 inches of organic matter into the existing spaded soil. Soak bareroot roses 12 to 24 hours prior to installing or use water-containerized plants. Dig a hole for the plant approximately 2 feet x 2 feet x 1 foot, making a cone-shaped pile of soil in the center of the hole that allows the crown to sit 1/2 inch below the surface. Place the rose plant in the hole over the mound, backfill, firm the soil, water to soak the area, and prune flowers or any damaged canes. Add 2 inches of loose organic bark mulch placed away from rose stems.

CARE AND MAINTENANCE

Beginning in mid-May, fertilize monthly with rose food, making a last application in mid-August. Never allow drought stress to occur. Water deeply in the morning, keeping foliage as dry as possible. Mulch 2 inches deep around perimeter of plant but not adjacent to canes. Prune to control unruly growth, removing dead stems, spent flowers, and any debris. To protect plants during winter, place 4 to 6 inches of loose organic bark mulch over crown, then cover with 4 inches of dense compost. Place several small tree branches over mound to eliminate erosion of mulch and compost. Gradually remove mulch after last frost and cut plant back to 12 to 15 inches. 'Frau Dagmar Hastrup' roses have fewer pest and disease problems than most rose varieties. Should a problem appear, properly identify and apply correct control as needed. Do not spray in the heat of day under any circumstances.

ADDITIONAL INFORMATION

'Frau Dagmar Hastrup' roses can be purchased bareroot dormant or actively growing in containers. Purchase only number 1 roses, the largest and healthiest available. Plants should have three green stems, each larger than your index finger and all pointing in different and upward directions. Potted roses should be in a 2-gallon pot. Flowers may be present, and look for full-size, dark green, unspotted leaves.

ADDITIONAL SPECIES, CULTIVARS, OR VARIETIES

There are none available.

Scarlet Meidiland

Rosa 'Keitoli' or 'Meikrotal'

Height: 4 feet
Growth Habit: Spreading
Bloom Period: Early summer
Flower Color: Scarlet red
Type: Shrub rose
Hardiness Zones: 4 through 7
Color photograph on page 250.

Light Requirements:

Beneficial Characteristics:

Scarlet Meidiland is suitable for several landscape tasks. Its multiple, very thorny stems create a barrier to unwanted foot traffic, and its low growing habit makes this rose an excellent ground covering for sunny slopes. The Meidiland's shiny dark green leaves glisten in the sun, providing dramatic background color for double petals of flashing scarlet red. The main flush will open and remain during most of June, with random clusters bursting forth until mid-fall. An all-around winner, the Scarlet Meidiland is an excellent member of a shrub border or makes a brilliant accent point all on its own.

WHEN TO PLANT

Purchase and plant Scarlet Meidiland roses spring through early summer.

WHERE TO PLANT

Site in full sun in very well-drained soil. Use for ground cover, to create a hedge, or plant free-standing. If creating a hedge of Scarlet Meidiland roses, allow 5 or more feet between plants.

HOW TO PLANT

Delineate the rose bed. Dig up any undesired plants or remove them with an herbicide. Spade or rototill the area, then blend a minimum of 6 inches of organic matter into the existing spaded soil. Soak bare-root roses 12 to 24 hours prior to installing or use water-containerized plants. Dig a hole for the plant approximately 2 ft. x 2 ft. x 1 ft., making a cone-shaped pile of soil in the center of the hole that allows the crown to sit 1/2 inch below the surface. Place the rose plant in the hole over the mound, backfill, firm the soil, water to soak the area, and prune flowers or any damaged canes. Add 2 inches of loose organic bark mulch placed away from rose stems.

CARE AND MAINTENANCE

Beginning in mid-May, fertilize monthly with rose food, making a last application in mid-August. Never allow drought stress to occur. Water deeply in the morning, keeping foliage as dry as possible. Mulch 2 inches deep around the perimeter of the plant but not adjacent to canes. Prune to control unruly growth, removing dead stems, spent flowers, and any debris. To protect plants during winter, place 4 to 6 inches of loose organic bark mulch over crown, then cover with 4 inches of dense compost. Place several small tree branches over mound to eliminate erosion of mulch and compost. Gradually remove mulch after last frost and cut plant back to 12 to 15 inches. Scarlet Meidiland roses have fewer pest and disease problems than most rose varieties. Should a problem appear, properly identify and apply correct control as needed. Do not spray in the heat of day under any circumstance.

ADDITIONAL INFORMATION

Scarlet Meidiland roses can be purchased bareroot dormant or actively growing in containers. Purchase only Grade Number 1 roses, the largest and healthiest available. Plants should have three green stems, each larger than your index finger and all pointing in different and upward directions. Potted roses should be in a 2-gallon pot. Flowers may be present; look for full-size, dark green, unspotted leaves.

ADDITIONAL SPECIES, CULTIVARS, OR VARIETIES

There are none available.

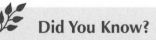 **Did You Know?**

The Scarlet Meidiland is a member of a newer series of shrub roses that have fewer problems than their close relatives but maintain the rugged usefulness, remarkable density, and brilliant fullness of their family with even more pizzazz.

Missouri lies at the heart of America, in a place rich in natural beauty . . . natives know the green banks along its waterways and treasure its quiet forests and sunny meadows . . .

Missouri

GARDENER'S GUIDE

Photographic Gallery
of Featured Plants

Balsam
Impatiens balsamina

Begonia
Begonia x Semperflorens-Cultorum

Blue Sage
Salvia farinacea

Cockscomb
Celosia cristata

Coleus
Solenostemon scutellarioides

Flowering Tobacco
Nicotiana alata

French Marigold
Tagetes patula

Geranium
Pelargonium x hortorum

Globe Amaranth
Gomphrena globosa

Impatiens
Impatiens wallerana

Pansy
Viola x wittrockiana

Periwinkle
Catharanthus roseus

Petunia
Petunia x hybrida

Snapdragon
Antirrhinum majus

Spider Flower
Cleome hassleriana

Toadflax
Linaria marocanna

Yellow Cosmos
Cosmos sulphureus

Zinnia
Zinnia elegans

Autumn Crocus
Colchicum autumnale

Caladium
Caladium x hortulanum

Canna
Canna x generalis

Crocus
Crocus spp.

Daffodil
Narcissus spp.

Dahlia
Dahlia hybrids

Elephant Ear
Colocasia esculenta

Giant Flowering Onion
Allium giganteum

Gladiolus
Gladiolus x hortulanus

Glory-of-the-Snow
Chionodoxa luciliae

Grape Hyacinth
Muscari spp.

Snowdrops
Galanthus nivalis

Snowflake
Leucojum aestivum

Tulip
Tulipa spp.

Winter Aconite
Eranthis hyemalis

Chinese or Kousa Dogwood
Cornus kousa

Donald Wyman Crabapple
Malus 'Donald Wyman'

Fringetree
Chionanthus virginicus

'Cherokee Princess' Dogwood
Cornus florida 'Cherokee Princess'

Improved Flowering Pear
Pyrus calleryana 'Aristocrat'

Redbud
Cercis canadensis

Red Japanese Maple
Acer palmatum 'Bloodgood'

Serviceberry
Amelanchier arborea

Tricolor Beech
Fagus sylvatica 'Purpurea Tricolor'

Washington Hawthorn
Crataegus phaenopyrum

Bishop's Weed
Aegopodium podograria 'Picta'

Bugle Weed
Ajuga reptans

Chamaleon Plant
Houttuynia cordata

Creeping Jenny
Lysimmachia nummularia

Creeping Juniper
Juniperus horizontalis

Creeping Phlox
Phlox subulata

Crown Vetch
Coronilla varia

Dead Nettle
Lamium maculatum

Dutch White Clover
Trifolium repens

English Ivy
Hedera helix

Hall's Honeysuckle
Lonicera japonica 'Halliana'

Lilyturf
Liriope spicata

Myrtle
Vinca minor

Stone Crop
Sedum spurium 'Dragon's Blood'

Sweet Woodruff
Galium ordoratum

Winter Creeper
Euonymus fortunei 'Colorata'

Blue Lyme Grass
Leymis arenarius

Feather Reed Grass
Calamagrostis x acutiflora 'Karl Foerster'

Fountain Grass
Pennisetum setaceum

Giant Reed Grass
Arundo donax

Japanese Blood Grass
Imperata cylindrica 'Red Baron'

Lemon Grass
Cymbopogon citratus

Maiden Grass
Miscanthus sinensis 'Gracillimus'

Prairie Dropseed Grass
Sporobolus heterolepsis

Red Fountain Grass
Pennisetum setaceum 'Rubrum'

Ribbon Grass
Phalaris arundinacea 'Picta'

Switch Grass
Panicum virgatum

Variegated Cord Grass
Spartina pectinata 'Aureomarginata'

Asparagus
Asparagus officinalis

Aster
Aster hybridus

Astilbe
Astilbe x arendsii

Balloonflower
Platycodon grandiflorus

Barrenwort
Epimedium x rubrum

Bleeding Heart
Dicentra spectablis

Chinese Peony
Paeonia lactiflora

Common Mallow
Hibiscus moscheutos

Common Yarrow
Achillea millifolium

Daylily
Hemerocallis ssp.

Fall Windflower
Anemone x hybrida

Fortune's Hosta
Hosta fortunei

Hardy Sage
Salvia x superba

Hollyhock
Alcea rosea

Iris
Iris spp. 'Bearded hybrids'

Lady's Mantle
Alchemilla mollis

Lily-of-the-Valley
Convallaria majalis

Liveforever
Hylotelephium spectabile

Mums
Chrysanthemum morifolium

Obedient Plant
Physostegia virginiana

Purple Coneflower
Echinacea purpurea

Shasta Daisy
Chrysanthemum x superbum

Spiked Speedwell
Veronica spicata

Tall Phlox
Phlox paniculata

Threadleaf Coreopsis
Coreopsis verticillata 'Zagreb'

249

Climbing 'Zephririne Drouhin'
Rosa 'Zephirine Drouhin'

Europeana Rose
Rosa 'Europeana'

'The Fairy' Rose
Rosa 'The Fairy'

'Frau Dagmar Hastrup' Rose
Rosa Rugosa 'Frau Dagmar Hastrup'

Scarlet Meidiland
Rosa 'Keitoli' or 'Meikrotal'

Amur Maple
Acer ginnala

Bald Cypress
Taxodium distichum

Black Gum
Nyssa sylvatica

Crimson King Maple
Acer platanoides 'Crimson King'

European Beech Tree
Fagus sylvatica

Hemlock
Tsuga canadensis

Littleleaf Linden
Tilia cordata

Maidenhair Tree
Ginkgo biloba

Norway Spruce
Picea abies

Red Oak
Quercus rubra

Red Sunset Maple
Acer rubrum 'Red Sunset'

River Birch
Betula nigra

Rosehill White Ash
Fraxinus americana 'Rosehill'

Serbian Spruce
Picea omorika

Tulip Tree
Liriodendron tulipifera

Upright Keteleeri Juniper
Juniperus chinensis 'Keteleeri'

Upright Techny Arborvitae
Thuja occidentalis 'Techny'

White Pine
Pinus strobus

Arrowwood Viburnum
Viburnum dentatum

251

Bayberry
Myrica pensylvanica

Bridalwreath Spiraea
Spiraea x vanhouttei

Burning Bush
Euonymus alatus

Deciduous Winterberry Holly
Ilex verticillata 'Winter Red'

Globe Arborvitae
Thuja occidentalis 'Woodwardi'

Hidcote St. Johnswort
Hypericum henryi 'Hidcote'

Inkberry Holly
Ilex glabra

Lantanaphyllum Viburnum
Viburnum x rhytidophylloides

Lilac
Syringa vulgaris

Pfitzer
Juniperus chinensis 'Pfitzeriana'

Purpleleaf Sand Cherry
Prunus x cistena

Pussy Willow
Salix caprea

Red Barberry
Berberis thunbergii var. atropurpurea

Red Twig Dogwood
Cornus sericea 'Kelseyi'

Snowball Bush
Hydrangea arborescens 'Annabelle'

Spring Witch Hazel
Hamamelis vernalis

Summersweet
Clethra alnifolia

Upright Yew
Taxus x media 'Hicksii'

Yellow False Cypress
Chamaecyparis pisifera 'Filifera Aurea'

Boston Ivy
Parthenocissus tricuspidata

Cardinal Climber
Quamoclit sloteri or Ipomoea quamoclit

Hyacinth Bean
Lablab purpureus

Jackman Clematis
Clematis x jackmanii

Japanese Wisteria
Wisteria floribunda

Moon Flower
Ipomoea alba

Morning Glory
Ipomoea tricolor

Scarlet Runner Bean
Phaseolus coccineus

Silver Lace Vine
Fallopia baldschuanica

Trumpet Honeysuckle
Lonicera sempervirens

Bee Balm
Monarda punctata

Big Bluestem Grass
Andropogon geradii

Bittersweet Vine
Celastrus scandens

Blue Bells
Martensia virginica

Blue Sage
Salvia azurea

Blue Star
Amsonia illustris

Butterfly Plant
Asclepias tuberosa

Canadian Columbine
Aquilegia canadensis

Celandine Poppy
Stylorphorum diphyllum

Coneflower
Ratibida pinnata

Crane's Bill Geranium
Geranium maculatum

False Blue Indigo
Baptisia australis

Goat's Beard
Aruncus dioicus

Primrose
Oenothera missouriensis

Rose Verbena
Verbena canadensis

Snakeroot
Cimicufuga racemosa

Sneezeweed
Helenium autumnale

Solomon's Seal
Polygonatum commutatum

Spiderwort
Tradescantia virginiana

Sweet William
Phlox divaricata

Trumpet Vine
Campsis radicans

USDA PLANT HARDINESS MAP

Missouri

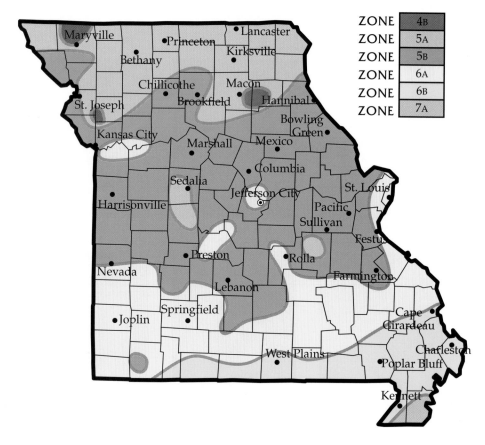

ZONE	4B
ZONE	5A
ZONE	5B
ZONE	6A
ZONE	6B
ZONE	7A

Maryville
Lancaster
Princeton
Kirksville
Bethany
Chillicothe
Macon
St. Joseph
Brookfield
Hannibal
Kansas City
Bowling Green
Marshall
Mexico
Columbia
Sedalia
St. Louis
Jefferson City
Harrisonville
Pacific
Sullivan
Festus
Preston
Rolla
Nevada
Farmington
Lebanon
Cape Girardeau
Joplin
Springfield
Charleston
West Plains
Poplar Bluff
Kennett

We walk Missouri's timbered ridges, gaze across its rolling plains of tall grass, and climb to the top of its rocky river bluffs with a sense of gratitude that so many of nature's gifts are here for us to share . . .

CHAPTER NINE

Shade Trees

ATREE IS VALUED FOR THE STRUCTURAL QUALITIES it
offers the landscape: it acts as a wall, a stage, a roof, a backdrop
for flowering shrubs, bulbs, and annuals. But trees have great
aesthetic properties in their own right, as well. A tree trunk covered
with blue lichens and green moss is a work of art. Its green boughs
filtered with sunlight can seem a spiritual emanation. The bird song
rising from its leafy branches is as uplifting as any symphony. The
tree you plant and nurture will bring any number of landscaping
and personal rewards.

A way to understand how deeply people value trees is to think
about how they grieve to lose one, especially one that has been a
part of their personal landscape for many years. It may be a tree
remembered from childhood, a maple that offered a branch for a
rope swing or held a rough tree house in its branches. Or an old oak
that gave its deep shade to relieve the summer heat and made a
cradle in its roots where a child could sit to read and dream. Even if
the tree is not an old familiar, its loss is felt in the way the house and
yard may look naked now without it, the way the garden at its feet is
no longer protected and must be replanted with sun-loving varieties,
and the way that the soft noise of its leaves outside the bedroom
window has vanished. Often when a tree is lost, the first impulse is
to replace it. Even if its grand form cannot be immediately recap-
tured, some satisfaction comes from seeing a young tree growing in
its place.

Before you select a tree, whether it is to replace one that has been
lost, or for any other reason, start by asking yourself some questions.
The answers will help you make the best choices, both for you and
for the tree. First, take a look around your yard and ask what are the
existing trees? Where are they located and how good is their health?
If there are older trees, it may be time to get the next generation

Chapter Nine

started. Even under ideal conditions, many years will go by before a newly installed tree begins to make a real landscape statement. While you are looking at the trees in your yard, examine the plants that are now growing there. How long will it be before they are affected by a new tree? Will the effect be beneficial or harmful? Think about how much sun you now enjoy. Is it just right? Too much? As the tree grows, it will certainly be less. Is there adequate room for the roots to spread? Will they damage a walk, patio, or driveway when they grow? Is the prospective site on a slope, in a low spot, or where the drying winter winds blow? Asking these and other species-related questions will help you complete a thorough site analysis in order to choose the best tree for your yard and your needs.

In addition to physically examining your site, ask what design benefits you expect the tree to provide. What will be the role of the new tree in the landscape? Is it to be a focal point all year round? Do you see it as a member of a mixed plant community? Do you want it primarily for shade in the summer, or perhaps to break winter winds? Compile a list of candidates based on your site analysis and design requirements. Check each candidate for rate of growth and mature height and width, silhouette, outline, and branching and rooting patterns. Several trees may fit the bill, and your choice may come down to one of personal taste.

When you plant a tree, you are making a statement that has some claim on permanence. You are already looking with satisfaction years down the road to the shade it will offer and the high roof of its branches against the sky. That happy anticipation is only the beginning of the many lasting gifts the tree will bring as years go by.

Amur Maple

Acer ginnala

Height and Width: 20 by 20 feet
Height in 10 Years: 10 feet
Type: Deciduous
Zones: 2 through 7
Color photograph on page 250.

Light Requirements:

The amur maple has a smaller but dynamic growth habit and many attractive qualities. It offers a rounded silhouette and usually suffers minimal storm damage. The small, glossy, trident-shaped leaves provide bright green color spring and summer, and the tree's fragrant flowers are followed by small, winged fruit that sail and twirl on currents of wind. In fall, the tree is ablaze with golden yellow and rich red foliage. You may choose an individual tree with a single or multiple trunks. The amur maple works beautifully as a specimen or grove planting.

WHEN TO PLANT

It is best to install the tree during dormancy, November through March. This minimizes a number of problems, from transplant shock to wind burn on the foliage.

WHERE TO PLANT

The growth habit of the amur maple's canopy and roots allows this tree to be sited in numerous locations, whether wetter or dry, urban or rural, in the ground or in large containers and elevated planters. Its low branching habit limits its use as a street tree.

HOW TO PLANT

Dig a hole three times the width and three-quarters the height of the rootball, and do not add amendments to the hole. If the tree is container grown, remove it from the pot and loosen the root mass if it is pot bound before placing the tree in the hole. If the tree is balled and burlapped, remove the rope after placing the tree in the hole, and then fold the burlap downward, but do not remove. Backfill the hole and firm the soil around the roots. Water the tree immediately and thoroughly, and cover the planting area with 2 to 3 inches of mulch.

If the tree is staked, the wiring must allow for some movement. Prune only dead or damaged branches.

CARE AND MAINTENANCE

Preventing drought stress during the first year is most critical. Prune during the summer months to minimize sap flow after the first year. Remove any staking wires after one year. Deep-root feed the second year after installation and then every third year.

ADDITIONAL INFORMATION

Amur maples can be container grown or balled and burlapped. Select a tree with a strong trunk and no open wounds; the branches should be fully budded or in leaf and flexible. The rootball should be proportional with the tree's height, approximately 3 inches in diameter for every foot of height. The smaller the tree, the faster it will establish in the landscape. If fall color is extremely important, select trees when they are at peak brilliance. Companion plantings to consider for drier locations are daffodils, dead nettle, hosta, and yews; for wetter sites, use Hall's honeysuckle, astilbe, and inkberry

ADDITIONAL SPECIES, CULTIVARS, OR VARIETIES

The compact amur maple *Acer ginnala* 'Compactum' or the 'Durand Dwarf', which grow 4 to 6 feet, work well in a rock garden or a condominium's tiny landscape.

Did You Know?

The amur maple is native to various environments in the Orient, from China and Mongolia to Korea. The small stature of this tree made it a keystone structural or container planting in many Chinese and Japanese gardens. Its multiple or single-trunked habit is easily controlled with pruning.

Bald Cypress N

Taxodium distichum

Height and Width: 50 by 30 feet	**Light Requirements:**
Height in 10 Years: 25 feet	
Type: Deciduous conifer	
Zones: 4 through 9	
Color photograph on page 250.	

Home territory for the bald cypress are the lowland swamps where alligators and egrets roam and Spanish moss and massive stands of lotus thrive. But this hardy tree can survive equally well in a high and dry location. The tall, straight trunk, pyramidal outline, and unusual root growth the cypress develops wetter areas, called "knees," command attention whatever its setting. Its fine-textured needles, yellow-green during the growing season and a rusty yellow just prior to dropping in the fall, and powdery blue cones make a spectacular contrast to the tree's parallel branching and cinnamon-colored bark. The bald cypress is an excellent lower maintenance tree for a home with a larger landscape.

WHEN TO PLANT

The best time to plant bald cypress is after the needles have fallen and before next year's growth has begun. This tree will appear awkward during its youth; select a tree to plant that is 10 feet or less tall.

WHERE TO PLANT

Because of its fast growth rate and mature height and width, it is best to plant a bald cypress in a larger yard where it will have plenty of room to develop.

HOW TO PLANT

Dig hole that is three times the width of the rootball; this will allow for better lateral root growth and faster establishment. Dig to a depth that ensures that when the tree is placed in the hole it will sit at surface level or slightly higher. Do not add amendments or fertilizer to the hole prior to installation. For balled and burlapped trees, remove all rope after placing the tree in the hole, and then fold the burlap downward. If the tree is container grown, remove it from the pot and loosen the root mass if it is pot bound before placing the tree in the hole. Backfill the hole and firm the soil around the roots. Water the tree immediately and thoroughly, and cover the planting area with 2 to 3 inches of mulch. If the tree is staked, the wiring must allow for some movement. Prune only dead or damaged branches.

CARE AND MAINTENANCE

Monitor rainfall and supplement it with irrigation for the first year after planting. In theory, there are potentially several insects and diseases that can impact the overall health of the baldcypress. However, this situation is very overstated and should not deter you from planting bald cypress. Remove any staking wires after one year.

ADDITIONAL INFORMATION

Select a tree with a strong trunk and no open wounds; the branches should be numerous, fully budded or in leaf, and flexible. The rootball should be proportional with the tree's height, approximately 3 inches in diameter for every foot of height. Balled and burlapped trees can be purchased in taller heights than container-grown trees, and will create an impact more quickly. Companion plantings to consider for wetter areas are big bluestem grass, inkberry, and summersweet; and for drier soil, try red fountain grass, giant flowering onion, dead nettle, and pfitzer.

ADDITIONAL SPECIES, CULTIVARS, OR VARIETIES

Two selections of the bald cypress offer different silhouettes: the thinner *Taxodium distichum* 'Shawnee Brave' or the more rotund *Taxodium distichum* 'Monarch of Illinois'.

Did You Know?

The bald cypress is the Midwest's cousin to the West Coast's sequoia and redwood trees. It has a long taproot which helps to stabilize the tree in swampy areas. The strong durable wood is used as construction material for decks and boat docks.

Black Gum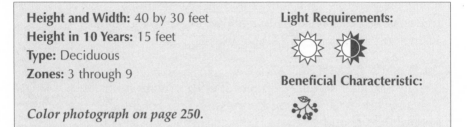

Nyssa sylvatica

Height and Width: 40 by 30 feet
Height in 10 Years: 15 feet
Type: Deciduous
Zones: 3 through 9

Color photograph on page 250.

Light Requirements:

Beneficial Characteristic:

The silhouette of the black gum tree changes many times over the course of its life, ranging from oval, to flat-topped, pendulous to rounded. What remains consistent over time is the small space between the tree's zigzag branches, which gives it a very twiggy appearance, and the darker shades of the bark. This combination makes the black gum striking against a clear blue winter or early spring sky, or when it is covered with snow. The elliptical, very polished, leather-like green leaves of summer change to yellows or scarlet in the fall, depending on the individual tree. The tree's small fruits are appealing to birds and wildlife.

When to Plant

The best time to plant the black gum is just after leaf drop in the fall or in the early spring. The extremes of summer or winter may be rough on the black gum if installed during those seasons.

Where to Plant

Although the black gum is considered to be a native swamp dweller, it is found in thin rocky soils. This slower-growing tree is happiest when planted in organic soils that have adequate moisture, and is best used as a lawn tree.

How to Plant

Dig hole that is three times the width of the rootball; this will allow for better lateral root growth and faster establishment. Dig to a depth that ensures that when the tree is placed in the hole it will sit at surface level or slightly higher. Do not add amendments or fertilizer to the hole prior to installation. For balled and burlapped trees, remove all rope after placing the tree in the hole, and then fold the burlap downward. If the tree is container grown, remove it from the pot and loosen the root mass if it is pot bound before placing the tree in the hole. Backfill the hole and firm the soil around the roots. Water the tree immediately and thoroughly, and cover the planting area with 2 to 3 inches of mulch. If the tree is staked, the wiring must allow for some movement. Prune only dead or damaged branches.

CARE AND MAINTENANCE

Monitor rainfall and supplement as needed during the first year. The durability, adaptability, and native heritage of the black gum usually enable it to take care of itself after it has been established for a year. Remove any staking wires after one year.

ADDITIONAL INFORMATION

When selecting a tree, look for a straight trunk and as few dead twigs as possible. The branches should be fully budded or in leaf and flexible. The rootball should be proportional with tree's height, approximately 3 inches in diameter for every foot of height. Black gum trees can be container grown, but it is best to purchase balled and burlapped trees because of this species' longer tap root. For the same reason, younger and smaller tree—one that is less than 10 feet in height—is the best size to transplant. The only way to ensure a specific fall color is to select the tree when it is in color. Companion plantings to consider for wet or dry locations are fringetree, red twig dogwood, variegated cord grass, and astilbe.

ADDITIONAL SPECIES, CULTIVARS, OR VARIETIES

There are none available.

Did You Know?

The black gum (which is not even in the same family with the dreaded sweet gum) is native to North America, with habitats from the East to the Midwest. The wood has been harvested for use in furniture making because of its hardness and excellent grain patterns.

'Crimson King' Maple

Acer platanoides 'Crimson King'

Height and Width: 30 by 20 feet and wider	**Light Requirements:**
Height in 10 Years: 15 feet	
Type: Deciduous	
Zones: 3 through 7	
Color photograph on page 250.	

The 'Crimson King' maple stands out among other large maples for several reasons. Its broad, rounded outline, smooth gray bark, and branching habit are all striking features. But what really turns heads is the tree's deep maroon leaf color. While its aesthetic qualities are very important, it hardiness should not be overlooked. This maple is one of the most versatile in terms of tolerance to various soil types, and to heat, dryness, and pollution. You'll find it also thrives when well watered and carefully nurtured.

WHEN TO PLANT

As with most deciduous trees, the best time to plant the 'Crimson King' maple is November through March.

WHERE TO PLANT

The main location requirement for a 'Crimson King' maple is that the site be well drained. This tree creates a focal point, so place accordingly. As all other large maples, the 'Crimson King' has a surface root and seeds that may be troublesome if the tree is not planted away from streets, walks, downspouts, and gutters.

HOW TO PLANT

Dig hole that is three times the width and three-quarters the height of the rootball; this will allow for better lateral root growth and faster establishment. Do not add amendments or fertilizer to the hole prior to installation. For balled and burlapped trees, remove all rope after placing the tree in the hole, and then fold the burlap downward. If the tree is container grown, remove it from the pot and loosen the root mass if it is pot bound before placing the tree in the hole. Backfill the hole and firm the soil around the roots. Water the tree

immediately and thoroughly, and cover the planting area with 2 to 3 inches of mulch. If the tree is staked, the wiring must allow for some movement. Prune only dead or damaged branches.

CARE AND MAINTENANCE

Trees that are allowed to go through severe and long (2 weeks or more) periods of drought stress during the summer can suffer leaf scorch. The 'Crimson King' maple is somewhat short lived, averaging a life span of approximately 30 years. Deep-root feed every 3 years. Take care not to bump the tree with mowing or other equipment, and do not weed whip around the trunk, which can open a wound near the ground. Prune only during the summer. Remove any staking wires after one year.

ADDITIONAL SPECIES, CULTIVARS, OR VARIETIES

The 'Crimson King' is a cultivar of the Norway maples, but others to consider would be the more narrow growing, columnar variety called *Acer platanoides* 'Crimson Sentry' or a green-leafed, wide-spreading cultivar, *Acer platanoides* 'Cleveland'.

ADDITIONAL INFORMATION

Select a tree whose rootball is approximately 3 inches in diameter for every foot of the tree's height. Look for a straight trunk free of open wounds, with short, flexible branches and not an abundance of buds, giving the tree a tall and gangly look. Crimson king maple is usually found balled and burlapped or in larger containers. Heights ranging from 6 to 10 feet are best to transplant. Companion plantings to consider using are serviceberry, yews, caladiums, English ivy, and hosta.

Did You Know?

Although the group of maples to which the 'Crimson King' maple belongs is called Norway maples, they are native to a widespread area that ranges from the mountains and valleys of eastern Europe through parts of the Middle East.

European Beech Tree

Fagus sylvatica

Height and Width: 40 by 30 feet
Height in 10 Years: 15 feet
Type: Deciduous
Zones: 4 through 7
Color photograph on page 238.

Light Requirements:

The soaring height of the European beech makes a regal landscape statement. It has a softly oval growing habit and remarkably soft gray bark that is great for carving initials. Spearhead-shaped buds appear during the winter and unfurl in the late spring, showing off a lustrous green foliage that turns bronze in the fall. Its low-branched habit makes it good for climbing, but the low branches and stout surface root system make it difficult to grow any plants under the tree. That said, however, it should be added that the dramatic European beech really does not need a supporting cast at its feet.

WHEN TO PLANT

The best time to transplant European beech is during the dormancy of late fall through early spring.

WHERE TO PLANT

The European beech requires a well-drained and highly organic planting site. Because this tree has a slower growth rate and is easily pruned, you can cheat a bit on its placement; in other words, with careful attention to its growth, the European beech can be placed near structures. However, this tree is most at home in a wide open lawn, where it can stretch and reach in all directions. Keep it out of low, poorly drained spots.

HOW TO PLANT

Dig a hole that is three times the width and three-quarters the height of the rootball; this will allow for better lateral root growth and faster establishment. Add organic matter, but no fertilizer, to the hole prior to installation. For balled and burlapped trees, remove all rope after placing the tree in the hole, and then fold the burlap downward. If the tree is container grown, remove it from the pot and loosen the root mass if it is pot bound before placing the tree in the hole. Backfill the hole and firm the soil around the roots. Water the tree immediately and thoroughly, and cover the planting area with 2 to 3 inches of mulch. If the tree is staked, the wiring must allow for some movement. Prune only dead or damaged branches.

CARE AND MAINTENANCE

Prevent any drought stress at any time throughout the life of the tree. Begin deep-root feeding two years after installation and every three years afterward. Prune beech trees from summer through early fall, but not during winter when the sap flow is heavy. Insect and disease problems are minimal. Remove any staking wires after 1 year.

ADDITIONAL INFORMATION

The trunks of European beech trees are usually bent or zigzag. When selecting a tree, be aware that the trunk will be sparsely branched, but all the branches should be flexible and fully budded or in leaf. The rootball should be approximately 3 inches in diameter for every foot of the tree's height. Trees that range from 4 to 8 feet in height, whether container grown or balled and burlapped trees, will have the least problems in transplantation. Consider these companion plantings, but do not place them under the tree's drip line: blue lyme grass, purple coneflower, false cypress, and Japanese maple.

ADDITIONAL SPECIES, CULTIVARS, OR VARIETIES

Two varieties that offer unusual growth habits and work well as foundation or patio plantings are the weeping beech, *Fagus sylvatica* 'Pendula', and the narrow, upright *Fagus sylvatica* 'Fastigata'.

Hemlock

Tsuga canadensis

Height and Width: 25 feet or
  taller by 20 feet
Height in 10 Years: 10 feet
Type: Coniferous evergreen
Zones: 3 through 8
Color photograph on page 250.

Light Requirements:

Beneficial Characteristic:

Open, animated, gracious, the hemlock tree can play a number of roles in various large and small landscapes. It has a pyramidal shape with bouncing pendulous branches that touch the ground surrounding the tree. The needles are short and very dark green, with white stripes on the underside of the needle that flash when exposed by the wind. Whether planted as a specimen tree, used as a backdrop for flowering plants or a seating area, or sited to screen an unwanted view, the hemlock makes a graceful landscape statement.

WHEN TO PLANT

The prime time of year to install a hemlock is mid-fall through late winter. This allows the plant to establish some root growth before the drought of the summer.

WHERE TO PLANT

Hemlocks require a well-drained and highly organic soil and do best in sunny, open locations. Although shade tolerant, they compete very poorly with larger established tree roots, so a woodland setting of smaller trees is best.

HOW TO PLANT

Dig hole that is three times the width and to a depth that ensures that the tree's crown will sit higher than the surrounding ground. Mix organic matter with the existing soil, but do not add fertilizer. For balled and burlapped trees, remove all rope after placing the tree in the hole, and then fold the burlap downward. If the tree is container grown, remove it from the pot and loosen the root mass if it is pot bound before placing the tree in the hole. Backfill the hole and firm the soil around the roots. Water the tree immediately and thoroughly, and cover the planting area with 2 to 3 inches of mulch. If the tree is staked, the wiring must allow for some movement. Prune only dead or damaged branches.

CARE AND MAINTENANCE

The hemlock's root system cannot be allowed to dry out at any time. If the ground is dry two inches below the surface, mulch the area and water thoroughly. Deep-root feed the tree the second year after installation and every 3 years thereafter. Insects and disease problems are minimal if the tree's health is maintained. Prune to shape and control growth in late winter or early spring. Remove any staking wires after one year.

ADDITIONAL INFORMATION

When selecting a hemlock, choose one that is dark green with no paleness whatsoever and not large dead patches. The best size to install is 3 to 8 feet tall, and the tree must have a moist, spongy rootball. Companion plantings to consider for a sunny spot are hollyhocks, bee balm, Chinese dogwood, and burning bush; in a shady area, plant lily of the valley, celandine poppy, Japanese maple, or witch hazel.

ADDITIONAL SPECIES, CULTIVARS, OR VARIETIES

For smaller landscapes or specialty gardens, consider using the weeping hemlock, *Tsuga canadensis* 'Sargentii', or the dwarf *Tsuga canadensis* 'Nana'.

Did You Know?

The hemlock is native to the region that lies east from Missouri and ranges from Nova Scotia to northern Alabama. This tree provides valuable timber and pulpwood. The small cones serve as food for some birds. Additionally, the evergreen habit offers birds the opportunity to nest and protection for roosting year round.

Littleleaf Linden

Tilia cordata

Height and Width: 40 by 30 feet
Height in 10 Years: 15 feet
Type: Deciduous
Zones: 3 through 7

Color photograph on page 250.

Light Requirements:

Beneficial Characteristic:

The littleleaf linden has an admirable toughness combined with a number of appealing aesthetic qualities. Its congenial ornamental value is evidenced in its frequent use as a shade tree, aligned along wide walks or streets, sited in the middle of parkways, or placed in large planters. Some situations require the removal of the linden's lower branches to improve access, but it takes pruning easily and can even be used for hedge planting. In spring the roundish buds open and heart-shaped, darker green leaves unroll. Then in early summer, the linden's fragrant white flowers fill the air and provide nectar for bees. Although the fall color is not spectacular, it does offer a rare yellow hue later in the season.

WHEN TO PLANT

The best time to plant lindens is after leaf drop; because the leaves hang on quite long, the tree may not be ready to plant until late fall. Installation through early spring is acceptable. If the tree is leafed out, protect the foliage from wind burn during transport.

WHERE TO PLANT

The littleleaf linden has a nearly endless list of uses, but it must be planted in moist, well-drained soil to accomplish any planting goal. When choosing a spot, consider the tree's size to minimize the need to prune.

HOW TO PLANT

Lindens are most often sold as balled and burlapped trees. Dig a hole three times the width and three-quarters the height of the rootball, a size that ensures better drainage away from the crown. Add 6 inches of organic matter to the existing soil, but do not add fertilizer. Place the tree in the hole, remove the rope, and fold burlap downward. Back fill the hole, firm soil around the roots, and water immediately and thoroughly. Cover the planting area with 2 to 3 inches of mulch. If staked, the wiring must be loose enough to allow for tree movement. Prune only dead or damaged branches. Keep the moisture level high.

CARE AND MAINTENANCE

Prevent any type of drought stress during the entire life of lindens, and monitor especially closely if planted in an elevated planter. The best defense against potential disease and insect problems is a healthy tree. Prune to control growth during the fall. Remove staking wires after 1 year.

ADDITIONAL INFORMATION

Choose a tree with a smooth, uninjured trunk that is full of lateral branches with either blunt buds on the ends or fully leafed, depending on the season. It is important to make sure the rootball is approximately 3 inches in diameter for every foot of the tree's height. Transplanting is quite easy at any size. Companion plantings to consider are globe arborvitae, Saint Johnswort, red fountain grass, tulips, and myrtle.

ADDITIONAL SPECIES, CULTIVARS, OR VARIETIES

Plant collectors will want to seek out the weeping dwarf variety, *Tilia cordata* 'Pendula Nana', or the narrow-growing cultivar, *Tilia cordata* 'Swedish Upright'.

Did You Know?

The littleleaf linden is the sophisticated European cousin of our native basswood or American linden. Its late spring to early summer blooming time produces nectar that is very important for bees. This means caution should be exercised when siting lindens in a landscape where bee activity may be problematic. The seed that results from pollination is quite distinctive: shaped like a flat spatula and with round fruits attached.

Maidenhair Tree

Ginkgo biloba

Height and Width: 50 by 40 feet
Height in 10 Years: 20 feet
Type: Deciduous
Zones: 3 through 8

Light Requirements:

Beneficial Characteristic:

Color photograph on page 251.

The ancient status of the ginkgo as a living fossil is only one of its many attractive characteristics. Also appealing are its distinctive bark furrows, wide-spreading branching habit, slippery fan-shaped leaves, and soft green summer and vibrant yellow fall color. Its leaves cascade to the ground over a very short period of time, reducing raking hours. The slow transformation of an awkward ginkgo sapling into a majestic shade tree is well worth the wait.

WHEN TO PLANT

The best time to plant a ginkgo tree is after leaf drop and before next year's growth sprouts, events which depend on the weather for that year.

WHERE TO PLANT

The ginkgo's slow rate of growth calls for patience, but the wait is made easier by thinking of the ultimate mature height and width of this magnificent tree. It must be planted where the soil is well drained, and is most efficiently used in larger landscapes, whether in the center of metropolitan areas, in the suburbs, or in the rural countryside.

HOW TO PLANT

Dig hole that is three times the width of the rootball, which allows for better lateral root growth and faster establishment. The depth of the hole should ensure that the crown of the tree will sit at surface level or slightly higher when the tree is placed in the hole. Do not add amendments or fertilizer to the hole prior to installation. For balled and burlapped trees, remove all rope after placing the tree in the hole, and then fold the burlap downward. If the tree is container grown, remove it from the pot and loosen the root mass if it is pot bound before placing the tree in the hole. Backfill the hole and firm the soil around the roots. Water the tree immediately and thoroughly, and cover the planting area with 2 to 3 inches of mulch. If the tree is staked, the wiring must allow for some movement. Prune only dead or damaged branches.

CARE AND MAINTENANCE
Prevent long-term drought stress during the first 2 years. Maintenance includes pruning in early spring and deep-root feeding the third year after installation. Remove any staking wires after 1 year.

ADDITIONAL INFORMATION
Select a tree that is 10 feet tall or less, with a strong trunk and no open wounds. Branching may appear to be sparse, short, and stubby, but the branches should be fully budded or in leaf and flexible. The rootball should be approximately 3 inches in diameter for every foot of the tree's height. The ginkgo is available in containers or balled and burlapped.

ADDITIONAL SPECIES, CULTIVARS, OR VARIETIES
In a smaller or more narrow landscape, consider using the columnar *Ginkgo biloba* 'Fastigata', or an architectural piece, the weeping, *Ginkgo billoba* 'Pendula'.

Did You Know?
The ginkgo is a rare gem of a tree, whose lineage can be traced back 150 million years by fossils found in southeast China. Children are always fascinated to look at a tree species that may have thrived when dinosaurs roamed the earth.

Norway Spruce

Picea abies

Height and Width: 30 feet or taller
  by 25 feet
Height in 10 Years: 10 to 20 feet
Type: Coniferous evergreen
Zones: 3 through 7
Color photograph on page 251.

Light Requirements:

Beneficial Characteristic:

This adaptable, tough, and graceful tree can meet many landscape needs. It works well planted as a specimen tree or in a mass planting. It provides an effective visual screen or weather barrier. Birds love to nest in it and children love to climb it. The overall shape is symmetrically pyramidal, and the branches produce short, dark green needles. Stiff and dense in appearance when young, the Norway spruce becomes more open and animated with age. When mature, the branches turn up at the tips and the branchlets weep and bear 4 to 6-inch cones. If given adequate space to grow and a little care, the Norway spruce grows fast in youth and remains admirably healthy for many years.

WHEN TO PLANT

The best time of year to plant Norway spruce is between November and March, when the tree is dormant and transplant shock is minimal. Successful planting during other times may require additional care to ensure a healthy tree.

WHERE TO PLANT

It is extremely important to plant the Norway spruce in a well-drained site, where water does not sit. The soil should have an average organic content and be slightly acidic. Soil modification can greatly expand the number of potential sites. Because of the tree's ultimate 30- to 40-foot height and 20- to 25-foot, do not plant it in smaller yards or near buildings, streets, drives, or walkways.

HOW TO PLANT

Dig a hole that is three times the width and three-quarters the height of the rootball; this will allow for better lateral root growth and reduces potential water problems. Mix organic matter with the existing soil. For balled and burlapped trees, remove all rope after placing the tree in the hole, and then fold the burlap downward. If the tree is container grown, remove it from the pot and loosen the root mass if it is pot bound before placing the tree in the hole. Backfill the hole and firm the soil around the roots. Water the tree immediately and thoroughly, and cover the planting area with 2 to 3 inches of mulch. If the tree is staked, the wiring must allow for some movement. Prune only dead or damaged branches.

CARE AND MAINTENANCE

It is recommended that drought stress be prevented for the entire life of the tree; supplement rainfall if the amount is less than 1 inch every 10 days. Checking for and controlling insect and disease problems during the first 2 years will have a tremendous impact on the future health of the tree, so don't hesitate to get a professional diagnosis. Prune to control size in the early spring, or as needed to remove dead or damaged branching.

ADDITIONAL INFORMATION

Select a tree that has a good dark green color covering the entire trunk, which should be straight, and flexible branches. The rootball should be approximately 3 inches in diameter for every foot of the tree's height. The best size for planting is from 3 feet to 12 feet tall. Companion plantings to consider are lilyturf, maiden grass, serviceberry, daylily, and bridalwreath.

ADDITIONAL SPECIES, CULTIVARS, OR VARIETIES

Consider using a dwarf *Picea abies* 'Pumila' or the spreader *Picea abies* 'Repens' for an unusual look or for smaller landscapes.

Red Oak

Quercus rubra

Height and Width: 60 by 40 feet	**Light Requirements:**
Height in 10 Years: Up to 20 feet	
Type: Deciduous	
Zones: 4 through 8	
	Beneficial Characteristic:
Color photograph on page 251.	

All the classic features of oak can be found in this one variety of the majestic family. The red is a faster growing oak and can be enjoyed for its mature qualities fairly soon after planting. The strong and sturdy trunk is covered with a handsome, dark brown and gray bark. The branches shoot out perpendicularly from the center, providing a very symmetrical outline. The foliage unrolls in the spring with a reddish hue. Leaves are divided into pointed segments and become a deep shiny shade of green on the upper surface and paler underneath. In fall, the leaves turn a rich brownish red, and the tree begins to drop the capped acorns loved by squirrels and children alike.

WHEN TO PLANT

The red oak's leaves hang on sometimes into the winter. Plant this tree at any time after the foliage has turned and before new growth begins in spring.

WHERE TO PLANT

Plant the red oak in well-drained soil that has a good organic content, and because of its mature height and spread, choose a larger, open area.

HOW TO PLANT

Dig a hole three times the width and three-quarters the height of the rootball to ensure better drainage away from the crown. Add organic matter but no fertilizer to the hole. For balled and burlapped trees, remove all rope after placing the tree in the hole, and then fold the burlap downward. If the tree is container grown, remove it from the pot and loosen the root mass if it is pot bound before placing the tree in the hole. Backfill the hole and firm the soil around the roots. Water the tree immediately and thoroughly, and cover the planting area with 2 to 3 inches of mulch. If the tree is staked, the wiring must allow for some movement. Prune only dead or damaged branches.

CARE AND MAINTENANCE

Prevent any drought stress during the first 2 years after planting; supplement rainfall as needed to equal 1 inch of moisture every 10 days. Remove staking wires after 1 year. The list of potential diseases and insect problems is minimal.

ADDITIONAL SPECIES, CULTIVARS, OR VARIETIES

For the oak connoisseur to consider are two close relatives of the red oak: the scarlet oak, *Quercus coccinea*, and the willow oak, *Quercus phellos*, which is at home in a lower wet area.

ADDITIONAL INFORMATION

Pick a tree with a strong central leader with numerous branches that are flexible and fully budded, at a height 4 to 15 feet. The rootball should be approximately 3 inches in diameter for every foot of the tree's height. This oak has no definite tap root and is sold balled and burlapped or container grown. If fall color is important, select the tree in when color is displayed. Companion plantings to consider are blue bells, serviceberries, lilac, crocus, and sweet woodruff.

Did You Know?

The red oak is native to the mountains, hills, and dales that lie between eastern Canada and Minnesota, south to Iowa. Its timber is used in construction because of its tough durability, and the acorns are sometimes used for hog feed.

Red Sunset Maple

Acer rubrum 'Red Sunset'

Height and Width: 50 feet or taller by 40 feet
Height in 10 Years: 20 feet
Type: Deciduous
Zones: 3 through 9
Color photograph on page 251.

Light Requirements:

Truly a four-season tree, this hybrid of the native red maples makes a dynamic landscape statement all year long. Its small, but showy red flowers are a harbinger of spring, and followed by equally pleasing red helicopter-like seeds. The foliage has red stems, with leaves that are pure green on top and pale underneath, and always eye-catching in the slightest breeze. On hot summer days, the red sunset maple offers a cool respite from the sun. And when the year turns toward fall, its vibrant red and yellow leaves burn in a brilliant swirl of sunset color. Come winter, the variously shaded gray bark stands out in the snow. This tree has all of the hard maple qualities, making it resistant to any type of storm damage, a potentially a tree with a long history.

WHEN TO PLANT

The best time to plant red sunset maple is during dormancy in the early spring.

WHERE TO PLANT

Plant red sunset maple in an open area to allow for the spreading of its branches and its aggressive surface roots. Do not site this tree near the driveway, nor beside a walk or patio.

HOW TO PLANT

The lack of a stabilizing tap root requires that the planting hole be dug to three times the width of the rootball, which allows for better lateral root growth, and to a depth that ensures that the tree is at surface level or slightly higher when placed in the hole. Do not add amendments or fertilizer to the hole prior to installation. For balled and burlapped trees, remove rope and fold burlap downward after placing the tree in the hole. Back fill the hole and firm the soil around the roots. Water immediately and thoroughly and cover the planting area with 2 to 3 inches of mulch. If the tree is staked, the wiring must be loose enough to allow for tree movement. Prune only dead or damaged branches.

CARE AND MAINTENANCE

Do not allow any drought stress for several years after installation. Deep root feed the second year after planting and every 3 years afterward. Prune during the summer because of the heavy winter sap flow. Remove any staking wires after 1 year.

ADDITIONAL INFORMATION

Pick an oval-shaped tree with a strong trunk and no new wounds. The quantity and placement of branches are not important, as long as they are flexible and well budded. The rootball should be approximately 3 inches in diameter for every foot of height. The red sunset maple is generally available only balled and burlapped. Choose a tree that is less than 12 feet in height. Companion plantings to consider are English ivy, lady's mantle, columbine, serviceberry, and lantana viburnum.

ADDITIONAL SPECIES, CULTIVARS, OR VARIETIES

Although its fall color is not quite as dramatic as the red sunset maple's, an upright *Acer rubrum* 'Columnare' fits in tighter spots. The globular *Acer rubrum* 'Globosum' works well in smaller gardens.

Did You Know?

The red maple is native to most of the eastern United States and Canada, where it can be found growing anywhere from river bottoms to rocky ledges. This indicates that the tree adapts to numerous soil situations, whether undernourished, poorly drained, rocky, or highly organic. The wood is considered top of the line for many uses.

River Birch

Betula nigra

Height and Width: 50 feet or taller by 40 feet	**Light Requirements:**
Height in 10 Years: 25 feet	
Type: Deciduous	
Zones: 4 through 9	
Color photograph on page 251.	

The river birch is native to Missouri, where its habitat ranges from river bottoms and low-lying flood plains to dry, rocky bluffs. It is best known for its wet-soil tolerance and its pale brown, thinly peeling bark, which exfoliates from any part of the tree that is greater than 2 inches in diameter. A multiple-trunked tree, the river birch makes a bold architectural statement from the time it is planted. Male flowers called catkins hang and bounce in the slightest breeze. Its fine-textured branching and the open spacing between leaves allow light to filter through the branches and strike the ground adjacent to the trunk. This sunlight is usually adequate to support numerous types of plants, making the river birch a good tree companion in shrub, perennial, and annual beds.

WHEN TO PLANT

The early fall leaf drop of the river birch makes it one of the first trees available to plant in the fall. Planting occurs from this time through the early spring.

WHERE TO PLANT

Because of its tolerance to wet soil, the river birch is often planted in low wet areas, but it also looks great planted in an open lawn. Do not plant it near an area where salt may be spread, such as a road or driveway, since exposure to salt can result in an iron deficiency.

HOW TO PLANT

Dig a hole three times the width of the rootball and to a depth that ensures that the crown of the tree is higher than the surrounding ground when the tree is placed in the hole. Do not add any organic matter or fertilizer to the hole. For balled and burlapped trees, remove all rope after placing the tree in the hole, and then fold the burlap downward. If the tree is container grown, remove it from the pot and loosen the root mass if pot bound before placing the tree in the hole. Backfill the hole and firm the soil around the roots. Water the tree immediately and thoroughly, and cover the planting area with 2 to 3 inches of mulch. If the tree is staked, the wiring must allow for some movement. Prune only dead or damaged branches.

CARE AND MAINTENANCE

Do not allow drought stress to occur for several years after installation. Prune during the summer to avoid excessive sap flow. Remove any staking wires after 1 year. There are no pest or disease problems.

ADDITIONAL INFORMATION

Look for a multi-trunked tree with good spacing between the trunks and very twiggy and flexible branches that are fully budded or in leaf. The rootball should be approximately 3 inches in diameter for every foot of height of the tallest trunk. River birches are sold in containers or balled and burlapped, with no advantage to either style. Companion plantings to consider in drier locations are any turf grass, bulbs, redbud, pfitzer, periwinkle, and bishop's weed; for the wetter areas, try inkberry, fringetree, chameleon plant, and ribbon grass.

ADDITIONAL SPECIES, CULTIVARS, OR VARIETIES

If you are trying to create a slightly more refined look in the landscape, consider an improved variety, the *Betula nigra* 'Heritage', which has salmon-colored bark.

Did You Know?

River birch wood has been used for furniture since the mid-1700s, a history which indicates the enduring strength of its qualities. The heat of summer, even if adequate moisture is available, will cause the river birch to drop leaves on a daily basis. This means the meticulous gardener should not plant it where it will cause frustration.

Rosehill White Ash

Fraxinus americana 'Rosehill'

Height and Width: 50 feet or
taller by 30 feet
Height in 10 Years: 20 feet
Type: Deciduous
Zones: 3 through 9
Color photograph on page 251.

Light Requirements:

Fast-growing white ash trees make an impact within a few years of installation. While the rosehill is an improved variety of white ash, its bark shows the same diamond pattern and varied shades of gray common to all white ash trees. The significant enhancements are seen in the rosehill's much darker green and more vibrant summer foliage, which turns a reddish gold in the fall and does not produce seeds. It is smaller in stature, which means that it can be used in settings other than parks. Additionally, its tolerance to poorer alkaline soils enables the rosehill to work well as a street tree.

WHEN TO PLANT

The rosehill ash colors in mid- to late September and drops its leaves within 10 days. This means it is available to plan quite early in the fall. Installation through the early spring is acceptable; if the tree is leafed out, protect it from wind burn during transport.

WHERE TO PLANT

Plant the rosehill white ash as a free-standing specimen lawn tree or in a plant community where the soil is well drained, but not overly dry.

HOW TO PLANT

Dig a hole three times the width and three-quarters the height of the rootball to ensure better drainage away from the crown. Do not add any organic matter or fertilizer to the hole. This tree is generally sold balled and burlapped. Remove all rope after placing the tree in the hole, and then fold the burlap downward. Backfill the hole and firm the soil around the roots. Water the tree immediately and thoroughly, and cover the planting area with 2 to 3 inches of mulch. If the tree is staked, the wiring must allow for some movement. Prune only dead or damaged branches.

CARE AND MAINTENANCE

Prevent any drought stress for several years after installation. Remove any staking wires after 1 year. The list of potential diseases and insect problems is lengthy.

ADDITIONAL INFORMATION

When selecting a tree, look for a straight trunk with a strong central leader which should be full of lateral symmetrical branches that either have blunt buds on the ends or are fully leafed, depending on the season. It is important that the rootball is approximately 3 inches in diameter for every foot of height. Transplanting is quite easy at any size. Companion plantings to consider are Washington hawthorn, bayberry, flowering tobacco, grape hyacinth, and sweet William.

ADDITIONAL SPECIES, CULTIVARS, OR VARIETIES

Varieties of white ash to consider for superior fall color are *Fraxinus americana* 'Autumn Purple' or a narrow upright cultivar called *Fraxinus americana* 'Greenspire'.

Did You Know?

White ash trees are native to the Midwest. The wood has been used by furniture and cabinet makers since it was first cultivated in the early 1700s, and has many additional uses today, including baseball bats.

Serbian Spruce

Picea omorika

Height and Width: 30 feet or taller by 15 feet	**Light Requirements:**
Height in 10 Years: 10 feet or taller	
Type: Coniferous evergreen	**Beneficial Characteristic:**
Zones: 4 through 7	
Color photograph on page 251.	

An attention getter in virtually all settings, the Serbian spruce can be a major player in almost size of landscape. Its thin, strongly pyramidal and symmetrical outline is a surprise whether seen from a distance or up close. The short, dark green needles, with white markings on the underside, give a look of fullness to the branches. The limbs cascade downward from the trunk, and then make an graceful upturn sweep. This unusual branching habit creates a feeling of movement even when the wind is not blowing. If stirred by branches, the animation is greater and more exciting. The bark, although hidden, has a warm and inviting brown tone. The cones are almost black when young and turn a warm brown color with age.

WHEN TO PLANT

Plant the Serbian spruce in late winter through early spring to give it a chance to establish root growth before the drying winds of summer.

WHERE TO PLANT

Like most of the shade-tolerant conifers, the Serbian spruce cannot compete for moisture where there are existing established trees. Place this tree beyond the drip line of larger trees or within a community of younger trees to reduce the chances of competition. The ideal spot is one that is protected from sun and winds for some period of the day.

HOW TO PLANT

The establishment of a healthy root system is essential to a successful planting. Dig a hole that is three times wider than the diameter of the rootball and deep enough to ensure that the crown of the tree is higher than the surrounding surface when the tree is placed in the hole. Mix organic matter with the soil removed from the hole, but do not add fertilizer. Serbian spruce are sold balled and burlapped. Remove the rope after placing the tree in the hole and then fold the burlap downward. Back fill the hole and firm the soil around the roots. Water immediately and thoroughly, and cover the planting area with 2 to 3 inches of mulch. Stake larger trees for stability, but the wiring must be loose enough to allow for some tree movement. Prune only dead or damaged branches.

CARE AND MAINTENANCE

Monitor the amount of rainfall and supplement water supply if there is less than 1 inch during a 10-day period. Keep the tree healthy to reduce the likelihood of insect and disease outbreaks. Remove any staking wires after 1 year.

ADDITIONAL INFORMATION

Purchase a tree that is fully branched and covered with dark green needles. Choose a balled and burlapped tree with a moist rootball, which indicates good health. The best size for installation is 4 to 8 feet. Companion plantings to consider are snowball bush, begonias, caladiums, bishop's weed, and bleeding heart.

ADDITIONAL SPECIES, CULTIVARS, OR VARIETIES

Smaller growing Serbian spruces that would be focal points in rock or collection gardens are the weeping variety, *Picea omorika* 'Pendula', and the dwarf *Picea omorika* 'Nana'.

🌿 Did You Know?

This tree is native to the valleys of eastern Europe, and in that region the strong light wood was used for making paper. The grace and beauty of this tree outshine many of its relatives, and it welcomes all birds whether resting, nesting, or seeking protection from the weather. Kills neighboring trees, such as "Bosnian Spruce."

Tulip Tree

Liriodendron tulipifera

Height and Width: 60 feet or taller by 40 feet	**Light Requirements:**
Height in 10 Years: 25 feet or taller	
Type: Deciduous	
Zones: 4 through 9	
Color photograph on page 251.	

The tulip is an immensely tall and wide-spreading tree. Its gray bark has a fissured texture that is distinctive from afar. Its unusual habit of sloughing off its lower branches as the tree grows makes the trunk appear to be even taller than it actually is. The few limbs are randomly spaced and support a very unusually shaped large leaf. The leaf is a cool pale green shade on top, and an even paler tone underneath, a contrast that is accentuated when the leaves move in the wind. The foliage turns a pure yellow during the fall. The orange, yellow, and green flowers that sit at ends of the branches drop their petals, but the fruiting structure remains through the winter.

WHEN TO PLANT

The only time that the tree can be installed is during the spring.

WHERE TO PLANT

The tulip tree's fast rate of growth calls for careful consideration on placement. It is most efficiently used in well-drained but moist open areas in larger landscapes. The nonaggressive roots do allow for siting near driveways, walks, and patios.

HOW TO PLANT

Dig a hole that is three times the width of the rootball; this will allow for better lateral root growth and faster establishment. Dig to a depth that ensures the tree will sit at a slightly higher than surface position when it is placed in the hole. Do not add amendments or fertilizer to the hole prior to installation. For balled and burlapped trees, remove all rope after placing the tree in the hole, and then fold the burlap downward. If the tree is container grown, remove it from the pot and loosen the root mass if pot bound before placing the tree in the hole. Backfill the hole and firm the soil around the roots. Water the tree

immediately and thoroughly, and cover the planting area with 2 to 3 inches of mulch. If the tree is staked, the wiring must allow for some movement. Prune only dead or damaged branches.

CARE AND MAINTENANCE
Prevent long-term drought stress during the first 2 years with supplemental watering. Be aware that no matter what the amount of rainfall or water has been, leaf drop will begin in June. Prune in winter. Although the list of potential insect and disease problems is lengthy, they are no more than an aggravation. Remove any staking wires after 1 year.

ADDITIONAL INFORMATION
Due to its fibrous root system, a young tree will appear leaning whether it is container grown or balled and burlapped. The sparsely spaced branches may be fully budded or leafed out and should be flexible. The rootball should be approximately 3 inches in diameter for every foot of the tree's height. Choose a specimen that is 6 feet or less in height. Companion plantings to consider are peonies, butterfly plant, tri-color beech, yew, and cockscomb.

ADDITIONAL SPECIES, CULTIVARS, OR VARIETIES
The tulip tree does have cultivars which can be used in smaller landscape settings, including the upright variety, *Liriodendron tulipifera* 'Fastigatum', and the dwarf form, *Liriodendron tulipifera* 'Compactum'.

Did You Know?
The yellow wood of this fast-growing member of the magnolia family has been use by furniture makers since the late 1600s. It is one of the tallest growing trees native to the East Coast. Found growing from Massachusetts to Florida, it has naturalized in other areas.

Upright Keteleeri Juniper

Juniperus chinensis 'Keteleeri'

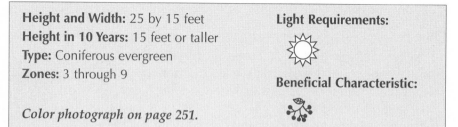

Height and Width: 25 by 15 feet
Height in 10 Years: 15 feet or taller
Type: Coniferous evergreen
Zones: 3 through 9

Color photograph on page 251.

Light Requirements:

Beneficial Characteristic:

Junipers belong to the cypress family and have almost limitless types of growing habits and uses in the landscape. 'Keteleeri' strikes a commanding pose with its rotundly pyramidal shape and branches that grow right down to the ground. The very pointed, shiny true green needles are so dense they conceal the entire woody interior. Small brown male and bluish female cones are found on each tree. The denseness of 'Keteleeri' makes it an excellent candidate for a larger hedging and screening situation, and its evergreen color increases its appeal as a solitary planting. It makes an excellent bird habitat.

WHEN TO PLANT

Mid-fall through mid-spring is the best time of year to install a 'Keteleeri' juniper, but their toughness allows for basically year-round planting.

WHERE TO PLANT

Depending upon the designated use, this juniper has only two very important requirements. The site must be in the full sun and be very well drained; no water can sit around the trunk.

HOW TO PLANT

Dig a hole that is three times the width of the rootball; this will allow for better lateral root growth and faster establishment. Dig to a depth that ensures the tree will sit at a slightly higher than surface position when it is placed in the hole. Do not add amendments or fertilizer to the hole prior to installation. For balled and burlapped trees, remove all rope after placing the tree in the hole, and then fold the burlap downward. If the tree is container grown, remove it from the pot and loosen the root mass if pot bound before placing the tree in the hole. Backfill the hole and firm the soil around the roots. Water the tree

immediately and thoroughly, and cover the planting area with 2 to 3 inches of mulch. If the tree is staked, the wiring must allow for some movement. Prune only dead or damaged branches.

CARE AND MAINTENANCE

The adaptability of 'Keteleeri' means that unless there is an extremely long and severe drought during the first year, no supplemental watering is needed. Pest and disease problems are not truly problematic for this variety of juniper, except for bagworms, which can simply be picked off. Prune according to usage during the winter. Remove any staking wires after 1 year.

ADDITIONAL INFORMATION

Picking out the best 'Keteleeri' juniper is not difficult. The tree needles should be a consistent medium-green color all over with no dead patches. The shape should be wider at the base and pointed at the top. Check to make sure there are no bag worm sacks any place on the tree. Container-grown or balled and burlapped trees are equal choices, and the best size for installation is 3 to 6 feet. Companion plantings to consider are snapdragons, gladiolas, creeping phlox, prairie drop seed, mums, and rose verbena.

ADDITIONAL SPECIES, CULTIVARS, OR VARIETIES

Numerous cultivars are available, including the compact spreader, *Juniperus chinensis* 'Mint Julep', or the ground-hugging *Juniperus chinensis* 'Nick's Compact'.

🌿 Did You Know?

The upright 'Keteleeri' juniper was introduced from China, and a major benefit of choosing a chinensis variety over the native species is that they do not transmit cedar apple rust and other diseases. This airborne disease can be aesthetically devastating to the crabapple, hawthorn, serviceberry, and apple, among other trees, and to the juniper as well.

Upright Techny Arborvitae

Thuja occidentalis 'Techny'

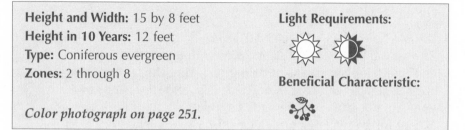

Height and Width: 15 by 8 feet
Height in 10 Years: 12 feet
Type: Coniferous evergreen
Zones: 2 through 8

Color photograph on page 251.

Light Requirements:

Beneficial Characteristic:

A n upright evergreen that is soft to the look and touch, 'Techny' arborvitae is a pleasing and effective tree in many landscapes. Its slower growth rate and shorter mature height are two important characteristics that make this tree useful in numerous ways, including as a backdrop for bird baths or statuary, as a screen to conceal an unpleasant view, and a wind and weather barrier for the patio. Its wick-and-flame shape allows for plantings adjacent to the trunk. 'Techny' has been popular for many years for the cool visual break it offers in the full sun of summer and the welcome greenery it supplies in winter.

WHEN TO PLANT

The best time of year to install a 'Techny' arborvitae is spring, which gives the tree a chance to become fully established before winter.

WHERE TO PLANT

Site in locations where the soil is well drained, but moist, and has a high organic content. 'Techny' tolerates exposures ranging from full sun to a fair amount of shade, which means it can fill many gaps in the landscape.

HOW TO PLANT

Dig a hole that is three times the width of the rootball; this will allow for better lateral root growth and faster establishment. Dig to a depth that ensures the tree will sit at a slightly higher than surface position when it is placed in the hole. Mix organic matter with the existing soil, but do not add fertilizer. For balled and burlapped trees, remove all rope after placing the tree in the hole, and then fold the burlap downward. If the tree is container grown, remove it from the pot and loosen the root mass if pot bound before placing the tree in the hole.

Backfill the hole and firm the soil around the roots. Water the tree immediately and thoroughly, and cover the planting area with 2 to 3 inches of mulch. If the tree is staked, the wiring must allow for some movement. Prune only dead or damaged branches.

CARE AND MAINTENANCE

Never allow any periods of extended drought. Supplement with water as needed to ensure the equivalent of 1 inch of rain every 10 days, summer and winter. Bagworms are a problem and should be removed if observed. Loosely wrap a rope around the tree during the winter to reduce problems from ice or snow storms. Prune during the winter. Remove any staking wires after one year.

ADDITIONAL INFORMATION

When selecting a tree, choose the densest, dark green foliage possible. The overall shape is flamelike, with the bottom 10 percent lacking needles. 'Techny' arborvitae is available in containers or ball and burlapped. The best size to purchase is between 3 and 6 feet. Check all over the tree for bag worm sacks and do not purchase if any are discovered. Companion plantings to consider for sites in the sun are fountain grass, balloon flower, false blue indigo, and crabapple; good companions in the shade are lily of the valley, spiderwort, and tri-color beech

ADDITIONAL SPECIES, CULTIVARS, OR VARIETIES

Thuja occidentalis 'Aurea' is a great yellow-needled tree for small gardens, and *Thuja occidentalis* 'Filiformis' has an attractive weeping habit.

Did You Know?

The soft, light, easily worked wood of the arborvitae first became popular with carpenters in the mid-sixteenth century. Its upright branch configuration offers today's landscapes an excellent place for many types of birds to nest, roost and/or seek protection from the weather.

White Pine

Pinus strobus

Height and Width: 40 by 25 feet
Height in 10 Years: 20 feet or taller
Type: Coniferous evergreen
Zones: 3 through 8

Color photograph on page 251.

Light Requirements:

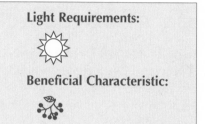

Beneficial Characteristic:

The white pine has a graceful majesty. Its exceptional height, dark gray bark softened by bluish green needles, and the large pine cones that hang at the ends of its branches combine in a singularly awesome impact on a landscape. The tree matures from a dense pyramid shape to an openly branched umbrella silhouette, a metamorphosis which occurs quite rapidly owing to the white pine's rapid rate of growth. Additionally, the white pine can be pruned and sheared to control its height, which opens up any number of possible design uses.

WHEN TO PLANT

The prime planting season for white pine is November through April, except when the ground is frozen.

WHERE TO PLANT

Plant white pine in a very well drained site, where water does not sit. The soil should have good organic content and be slightly acidic. Depending on the anticipated use and your willingness to prune, a white pine can fit many different landscapes.

HOW TO PLANT

Its lack of a substantial root system makes the white pine appear unstable in a container or wrapped in burlap. Dig a hole that is three times wider and three-quarters the height of the rootball to allow for better lateral root growth and to reduce potential water problems. Mix organic matter with the existing soil, but do not add fertilizer. Be aware that when the tree is removed from the container or when the burlap is loosened, the soil may fall away. Regardless of this loss of soil, place the tree in the hole and then remove the rope and fold the burlap downward. Back fill the hole and firm the soil around the roots. Water immediately and thoroughly and cover with 2 to 3 inches of mulch. If the tree is staked, the wiring must be loose enough to allow for tree movement. Prune only dead or damaged branches.

CARE AND MAINTENANCE

Prevent drought stress year round. Prune to control size in the early spring, or as needed to remove dead or damaged branching. Pest and disease problems are somewhat of a concern during the first 5 years after installation. Monitor the tree closely and seek proper diagnosis and control if any problems are observed.

ADDITIONAL INFORMATION

Choose a tree with a straight trunk with branches radiating from multiple, equally spaced spots along the trunk's entire length. This form gives an obvious pyramidal outline, particularly if the tree is sheared many times while growing. If a more natural look is preferred, select a specimen that is park grade or unsheared. White pines are available as container grown or balled and burlapped. The best size for planting is from 3 to 12 feet. Companion plantings to consider are bee balm, flowering pear, lilac, lemon grass, winter aconite, and switch grass.

ADDITIONAL SPECIES, CULTIVARS, OR VARIETIES

Any size or shaped yard can house a type of white pine. Consider, for instance, the shorter more rotund variety *Pinus strobus* 'Pumila', or the narrow upright type, the *Pinus strobus* 'Fastigata'.

 Did You Know?

The native habitat of the white pine is to the east and north of the Missouri River. The wood has been used by carpenters since the early 1700s. Mature tree needles make a soft music in the wind and grow on the outer two-thirds of the branch, which makes the white pine an excellent climbing tree for children.

Shrubs

S HRUB IS A HOMELY NAME, not a word that inspires poetry. It fits the accurate notion that these plants are the landscape's work-horses: sturdy, reliable, adaptable, and enduring. But once you come to know the individual members of this family, other words will come to mind as well, words like amiable, versatile, splendid, and graceful. The common names of shrubs sing of their beauty: sweet, burning, snowball, bridal. And who can deny that there is poetry in the fragrance of the blooming lilac, the perfect blossom of the snow-ball bush, or the sight of birds making a winter feast of bright red holly berries? Deciduous shrubs are living calendars, providing markers of the ever-changing seasons, from spring flowers and sum-mer fruits, to fall color and winter branching habits. Evergreen shrubs establish a sense of enduring landscape stability.

The native homes of shrubs which thrive in Missouri today stretch from the Orient across North America and reach into the interior of Europe and Asia. Many have altered very little over time, and others are new varieties which have improved on the beauty and enlarged the usefulness of this remarkably diverse group of plants. Shrubs are especially quick to fulfill an aesthetic or functional need in a land-scape, and they require minimal care. They can screen an unwanted view or provide privacy from the street, frame any side of a house, mark a drive, create a backdrop for a garden, offer a bird habitat, perfume the patio, and lend cutting flowers for your table. Some varieties thrive in the hot sun, some in the shade, some like a dry soil, and some prefer wet. Whatever your need, there is a shrub that can do the job.

It is well known that shrubs are a tough bunch, but they still do better when placed in the most suitable sites for their kind. Before any holes are dug or any shrubs are purchased, a thorough site evaluation and review of possible shrub candidates should be undertaken. Take a stroll around the yard, keeping in mind how the landscape changes with each season. Be aware of which areas get the most sun and for how long during the various seasons. Consider the existing plants, their health, and habits. Rough out a map of the slopes, low spots, and drainage patterns. Mark the walks, driveway, deck, patio, downspouts, doors, garage, and any other outstanding structures. Compile a list of shrub candidates that indicates their mature size, shape, rate of growth, invasiveness, and season of bloom, fruits, thorns, or suckering. This preparatory work will eliminate future frustration with a shrub that does poorly because it is in the wrong spot and will also reduce the amount of maintenance the shrub requires.

Once the research is completed, you can begin the enjoyable work of preparing the site, choosing the shrubs, and planting them. Whether your project is a small city courtyard, an ample suburban patio, or a wide expanse of country estate, your well-chosen shrubs will bring immediate and lasting pleasure.

Arrowwood Viburnum

Viburnum dentatum

Height and Width: 8 by 8 feet, and larger
Bloom Time: Late spring
Flower Color: White
Type: Deciduous
Zones: 2 through 8
Color photograph on page 251.

Light Requirements:

Beneficial Characteristic:

The arrowwood viburnum has not received as much press for glamour as some other shrubs, but it is hard to beat this deciduous shrub for versatility and adaptability. Its dense and numerous stems shoot up and out from the center growth point, forming a large, graceful vase-shaped bush. The foliage is a medium-dark, glossy green on top, with a contrasting underside. While the white flowers are not fragrant, they open as early as the warm days of late May or early June. When the flowering season ends, the viburnum produces a darkish fruit that is enjoyed by many bird species, whose presence makes the fall even more delightful.

When to Plant

Plant arrowwood viburnum in the late fall through mid-spring.

Where to Plant

Arrowwood viburnum requires a larger, well-drained site in the full sun or lightly shaded. Allow for space to colonize as the arrowwood will sucker at the base.

How to Plant

For a previously prepared bed, dig a hole three times the diameter and slightly less than the height of the rootball. For a new bed or a single planting space, delineate the planting area and remove any undesirable plants by digging or with an herbicide. Rototill or spade the soil to a depth of 6 to 8 inches, mix 6 inches of organic matter with the existing soil, and level the planting area. Do not add fertilizer. Water shrubs thoroughly prior to installation. If planting a containerized shrub, remove from pot, loosen roots if pot bound, and place in hole. If planting a balled and burlapped shrub, lower it into the hole, cut all rope, and fold burlap downward. Backfill the hole and firm the soil around the root system. Water immediately and cover the planting area with 2 to 3 inches of mulch. Prune only to remove dead or damaged branches.

CARE AND MAINTENANCE

Fertilize monthly with an all-purpose tree and shrub food, beginning with the emergence of new growth and stopping in mid-August. Prevent any drought stress during the first growing season. Prune as needed within 12 weeks of flower drop. Pest and disease problems are virtually nonexistent.

ADDITIONAL INFORMATION

Arrowwood viburnums are priced by their height, and sold in containers or balled and burlapped; either is acceptable. If the shrub is dormant, look for numerous buds on flexible stems and a moist rootball. The rootball should be 3 inches wide for every foot of the tallest stem. If the shrub is leafed out, check the quantity of leaves, and look for a consistent color and size of leaf. If fall leaf color is important for your planting site, select the shrub during the fall. Companion plantings to consider are blue sage, snapdragons, gladiola, creeping phlox, and Chinese dogwood.

ADDITIONAL SPECIES, CULTIVARS, OR VARIETIES

There are none available.

Did You Know?

Viburnums can be found in the temperate climates of North America, Europe, and Asia. The arrowwood viburnum is native to the eastern half of the United States, north to the Canadian border and south to Texas and was first used in gardens and residential landscapes in the early 1700s.

Bayberry

Myrica pensylvanica

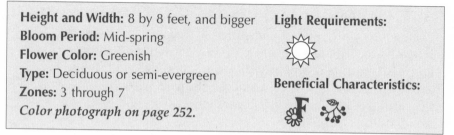

Height and Width: 8 by 8 feet, and bigger
Bloom Period: Mid-spring
Flower Color: Greenish
Type: Deciduous or semi-evergreen
Zones: 3 through 7
Color photograph on page 252.

Light Requirements:

Beneficial Characteristics:

This remarkable shrub can be found growing along the rocky coast from Maine to North Carolina, evidence of its ability to thrive in poor, sterile, and rugged hilltop soils. It has proven itself a winner, as well, in heavy compacted soils. Hardiness and adaptability are important to any shrub, but the bayberry also creates a sophisticated look in most settings. Its upright, somewhat open, twiggy habit is softly mounded at the top, giving the shrub an umbrella-like form. This shape and its fragrant leaves offer annuals, perennials, and ground covers plenty of light while also providing protection from the most intense midday sun. A bayberry works well as a streetside planting, can create attractive screening, or can stand quite well all on its own in a far corner of the backyard.

WHEN TO PLANT
It is best to plant bayberry in the spring

WHERE TO PLANT
Plant bayberry in a sunny, well-drained location, anywhere from a roadside setting to framing a garden.

HOW TO PLANT
For a previously prepared bed, dig a hole three times the diameter and slightly less than the height of the rootball. For a new bed or a single planting space, delineate the planting area and remove any undesirable plants by digging or with an herbicide. Rototill or spade the soil to a depth of 6 to 8 inches, mix 6 inches of organic matter with the existing soil, and level the planting area. Do not add fertilizer. Water shrubs thoroughly prior to installation. If planting a containerized shrub, remove from pot, loosen roots if pot bound, and place in hole. If planting a balled and burlapped shrub, lower it into

the hole, cut all rope, and fold burlap downward. Backfill the hole and firm the soil around the root system. Water immediately and cover the planting area with 2 to 3 inches of mulch. Prune only to remove dead or damaged branches.

CARE AND MAINTENANCE
Fertilize monthly with an all-purpose tree and shrub food, beginning with the emergence of new growth and stopping in mid-August. Prevent any drought stress during the first growing season. Prune by mid-summer to control size or to shape. There are no pest or disease problems.

ADDITIONAL INFORMATION
The best size of bayberry to plant is 2 to 6 feet tall, either in a container or balled and burlapped. If the shrub is dormant, look for numerous tiny buds along flexible stems and a moist rootball. The rootball should be 2 to 3 inches wide for every foot of the tallest stem. If the shrub is leafed out, check the quantity of leaves, and look for a consistent color and size of leaf. One male shrub is needed for every five females. Companion plantings to consider are obedient plant, cranesbill, toadflax, cannas, and English ivy.

ADDITIONAL SPECIES, CULTIVARS, OR VARIETIES
There are none available.

Did You Know?
Bayberries are native to the east coast from Canada to Florida. The females produce a gray-colored fruit used in the production of bayberry candles.

Bridalwreath Spiraea

Spiraea × vanhouttei

Height and Width: 8 by 8 feet
Bloom Period: Mid-spring
Flower Color: White
Type: Deciduous
Zones: 3 through 8
Color photograph on page 252.

Light Requirements:

Beneficial Characteristic:

Bridalwreath spiraea springs from the ground in a fountain of growth that shoots high into the air and then gently cascades to earth. When in bloom in the spring, it makes a trailing bouquet of fragrant, double, white flowers that ripple in the slightest breeze. An unusual trait of this shrub is that the mature branches maintain their very slim width for many years, so that the shrub's graceful flowing line does not thicken and stiffen with time. The small, dark green leaves that cover almost the entire length of the stem turn a pale orange color in the fall. Bridalwreath spiraea provides an excellent backdrop for summer- and fall-blooming plants, and works well in smaller yards or larger planting areas.

WHEN TO PLANT
Plant bridalwreath spiraea in the spring or fall.

WHERE TO PLANT
Bridalwreath spiraea requires full sun in a well-drained location. Grouped or specimen plantings work well.

HOW TO PLANT
For a previously prepared bed, dig a hole three times the diameter and slightly less than the height of the rootball. Add 6 inches of organic matter to the soil and blend together, do not add fertilizer. For a new bed or a single planting space, delineate the planting area and remove any undesirable plants by digging or with an herbicide. Rototill or spade the soil to a depth of 6 to 8 inches, mix 6 inches of organic matter with the existing soil, and rake smooth. Water shrubs thoroughly prior to installation. Remove shrub from pot, loosen the roots if pot bound, and place the shrub in the hole. Backfill the hole

and firm the soil around the root system. Water immediately and cover the planting area with 2 to 3 inches of mulch. Prune only to remove dead or damaged branches.

CARE AND MAINTENANCE
Fertilize monthly with an all-purpose tree and shrub food, beginning with the emergence of new growth and stopping in mid-August. Prevent any drought stress during the first growing season. Prune by early summer to control size or to shape. There are no pest or disease problems.

ADDITIONAL INFORMATION
Select a container-grown plant that is 1 to 4 feet in height. Dormant plants should be full of limber twigs with buds the entire length. If leafed out, check for consistent color and size of leaf. The rootball should be 2 to 3 inches wide for every foot of the tallest stem. Companion plantings to consider are blue sage, French marigold, crocus, creeping juniper, and Japanese blood grass.

ADDITIONAL SPECIES, CULTIVARS, OR VARIETIES
The bridalwreath spiraea has no additional types, but other varieties of spiraeas to consider are the red-flowering *Spiraea* × *bumalda* 'Anthony Waterer', and the low-growing, yellow-leafed *Spiraea* × *bumalda* 'Limemound'.

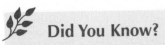

Did You Know?

Bridalwreath spiraea was originally hybridized and propagated in the 1800s from one parent that is native to Northern China and Siberia and the other from Southern China and Japan. This shrub is easily grown from seed if the seed is gathered, placed in a container with plant-starter potting-soil mix, and left outside during the winter.

Burning Bush

Euonymus alatus

Height and Width: 12 by 10 feet
Bloom Period: Late spring
Flowers Color: Greenish
Type: Deciduous
Zones: 4 through 9
Color photograph on page 252.

Light Requirements:

Beneficial Characteristic:

Where there is a need for screening, hedging, or bookends to frame a garden, specimen, or clustered plantings, burning bush is an excellent candidate to consider. This shrub possesses many diverse and admirable characteristics. The shrub's ball-like outline is built upon a series of impenetrable horizontal twigs and stems which have an extra corky flap running their entire length. The branching arrangement is ideal for birds that are nesting or seeking a protected place to land. Its circular form is a tremendous foil when it is sited as a companion beside plants with a vertical or upright presence. In the fall, burning bush earns its name with brilliant red foliage, and in the winter its rounded shape stands out boldly in snow.

WHEN TO PLANT

Install burning bush from early fall through mid-spring.

WHERE TO PLANT

Burning bush requires full sun and a well-drained spot. Allow it adequate room to grow to minimize the need to prune.

HOW TO PLANT

For a previously prepared bed, dig a hole three times the diameter and slightly less than the height of the rootball. For a new bed or a single planting space, delineate the planting area and remove any undesirable plants by digging or with an herbicide. Rototill or spade the soil to a depth of 6 to 8 inches, mix 6 inches of organic matter with the existing soil, but no fertilizer, and rake smooth. Water shrubs thoroughly prior to installation. Remove containerized shrub from pot, loosen the roots if pot bound, and place the shrub in the hole. Place balled and burlapped shrub in the hole, cut ropes, and fold burlap downward. Backfill the hole and firm the soil around the

root system. Water immediately and cover the planting area with 2 to 3 inches of mulch. Prune only to remove dead or damaged branches.

CARE AND MAINTENANCE

Fertilize monthly with an all-purpose tree and shrub food, beginning with the emergence of new growth and stopping in mid-August. Prevent any drought stress during the first growing season. Prune after leaf drop in the fall to control size and habit. Pest and disease problems are virtually nonexistent.

ADDITIONAL INFORMATION

Burning bush is available either in a container or balled and burlapped, with the potted plants generally being the smaller. This shrub is relatively slow growing, so select the size accordingly. Pick a shrub that is roundly symmetrical, full of flexible stems, and well budded if dormant. If actively growing, check the quantity of leaves and look for consistent color and size of leaf. The rootball should be moist and 2 to 3 inches wide for every foot of the tallest stem. Companion plantings to consider are blue lyme grass, daylily, coneflower, petunias, and bugle weed.

ADDITIONAL SPECIES, CULTIVARS, OR VARIETIES

Although called compact, *Euonymus alatus* 'Compactus' is not dramatically smaller in size. Another possible type for smaller spaces is *Euonymus alatus* 'Rudy Haag', which may grow only 5 feet high and wide.

Did You Know?

Burning bush was discovered in the mid 1800s in Asia, although close relatives can be found throughout much of the world, all with very different growth habits. A purplish-flowered variety called the "wahoo" is found along the edges of woodlands in eastern Canada and the United States.

Deciduous Winterberry Holly

Ilex verticillata 'Winter Red'

Height and Width: 9 by 9 feet
Bloom Period: Mid-spring
Flower Color: Whitish
Type: Deciduous
Zones: 3 through 9
Color photograph on page 252.

Light Requirements:

Beneficial Characteristics:

If you have been frustrated by a low wet spot in the landscape that has resisted and weakened or killed off a wide variety of plants, you can fight back with winterberry holly. This deciduous shrub will not only survive, but actually prefers this type of planting area. In fact, winterberry holly appears to welcome extremes. It is equally successful sitting in the day-long sun. The winterberry's abundance of almost black stems, branches, twigs, and suckers form a thicket that is wider at the top than at the bottom. Its rough and twisting demeanor suggests this shrub should be allowed a natural setting. When the winterberry's dark green leaves begin to yellow in mid-fall, the scarlet holly berries appear and they persist through much of the winter. Male and female plants must be planted together for the pollination to occur which enables the females to produce their brilliant red fruit.

WHEN TO PLANT

Plant winterberry holly in the mid-fall through mid-spring.

WHERE TO PLANT

Site winterberry holly in a larger area in almost any soil except highly alkaline. Allow this shrub space to spread as suckering at the base will occur.

HOW TO PLANT

For a previously prepared bed, dig a hole three times the diameter and slightly less than the height of the rootball. For a new bed or a single planting space, delineate the planting area and remove any undesirable plants by digging or with an herbicide. Rototill or spade the soil to a depth of 6 to 8 inches, mix 6 inches of organic matter with the existing soil, but no fertilizer, and rake smooth. Water shrubs thoroughly prior to installation. Remove containerized shrub from pot, loosen the roots if pot bound, and place the shrub in the hole. Place balled and burlapped shrub in the hole, cut ropes, and fold burlap downward. Backfill the hole and firm the soil around the root system. Water immediately and cover the planting area with 2 to 3 inches of mulch. Prune only to remove dead or damaged branches.

CARE AND MAINTENANCE

Fertilize monthly with an all-purpose tree and shrub food, beginning with the emergence of new growth and stopping in mid-August. Prevent any drought stress during the first growing season. Prune by mid-summer to control size. Pest and disease problems are virtually nonexistent.

ADDITIONAL INFORMATION

Winterberry hollies are available in numerous sizes, in containers or balled and burlapped, with no advantage to either style. Look for numerous buds on flexible stems and a moist rootball that is 3 inches in diameter for every foot of the tallest stem. If the plant is in leaf, check the leaf quantity and look for consistent color and size of leaves. Companion plantings consider are Hall's honeysuckle, ribbon grass, astilbe, and snakeroot.

ADDITIONAL SPECIES, CULTIVARS, OR VARIETIES

Smaller-sized varieties are *Ilex verticillata* 'Fairfax' or *Ilex verticillata* 'Bonfire'. *I. Verticillata* 'Sparkleberry' received the Styer award in 1987.

Did You Know?

The unimproved variety of holly which is native to North America has the widest range of any type of holly in the world, growing from eastern Canada through much of the American Midwest and South. Another common name is black alder, which refers to the dark color of the winterberry holly's bark.

Globe Arborvitae

Thuja occidentalis 'Woodwardi'

Height and Width: 5 by 5 feet
Flowers: Insignificant
Type: Coniferous Evergreen
Zones: 2 through 7
Color photograph on page 252.

Light Requirements:

The globe arborvitae possesses the supreme virtue of achieving a globular shape without pruning. Its small, dark green, closely overlapping leaves obscure the shrub's dense thicket of branches, so that it appears to be more sculpted than grown. This shrub is often used in traditional foundation plantings, where it is planted at equal intervals along the house, or clustered to highlight windows and other architectural features, or set at a corner to carry a theme into the side yard. Globe arborvitae are sometimes placed at all the corners of a garden, whether vegetable, herb, or flower, to create a kind of outdoor room. This evergreen shrub also works well if planted at the edge of the lawn to smooth the movement into the tree line. It can be dotted in spots in a shade garden to increase the winter appeal of this area of the yard.

WHEN TO PLANT

Plant globe arborvitae in the fall through mid-spring.

WHERE TO PLANT

Globe arborvitae do well in a sunny or lightly shaded location which is very well drained.

HOW TO PLANT

For a previously prepared bed, dig a hole three times the diameter and slightly less than the height of the rootball, and do not add fertilizer. For a new bed or a single planting space, delineate the planting area and remove any undesirable plants by digging or with an herbicide. Rototill or spade the soil to a depth of 6 to 8 inches, mix 6 inches of organic matter with the existing soil, but no fertilizer, and rake smooth. Water shrubs thoroughly just prior to removing from pots. Remove shrub from pot, loosen the roots if pot bound, and place the shrub in the hole. Backfill the hole and firm the soil around the root system. Water immediately and cover the planting area with

308

2 to 3 inches of mulch. Prune only to remove dead or damaged branches.

CARE AND MAINTENANCE
Fertilize monthly with an all-purpose evergreen tree and shrub food, beginning with the emergence of new growth and stopping in mid-August. Prevent any drought stress during the first growing season. No pruning is needed. Pest and disease problems are minimal.

ADDITIONAL INFORMATION
Globe arborvitae are sold as container-grown shrubs of various sizes. Check the stems for flexibility, fullness, consistent color, and an overall symmetrical shape. The rootball's diameter should be equal to half the plant's height. Companion plantings to consider are spiderwort, blue sage, autumn crocus, bishop's weed, and Japanese blood grass.

ADDITIONAL SPECIES, CULTIVARS, OR VARIETIES
A smaller-growing, globe-shaped variety is *Thuja occidentalis* 'Little Gem'; a cone-shaped variety is *Thuja occidentalis* 'Rheingold'.

Did You Know?
Globe arborvitae is a naturally occurring mutation of the American or white cedar whose native habitat ranges from southeastern Canada to the Mississippi. The wood of the larger growing types is prized because it is easy to work and has been harvested since the mid-1500s.

Hidcote St. Johnswort

Hypericum henryi 'Hidcote'

Mature and Width: 3 by 3 feet
Bloom Period: Midsummer
Flower Color: Yellow
Type: Deciduous
Zones: 3 through 8
Color photograph on page 252.

Light Requirements:

Beneficial Characteristics:

Hidcote St. Johnswort is abuzz with insects from late May through all of June and then again in August. Butterflies, moths, honeybees—all are drawn to this smaller-growing, long-flowering shrub. The fine-textured structural properties of the stems, regardless of their age, make St. Johnswort stand out from many of the other sun-dwelling bushes. The twig sprouts grayish green leaves, and sitting at the twig's end is a highly unusual flower, a saucer of leaves supporting a cone which bursts open to reveal a deeply vivid yellow blossom. St. Johnswort will benefit if it is sited in a fully sunny location with protection from the worst winter's wind chills.

WHEN TO PLANT
Plant St. Johnswort during the spring.

WHERE TO PLANT
Hidcote St. Johnswort requires a sunny well-drained spot, possibly away from seating areas if bees are a problem.

HOW TO PLANT
For a previously prepared bed, dig a hole three times the diameter and slightly less than the height of the rootball, and do not add fertilizer. For a new bed or a single planting space, delineate the planting area and remove any undesirable plants by digging or with an herbicide. Rototill or spade the soil to a depth of 6 to 8 inches, mix 6 inches of organic matter with the existing soil, but no fertilizer, and rake smooth. Water shrubs thoroughly just prior to removing from pots. Remove shrub from pot, loosen the roots if pot bound, and place the shrub in the hole. Backfill the hole and firm the soil around the root system. Water immediately and cover

the planting area with 2 to 3 inches of mulch. Prune only to remove dead or damaged branches.

CARE AND MAINTENANCE

Fertilize monthly with an all-purpose tree and shrub food, beginning with the emergence of new growth and stopping in mid-August. Prevent any drought stress during the first growing season. Prune after leaf drop to control size and shape. Pest and diseases are little trouble.

ADDITIONAL INFORMATION

St. Johnswort shrubs are grown in containers of various sizes. If the plant is dormant, carefully check the stems for flexibility and fullness. If it is in leaf, check for an abundance of leaves, and look for consistent leaf color and size. The rootball should be 2 to 3 inches wide for every foot of the tallest stem. Companion plantings to consider are fall windflower, blue lyme grass, cockscomb, elephant ears, and creeping juniper.

ADDITIONAL SPECIES, CULTIVARS, OR VARIETIES

There are none available.

 Did You Know?

Some people mistakenly believe that St. Johnswort will give them warts. The word "wort" is simply an old English term that means "plant." One of the parents of this hardy variety can be found growing in southeastern Europe and Asia Minor, but the lineage of the other parent is a controversial subject.

Inkberry Holly

Ilex glabra

Height and Width: 8 by 8 feet
Bloom Period: Late spring
Flowers Color: Whitish
Type: Broadleaf evergreen
Hardiness Zones: 4 through 9
Color photograph on page 252.

Light Requirements:

Beneficial Characteristic:

The inkberry holly is a broadleaf evergreen holly with small, ink-black berries which is native to the low wetlands of Missouri. This shrub is quite impressive in its ability not only to survive in its native habitat, but also to colonize and stake out a substantial amount of territory. It is quite easy to make use of the inkberry in home landscapes if a few simple facts about this shrub are kept in mind. First, although the inkberry has evergreen oblong leaves, its growing habit is to spread wider at the top of the shrub which causes the bottom quarter of the plant to be leafless. This habit can be managed by pruning the top to reduce its width, or by removing a third of the oldest stems each year. Second, the leafless lower stems make this plant suitable as a companion for many shade-loving perennials and annuals.

WHEN TO PLANT
Plant inkberry in the spring or fall.

WHERE TO PLANT
If inkberry is not planted where there is an adequate or abundant supply of water, it will lose some of its luster.

HOW TO PLANT
For a previously prepared bed, dig a hole three times the diameter and slightly less than the height of the rootball, and do not add fertilizer. For a new bed or a single planting space, delineate the planting area and remove any undesirable plants by digging or with an herbicide. Rototill or spade the soil to a depth of 6 to 8 inches, mix 6 inches of organic matter with the existing soil, but no fertilizer, and rake smooth. Water shrubs thoroughly just prior to removing from pots. Remove shrub from pot, loosen the roots if pot bound, and place the shrub in the hole. Backfill the hole and firm the soil around

the root system. Water immediately and cover the planting area with 2 to 3 inches of mulch. Prune only to remove dead or damaged branches.

CARE AND MAINTENANCE

Fertilize monthly with an all-purpose evergreen tree and shrub food, beginning with the emergence of new growth and stopping in mid-August. Prevent any drought stress during the first growing season. Prune during the late winter to control size or shape. Pest and disease problems are minimal.

ADDITIONAL INFORMATION

Inkberry is sold as container-grown shrubs of various sizes. Check the stems for flexibility and the leaves for consistent color and size. The rootball should be 2 to 3 inches wide for every foot of the tallest stem. Companion plantings to consider are ribbon grass, astilbe, goatsbeard, red fountain grass, and chameleon plant.

ADDITIONAL SPECIES, CULTIVARS, OR VARIETIES

Two compact varieties are the 'Nordic' and 'Shamrock'.

Did You Know?

Inkberry was first cultivated for gardens in the mid 1700s. This is the only holly that spreads by underground runners.

Lantanaphyllum Viburnum

Viburnum × rhytidophylloides

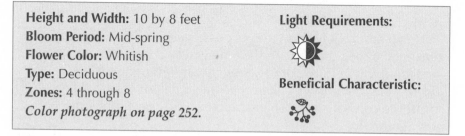

Height and Width: 10 by 8 feet
Bloom Period: Mid-spring
Flower Color: Whitish
Type: Deciduous
Zones: 4 through 8
Color photograph on page 252.

Light Requirements:

Beneficial Characteristic:

The superb foliage and astounding fruit production of the larger-growing lantanaphyllum viburnum make it an excellent choice for planting under the shadows of large trees. Its large, spearhead-shaped leaves have a dark green upper surface and a paler lower surface. This two-toned characteristic makes the foliage quite showy when the wind blows. The leaves persist well into the fall, offering a last glimpse of the previous growing season. This viburnum's coarse texture works beautifully when surrounded in the shade setting by plants with contrasting finer textures. Though the shading is not required, the shrub's aesthetic qualities are enhanced by shady conditions.

WHEN TO PLANT

Plant lantanaphyllum viburnum in the fall or early to mid-spring.

WHERE TO PLANT

Site lantanaphyllum viburnum in a larger landscape where the soil is well drained and there is some protection from midday sun. Allow this shrub space to mature.

HOW TO PLANT

For a previously prepared bed, dig a hole three times the diameter and slightly less than the height of the rootball. For a new bed or a single planting space, delineate the planting area and remove any undesirable plants by digging or with an herbicide. Rototill or spade the soil to a depth of 6 to 8 inches, mix 6 inches of organic matter with the existing soil, but no fertilizer, and rake smooth. Water shrubs thoroughly prior to installation. Remove containerized shrub from pot, loosen the roots if pot bound, and place the shrub in the hole. Place balled and burlapped shrub in the hole, cut ropes, and fold burlap downward. Backfill the hole and firm the soil around the

root system. Water immediately and cover the planting area with 2 to 3 inches of mulch. Prune only to remove dead or damaged branches.

Care and Maintenance

Fertilize monthly with an all-purpose tree and shrub food, beginning with the emergence of new growth and stopping in mid-August. Prevent any drought stress during the first growing season. Avoid pruning in late summer because the flower buds will be pruned out. Pest and disease problems are virtually nonexistent.

Additional Information

Lantanaphyllum viburnums are priced by height, and sold in containers or balled and burlapped; either style is acceptable. If the plant is dormant, look for numerous buds on flexible stems, and a moist rootball which is 3 inches in diameter for every foot of the tallest stem's height. If the plant is in leaf, check the leaf quantity, and look for consistent color and size of leaves. Companion plantings to consider are sweet woodruff, Solomon's seal, begonias, and caladiums.

Additional Species, Cultivars, or Varieties

Varieties with more pronounced habits are *Viburnum × rhytidophylloides* 'Alleghany' or *Viburnum rhytidophylloides × V. lantana* 'Willowwood'.

🌿 Did You Know?

The fruits, which are aesthetically rewarding and also serve to feed various birds, may be more abundant if different types of viburnum are planted in the landscape. Though sometimes called semi-evergreen, the leaves will drop by Thanksgiving unless the late fall is extremely mild.

Lilac

Syringa vulgaris

Height and Width: 12 feet
  or taller by 12 feet
Bloom Period: Mid-spring
Flower Color: Lavender
Type: Deciduous
Zones: 3 through 7
Color photograph on page 252.

Light Requirements:

Beneficial Characteristics:

The lilac is most often remembered and adored for its distinctive, sweet spring fragrance and drooping spikes of lavender blooms. People often plant it out of a nostalgia for favorite gardens remembered from the past. Its thicket of limbs, persistent suckering, and salt tolerance make it a superior shrub for screening the house and yard from the street, although its spring blooms are sure to stop passersby. This shrub does well just about anywhere, as long as it is placed in the sun. To keep a lilac healthy, remove the limbs near the ground when they exceed the width of your wrist.

WHEN TO PLANT

Lilacs can be planted from the fall through the mid-spring.

WHERE TO PLANT

Site a lilac in a larger area which is well drained and in the full sun. This shrub's salt tolerance allows for placement near roads.

HOW TO PLANT

For a previously prepared bed, dig a hole three times the diameter and slightly less than the height of the rootball. For a new bed or a single planting space, delineate the planting area and remove any undesirable plants by digging or with an herbicide. Rototill or spade the soil to a depth of 6 to 8 inches, mix 6 inches of organic matter with the existing soil, but no fertilizer, and rake smooth. Water shrubs thoroughly prior to installation. Remove containerized shrub from pot, loosen the roots if pot bound, and place the shrub in the hole. Place balled and burlapped shrub in the hole, cut ropes, and fold burlap downward. Backfill the hole and firm the soil around the

root system. Water immediately and cover the planting area with 2 to 3 inches of mulch. Prune only to remove dead or damaged branches.

CARE AND MAINTENANCE
Fertilize monthly with an all-purpose tree and shrub food, beginning with the emergence of new growth and stopping in mid-August. Powdery mildew is the most common problem of lilacs. Prevent any drought stress during the first growing season. Prune as needed within 12 weeks of flower drop. Keeping the plant healthy is the best approach to eliminating the many potential pest and disease problems untended lilacs can face.

ADDITIONAL INFORMATION
Lilacs are priced by height, and sold in containers or balled and burlapped; either style is acceptable. If the plant is dormant, look for numerous buds on flexible stems and a moist rootball, which is 3 inches in diameter for every foot of the tallest stem's height. If the plant is in leaf, check the leaf quantity, and look for consistent color and size of leaves. If flower color is important, select the plant when in bloom. Companion plantings to consider are creeping phlox, feather reed grass, purple coneflower, and rose verbena.

ADDITIONAL SPECIES, CULTIVARS, OR VARIETIES
Varieties of lilacs with different colored blooms are: white *Syringa vulgaris* 'Edith Cavell' and purple *Syringa vulgaris* 'Night'.

Did You Know?
The lilac belongs to the olive family, and close inspection of the shrub a few months after flowering will reveal clusters of small greenish fruits. This particular species has roots in southeast Europe, with relatives scattered from Asia across the Himalayas and back to Europe.

Pfitzer

Juniperus chinensis 'Pfitzeriana'

Height and Width: 8 by 12 feet, and bigger
Flowers: Insignificant
Type: Coniferous evergreen
Zones: 3 through 9
Color photograph on page 252.

Light Requirements:

Beneficial Characteristic:

The softly layered limbs of the pfitzer, covered with shorter green needles, stretch very wide to fill any number of landscape voids. This shrub's wider-than-tall growth habit means that fewer plants are needed if the pfitzer is planted as an evergreen screen or large hedge. Its pale bluish fruits add a delicate touch of color when the shrub's long arms gently move in the wind and make the pfitzer highly attractive to birds. If allowed adequate room to grow, this evergreen shrub will pay dividends for many years.

WHEN TO PLANT
Plant pfitzer from the fall through the spring.

WHERE TO PLANT
Pfitzer requires a sunny location which is very well drained.

HOW TO PLANT
For a previously prepared bed, dig a hole three times the diameter and slightly less than the height of the rootball, and do not add fertilizer. For a new bed or a single planting space, delineate the planting area and remove any undesirable plants by digging or with an herbicide. Rototill or spade the soil to a depth of 6 to 8 inches, mix 6 inches of organic matter with the existing soil, but no fertilizer, and rake smooth. Water shrubs thoroughly just prior to removing from pots. Remove shrub from pot, loosen the roots if pot bound, and place the shrub in the hole. Backfill the hole and firm the soil around the root system. Water immediately and cover the planting area with 2 to 3 inches of mulch. Prune only to remove dead or damaged branches.

CARE AND MAINTENANCE
Fertilize monthly with an all-purpose evergreen tree and shrub food, beginning with the emergence of new growth and stopping in mid-August. Prevent any drought stress during the first growing season. Prune during the late winter to control size. Diseases are not problematic, but watch for bagworms.

ADDITIONAL INFORMATION
Pfitzers are sold as container-grown shrubs of various sizes. Check the stems for flexibility, fullness, consistent color, and an overall symmetrical shape. Make sure that bagworms are not present. The rootball's diameter should be equal to half the plant's height. Companion plantings to consider are primrose, geraniums, dahlias, feather reed grass, and creeping phlox.

ADDITIONAL SPECIES, CULTIVARS, OR VARIETIES
A blue-needled, smaller growing variety is *Juniperus chinensis* 'Blue Vase', and yellow spreading variety is *Juniperus chinensis* 'Gold Coast'.

Did You Know?
While it is nearly unknown today, the pfitzer was an extremely popular plant in the 1950s. Its wide-reaching branches highlighted homes for an entire generation. Perhaps the current return of 1950s-style furniture and clothing will signal the return of the pfitzer from the depths of landscape obscurity.

Purpleleaf Sand Cherry

Prunus × cistena

Height and Width: 10 by 8 feet
Bloom Period: Mid-spring
Flower Color: Pinkish
Type: Deciduous Shrub
Zones: 2 through 8
Color photograph on page 252.

Light Requirements:

Beneficial Characteristic:

The purpleleaf sand cherry's vibrant reddish purple foliage and upright habit makes it a landscape standout. Because it is so eye-catching, it's can be used to direct the view toward a seating area, or statuary, or bird feeders and baths. Planted in a mass, it works to draw the eye in a different direction and away from less attractive views. Planted along the house, it jazzes up a dull expanse of foundation. This shrub's dark-colored bark and branching habit make a striking silhouette in the winter when placed against a light background, an outline that is made even more attractive by a heavy frost or freshly fallen snow. Nesting birds are attracted by the dense branches.

WHEN TO PLANT

Plant purpleleaf sand cherry in the spring or the fall.

WHERE TO PLANT

Purpleleaf sand cherry requires the full sun in a well-drained location, and can be planted in a group or as a free-standing specimen.

HOW TO PLANT

For a previously prepared bed, dig a hole three times the diameter and slightly less than the height of the rootball. For a new bed or a single planting space, delineate the planting area and remove any undesirable plants by digging or with an herbicide. Rototill or spade the soil to a depth of 6 to 8 inches, mix 6 inches of organic matter with the existing soil, but no fertilizer, and rake smooth. Water shrubs thoroughly prior to installation. Remove containerized shrub from pot, loosen the roots if pot bound, and place the shrub in the hole. Place balled and burlapped shrub in the hole, cut ropes, and fold burlap downward. Backfill the hole and firm the soil around the root system. Water immediately and cover the planting area with 2 to 3 inches of mulch. Prune only to remove dead or damaged branches.

CARE AND MAINTENANCE

Fertilize monthly with an all-purpose tree and shrub food, beginning with the emergence of new growth and stopping in mid-August. Prevent any drought stress during the first growing season. Prune by midsummer to control the size and shape.

ADDITIONAL INFORMATION

The purpleleaf sand cherry is available in containers or balled and burlapped, usually in heights from 1 to 4 feet. Dormant plants should be full of limber twigs with buds the entire length. If the plant is leafed out, check for consistent leaf color and size. The rootball's diameter should be equal to half the plant's height. Companion plantings to consider are Dutch white clover, giant reed grass, sneezeweed, and glory of the snow.

ADDITIONAL SPECIES, CULTIVARS, OR VARIETIES

There are none available.

🌿 Did You Know?

Purpleleaf sand cherry belongs to the rose family, which includes most of the stone-fruit trees (that is, trees whose fruit have large pits). This shrub is a cross between the purpleleaf flowering plum that is native to the Balkan Mountains of Europe and the sand cherry which is native to the Great Lakes region.

Pussy Willow

Salix caprea

Other Name: Goat Willow
Height and Width: 15 by 10, and bigger
Bloom Period: Early Spring
Flower Color: Yellow/Gray
Type: Deciduous
Zones: 4 through 8
Color photograph on page 252.

Light Requirements:

Beneficial Characteristic:

The pussy willow's growing habit is somewhat treelike. Branches emerge very near the ground from a single trunk and are easily removed to permit easier access around the plant. The leaves have a true green upper surface and a whitish underside. Highly tolerant of wet soil, the pussy willow is a good candidate for swampy spots. This shrub is best known and loved for its fuzzy catkins, the male flowers, which invite petting. Children are especially intrigued by the fuzzy flowers, and so this shrub offers parents a chance to teach lessons in plant development.

WHEN TO PLANT

Plant pussy willows from mid-fall through mid-spring.

WHERE TO PLANT

Site pussy willows in a sunny larger area in almost any soil from dry to swampy. Allow the shrub ample space for growth.

HOW TO PLANT

For a previously prepared bed, dig a hole three times the diameter and slightly less than the height of the rootball. For a new bed or a single planting space, delineate the planting area and remove any undesirable plants by digging or with an herbicide. Rototill or spade the soil to a depth of 6 to 8 inches, mix 6 inches of organic matter with the existing soil, but no fertilizer, and rake smooth. Water shrubs thoroughly prior to installation. Remove containerized shrub from pot, loosen the roots if pot bound, and place the shrub in the hole. Place balled and burlapped shrub in the hole, cut ropes, and fold burlap downward. Backfill the hole and firm the soil around the root system. Water immediately and cover the planting area with 2 to 3 inches of mulch. Prune only to remove dead or damaged branches.

CARE AND MAINTENANCE

Fertilize monthly with an all-purpose tree and shrub food, beginning with the emergence of new growth and stopping in mid-August. Prevent any drought stress during the first growing season. Prune by early summer to control the size and shape. The list of pests and diseases is extensive, but none are problematic to control.

ADDITIONAL INFORMATION

Pussy willows are available in numerous sizes, in containers or balled and burlapped, with no advantage to either style. Look for numerous buds on flexible stems, and a moist rootball that is 3 inches in diameter for every foot of the tallest stem's height. If the plant is in leaf, check the leaf quantity of leaves, and look for consistent color and size of leaves. Companion plantings to consider are big blue stem, balloon flower, and winter creeper.

ADDITIONAL SPECIES, CULTIVARS, OR VARIETIES

A weeping variety is the *Salix caprea* 'Pendula' or *Salix caprea* 'Weeping Sally'.

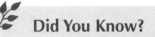 **Did You Know?**

Pussy willows come from a very widespread family that can be found in almost every corner of the world in the cooler temperate regions. Cuttings placed in a vase last for an extremely long time; when roots emerge and grow in the water, then the branchlets can be planted in low wet areas.

SHRUBS

Red Barberry

Berberis thunbergii var. *atropurpurea*

Height and Width: 6 by 6 feet	**Light Requirements:**
Bloom Period: Mid-spring	
Flower Color: Yellow	
Type: Deciduous	**Beneficial Characteristic:**
Zones: 4 through 7	
Color photograph on page 253.	

The colorful red barberry shrub makes an attractive focal point in nearly any size of landscape. Its smallish, lemon-colored flowers bloom between late April and early May, providing an attractive contrast to the shrub's intense reddish-purple leaves. After the leaf drop occurs in October, brilliant ruby fruits appear on the dense and thorny branches, whose thickness is magnified by the zigzag growth pattern of the stems. Red barberries work well as a hedge or in a mass planting, but remember not to place this very thorny shrub near walks, entrances, or seating areas.

WHEN TO PLANT

Plant red barberries in any season: they will require a little more care if installed in the summer.

WHERE TO PLANT

Red barberries do well in a sunny, well-drained location.

HOW TO PLANT

For a previously prepared bed, dig a hole three times the diameter and slightly less than the height of the rootball, and do not add fertilizer. For a new bed or a single planting space, delineate the planting area and remove any undesirable plants by digging or with an herbicide. Rototill or spade the soil to a depth of 6 to 8 inches, mix 6 inches of organic matter with the existing soil, but no fertilizer, and rake smooth. Water shrubs thoroughly just prior to removing from pots. Remove shrub from pot, loosen the roots if pot bound, and place the shrub in the hole. Backfill the hole and firm the soil around the root system. Water immediately and cover the planting area with 2 to 3 inches of mulch. Prune only to remove dead or damaged branches.

CARE AND MAINTENANCE

Fertilize monthly with an all-purpose tree and shrub food, beginning with the emergence of new growth and stopping in mid-August. Prevent any drought stress during the first growing season. Prune after leaf drop to control size or shape. Pests and diseases are little trouble.

ADDITIONAL INFORMATION

Red barberries are grown in containers of various sizes. If plant is dormant, carefully check the stems for flexibility and fullness. If in leaf, check for an abundance of leaves, and look for consistent color and size of leaves. The rootball diameter should equal half the plant's height. Companion plantings consider are cosmos, dahlia, stone crop, fountain grass, and liveforever.

ADDITIONAL SPECIES, CULTIVARS, OR VARIETIES

A species which is excellent for a smaller location is the crimson pygmy barberry, *Berberis thunbergii* var. *atropurpurea* 'Crimson Pygmy' or the mid-sized yellow-leafed variety *Berberis thunbergii* 'Aurea'.

SHRUBS

 Did You Know?

Although the barberry family is quite extensive, no member equals the popularity of the red barberry. This species is native to Japan and has been used elsewhere in the world in a variety of garden settings since the mid-1800s. The barberry is one of the easiest shrubs to hybridize, and new varieties become available each year.

Red Twig Dogwood

Cornus sericea 'Kelseyi'

Height and Width: 3 by 3 feet
Bloom Period: Late spring
Flower Color: Whitish
Type: Deciduous
Zones: 2 through 8
Color photograph on page 253.

Light Requirements:

The red twig dogwood commands a front and center spot in nearly any landscape where it is planted. It is accomplished at masking background plants that are overly woody at their base and at marking the distant reaches of the lawn. Its clusters of small white flowers pop out in mid- to late spring, giving way to white fruits in the late summer to early fall. The main attraction, however, comes after leaf drop, when this dogwood's red twigs make a highly dramatic and very unusual show of color all winter long. The Kelsey is a smaller-growing variety which will work in a very small landscape or, if massed, will create the desired results in any larger yard.

WHEN TO PLANT

Plant red twig dogwood at any time from the fall through mid-spring.

WHERE TO PLANT

Site red twig dogwood in a larger, sunny or shaded area in almost any soil, from dry to very wet.

HOW TO PLANT

For a previously prepared bed, dig a hole three times the diameter and slightly less than the height of the rootball. For a new bed or a single planting space, delineate the planting area and remove any undesirable plants by digging or with an herbicide. Rototill or spade the soil to a depth of 6 to 8 inches, mix 6 inches of organic matter with the existing soil, but no fertilizer, and rake smooth. Water shrubs thoroughly prior to installation. Remove containerized shrub from pot, loosen the roots if pot bound, and place the shrub in the hole. Place balled and burlapped shrub in the hole, cut ropes, and fold burlap downward. Backfill the hole and firm the soil around the root system. Water immediately and cover the planting area with 2 to 3 inches of mulch. Prune only to remove dead or damaged branches.

CARE AND MAINTENANCE
Fertilize monthly with an all-purpose tree and shrub food, beginning with the emergence of new growth and stopping in mid-August. Prevent any drought stress during the first growing season. Prune as needed to control size. Twig canker is a serious problem.

ADDITIONAL INFORMATION
Red twig dogwoods are available in containers or balled and burlapped, with no advantage to either style. On a dormant plant, look for numerous buds on flexible stems, and a moist rootball which is 3 inches in diameter for every foot of the tallest stem's height. If plant is in leaf, check the leaf quantity, and look for consistent color and size of leaves. Companion plantings to consider are Hall's honeysuckle, spiderwort, red fountain grass, and hollyhocks.

ADDITIONAL SPECIES, CULTIVARS, OR VARIETIES
A compact grower is *Cornus sericea* 'Isanti' , and a bright-red-stemmed type is *Cornus sericea* 'Cardinal'.

Did You Know?
Members of the dogwood family can be found in North America, Asia, and Europe and can range from perennial ground covers to the traditional tree of the American Midwest. The parents of the red twig dogwood are found from New England to Manitoba and south to Kentucky. This shrub has been domesticated since the mid 1600s.

Snowball Bush

Hydrangea arborescens 'Annabelle'

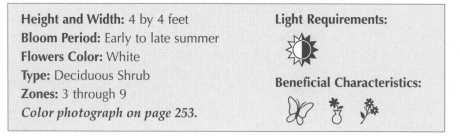

Height and Width: 4 by 4 feet
Bloom Period: Early to late summer
Flowers Color: White
Type: Deciduous Shrub
Zones: 3 through 9
Color photograph on page 253.

Light Requirements:

Beneficial Characteristics:

What! Snowballs in the summer! The almost storybook characteristics of this shrub make it an instant attraction and a hit in the summer garden. Its thick, somewhat willowy stems shoot straight up from the ground, carrying huge, pure white, globular clusters of flowers that weigh down the branches. The clusters fade through a series of browns and persist into the winter. Placing this shrub in a partly shaded setting will add to its drama. It works well planted as a single specimen, aligning the house foundation, or delineating the lawn from the tree line.

WHEN TO PLANT

Plant snowball bush in the spring.

WHERE TO PLANT

Site snowball bush where the soil is well drained and there is some protection from the midday sun. Allow this shrub adequate space to mature.

HOW TO PLANT

For a previously prepared bed, dig a hole three times the diameter and slightly less than the height of the rootball, and do not add fertilizer. For a new bed or a single planting space, delineate the planting area and remove any undesirable plants by digging or with an herbicide. Rototill or spade the soil to a depth of 6 to 8 inches, mix 6 inches of organic matter with the existing soil, but no fertilizer, and rake smooth. Water shrubs thoroughly just prior to removing from pots. Remove shrub from pot, loosen the roots if pot bound, and place the shrub in the hole. Backfill the hole and firm the soil around the root system. Water immediately and cover the planting area with 2 to 3 inches of mulch. Prune only to remove dead or damaged branches.

CARE AND MAINTENANCE

Fertilize monthly with an all-purpose tree and shrub food, beginning with the emergence of new growth and stopping in mid-August. Prevent any drought stress during the first growing season. Flowers are produced on current-season's growth, so prune as needed during fall, winter, or very early spring by removing up to $3/4$ of the stem length. Pest and disease problems are virtually nonexistent.

ADDITIONAL INFORMATION

Snowballs are sold in containers. If the shrub is dormant, look for numerous buds on flexible stems and a moist root ball which is 3 inches in diameter for every foot of the tallest stem's height. If in leaf, check the leaf quantity and look for consistent color and size of leaves. Companion plantings to consider are lilyturf, celandine poppy, grape hyacinth, toadflax, and lady's mantle.

ADDITIONAL SPECIES, CULTIVARS, OR VARIETIES

A variety with a larger flower cluster is *Hydrangea arborescens* 'Grandiflora'.

Did You Know?

The snowball bush belongs to the hydrangea family, which also includes currants and gooseberries. Its parents are native to the mid-coastal and southern areas of the United States, where they range in habitat from rocky outcroppings to deeply shaded groves. Cut the flowers just after the white is gone for seasonal arrangements.

Spring Witch Hazel

Hamamelis vernalis

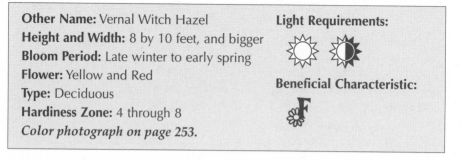
The witch hazel can fill many niches in the landscape while making very few demands. Witch hazel is a very early harbinger of spring and truly a welcome sight when the red and yellow flowers unfurl and fill the air with fragrance. During the summer, this shrub's vaselike shape, dark green leaves, and gray colored bark add character to any annual or perennial garden. Its bright yellow late fall foliage is a spectacular signal that winter is on the way. This large-growing dense shrub colonizes an area with new growth from its base, making it a good candidate for woodland gardens, informal screenings, or shrub borders. Although witch hazel has a medium growth rate, this shrub should be given ample room to grow from the beginning.

WHEN TO PLANT
The best time to plant witch hazel is in the late fall through mid-spring.

WHERE TO PLANT
Plant witch hazel in a larger well-drained site in the full sun or where it is lightly shaded. Because this shrub suckers at the base, allow it adequate space in which to colonize.

HOW TO PLANT
For a previously prepared bed, dig a hole three times the diameter and slightly less than the height of the rootball. For a new bed or a single planting space, delineate the planting area and remove any undesirable plants by digging or with an herbicide. Rototill or spade the soil to a depth of 6 to 8 inches, mix 6 inches of organic matter with the existing soil, but no fertilizer, and rake smooth. Water shrubs thoroughly prior to installation. Remove containerized shrub

from pot, loosen the roots if pot bound, and place the shrub in the hole. Place balled and burlapped shrub in the hole, cut ropes, and fold burlap downward. Backfill the hole and firm the soil around the root system. Water immediately and cover the planting area with 2 to 3 inches of mulch. Prune only to remove dead or damaged branches.

CARE AND MAINTENANCE

Fertilize monthly with an all-purpose tree and shrub food, beginning with the emergence of new growth and stopping in mid-August. Prevent any drought stress during the first growing season. Prune as needed within 12 weeks of flower drop. Pest and disease problems are virtually nonexistent.

ADDITIONAL INFORMATION

Spring witch hazels are priced by height, and sold in containers or balled and burlapped; either style is acceptable. If the plant is dormant, look for numerous buds on flexible stems and a moist rootball which is 3 inches in diameter for every foot of the tallest stem's height. If in leaf, check the leaf quantity and look for consistent color and size of leaves. If fall leaf color is important, select the shrub at that time. Companion plantings to consider are winter creeper, ribbon grass, goatsbeard, and bluebells.

ADDITIONAL SPECIES, CULTIVARS, OR VARIETIES

A fall-blooming variety of witch hazel is *Hamamelis virginiana*.

Summersweet N

Clethra alnifolia

Height and Width: 8 by 8 feet
Bloom Period: Mid- to late summer
Flowers Color: White
Type: Deciduous
Zones: 3 through 9
Color photograph on page 253.

Light Requirements:

Beneficial Characteristics:

The perfume of witch hazel spices the air in February, and sweet lilac permeates the days and nights of later spring. Then comes the lovely aroma of summersweet. This shrub suckers from the base, making it a good candidate for a larger-growing hedge or screen. Summersweet's white flowers stand in tall spikes at the ends of its densely leafed branches, emitting their sweet perfume for several weeks in the summer. It does well in a variety of sites, whether located in the full sun or a quite deep shade, and prefers a wetter growing area. When choosing a site for summersweet, remember that its strong fragrance is very attractive to bees.

WHEN TO PLANT

The best time to plant summersweet is from mid-fall through mid-spring.

WHERE TO PLANT

Site summersweet in sunny or shaded, dry or wet locations. Allow this shrub ample space for growth.

HOW TO PLANT

For a previously prepared bed, dig a hole three times the diameter and slightly less than the height of the rootball. For a new bed or a single planting space, delineate the planting area and remove any undesirable plants by digging or with an herbicide. Rototill or spade the soil to a depth of 6 to 8 inches, mix 6 inches of organic matter with the existing soil, but no fertilizer, and rake smooth. Water shrubs thoroughly prior to installation. Remove containerized shrub from pot, loosen the roots if pot bound, and place the shrub in the hole. Place balled and burlapped shrub in the hole, cut ropes, and fold burlap downward. Backfill the hole and firm the soil around the

root system. Water immediately and cover the planting area with 2 to 3 inches of mulch. Prune only to remove dead or damaged branches.

CARE AND MAINTENANCE

Fertilize monthly with an all-purpose tree and shrub food, beginning with the emergence of new growth and stopping in mid-August. Prevent any drought stress during the first growing season. Flowers are produced on current-season's growth, so prune as needed during fall, winter, or very early spring by removing up to 3/4 of the stem length. Pest and disease problems are virtually nonexistent.

ADDITIONAL INFORMATION

Summersweet is available in numerous sizes of containers or balled and burlapped; there is no advantage to either style. If plant is dormant, look for numerous buds on flexible stems and a moist rootball which is 3 inches in diameter for every foot of the tallest stem's height. If in leaf, check the leaf quantity and look for consistent color and size of leaves. Companion plantings to consider are hosta, impatiens, cannas, columbine, and myrtle.

ADDITIONAL SPECIES, CULTIVARS, OR VARIETIES

The *Clethra alnifolia* 'Paniculata' variety has larger clusters of flowers. A pink-budded variety is the *Clethra alnifolia* 'Rosea'. "Hummingbird" has received the Pennsylvania Horticultural Society Gold Medal (Styer Award).

Did You Know?

A coastal dweller from Maine to Florida, this native to the eastern seaboard was first cultivated in the 1700s and has found its way into many landscapes. Summersweet belongs to a very small family and has close relatives in Asia and South and North America.

Upright Yew

Taxus × media 'Hicksii'

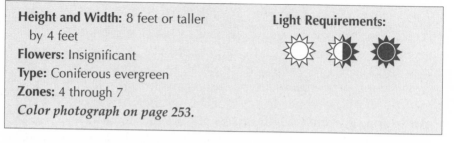

Height and Width: 8 feet or taller
   by 4 feet
Flowers: Insignificant
Type: Coniferous evergreen
Zones: 4 through 7
Color photograph on page 253.

Light Requirements:

Yews have become the standard evergreen shrub by which all others are measured. Their preferred status rests on several attractive qualities. First, they are highly amenable to pruning and take nearly any shape that the gardener can imagine and achieve with pruning shears. Second, their rate of growth is fairly consistent, which means that plantings sited in both the sun and full shade will grow at approximately the same rate. This makes yews particularly useful for hedges and foundation plantings. The yew's foliage is a darker shade of green, and some varieties pale in the winter. The female yews produce red berries, which are cones, and when the males are in flower their yellow pollen will float in the air if shaken from the shrub. The Hicks yew is a darker-needled variety of upright yew that is particularly useful for very narrow planting spaces. It offers a perfect backdrop for rose, annual, or perennials gardens. A pair planted side by side establishes a symbolic gateway to the woodland or shade garden or a seating area.

WHEN TO PLANT
The fall through the spring is the best time to plant the upright yew.

WHERE TO PLANT
Plant the upright yew in a sunny or shaded, very well-drained location.

HOW TO PLANT
For a previously prepared bed, dig a hole three times the diameter and slightly less than the height of the rootball. For a new bed or a single planting space, delineate the planting area and remove any undesirable plants by digging or with an herbicide. Rototill or spade the soil to a depth of 6 to 8 inches, mix 6 inches of organic matter with the existing soil, but no fertilizer, and rake smooth. Water

shrubs thoroughly prior to installation. Remove container-ized shrub from pot, loosen the roots if pot bound, and place the shrub in the hole. Place balled and burlapped shrub in the hole, cut ropes, and fold burlap downward. Backfill the hole and firm the soil around the root system. Water immediately and cover the planting area with 2 to 3 inches of mulch. Prune only to remove dead or damaged branches.

CARE AND MAINTENANCE

Fertilize monthly with an all-purpose evergreen tree and shrub food, beginning with the emergence of new growth and stopping in mid-August. Prevent any drought stress during the first growing season. Prune as needed during the spring or early fall. Pests and diseases are little trouble.

ADDITIONAL INFORMATION

Upright yews are sold as container-grown or balled and burlapped shrubs of various sizes; there is no advantage to one style. Check the stems for flexibility, fullness, consistent color, and an overall symmetrical shape. The rootball's diameter should be equal to half the plant's height. Companion plantings to consider are bishop's weed, sweet William, snowflake, pansy, and hollyhocks.

ADDITIONAL SPECIES, CULTIVARS, OR VARIETIES

Different growth habits are found in the pyramidal *Taxus × media* 'Hatfieldii' and the low-growing *Taxus × media* 'Tauntonii'.

Did You Know?

In a family all to themselves, the yews can be found mainly in the northern hemisphere, from northern Africa and Europe to Japan. The parentage of the typical plant used in the midwestern landscape is a cross of the English and Japanese yew. Keep in mind that the foliage can be poisonous if eaten.

Yellow False Cypress

Chamaecyparis pisifera 'Filifera Aurea'

Height and Width: 6 by 8 feet
Flowers: Insignificant
Type: Coniferous evergreen
Zones: 4 through 8
Color photograph on page 253.

Light Requirements:

The yellow false cypress is a prime example of the fact that "evergreen" does not always mean green. The color of its needles is not the only characteristic that sets this evergreen apart from others. It also has long, thin, weeping branches which give it an unusual cascading stature in the garden. This shrub is a "collector's specimen," for sure, but it also proves itself useful in a variety of full-sun sites. It provides an eye-catching contrast when sited near green shrubs other plants. A more subtle effect is achieved when the yellow false cypress is planted in a rock garden or near larger, earth-toned boulders. Wherever it is placed, this shrub is guaranteed to be a conversation piece.

WHEN TO PLANT

The best time to plant yellow false cypress is from the fall through mid-spring.

WHERE TO PLANT

Plant yellow false cypress in a bright, sunny location which is very well drained.

HOW TO PLANT

For a previously prepared bed, dig a hole three times the diameter and slightly less than the height of the rootball, and do not add fertilizer. For a new bed or a single planting space, delineate the planting area and remove any undesirable plants by digging or with an herbicide. Rototill or spade the soil to a depth of 6 to 8 inches, mix 6 inches of organic matter with the existing soil, but no fertilizer, and rake smooth. Water shrubs thoroughly just prior to removing from pots. Remove shrub from pot, loosen the roots if pot bound, and place the shrub in the hole. Backfill the hole and firm the soil around the root system. Water immediately and cover the planting area with

2 to 3 inches of mulch. Prune only to remove dead or damaged branches.

CARE AND MAINTENANCE
Fertilize monthly with an all-purpose evergreen tree and shrub food, beginning with the emergence of new growth and stopping in mid-August. Prevent any drought stress during the first growing season. No pruning is needed. Pests and diseases are little trouble.

ADDITIONAL INFORMATION
Yellow false cypresses are sold as container-grown shrubs of various sizes. Check the stems for flexibility, fullness, consistent color, and an overall symmetrical shape. The rootball diameter should be equal to half the plant's height. Companion plantings to consider are Shasta daisy, prairie dropseed, snapdragon, crocus, and false blue indigo.

ADDITIONAL SPECIES, CULTIVARS, OR VARIETIES
Varieties that provide a different colored foliage are: the silvery bluish *Chamaecyparis pisifera* 'Boulevard', and the gray-green *Chamaecyparis pisifera* 'Squarrosa'.

 Did You Know?

The yellow false cypress belongs to the Japanese cypress family, and its larger growing relatives were first cultivated for commercial lumber in the mid 1800s. This naturally occurring mutation with its unusual growth habit and color brings much needed color to the winter landscape.

CHAPTER ELEVEN

Vines

T HE GRAPE VINE, A SOURCE OF FRUIT AND WINE, has long figured in our imagination as a symbol of nature's bounty. But anyone who comes to know the varied group of plants called vines will soon imagine their enduring beauty, as well, when speaking of the fruits of the vine. Vines solve any number of landscape problems, and always with graceful, often colorful, and sometimes deliciously fragrant results.

Generally speaking, a vine is a plant whose stem requires support and which climbs with the aid of tendrils, or by twining around a structure, or by creeping along the ground. Hardy or perennial varieties are native to northern temperate regions, while annual varieties originate in the tropics. Some vines are evergreen and some deciduous. As a group they possess a wide variety of textures, foliage, and flowering habits. Some are fragrant and produce fruits, some offer a brilliant change in fall color. Most are a year-round source of pleasure.

The two basic categories of vines are clinging and nonclinging. Clinging vines use an adaptation of their stems—small suction cups, or rootlets, that adhere to almost any rough surface—to cling to a wall, foundation, tree trunk, trellis, arbor, post, or nearly anything else within reach. Nonclinging vines gain support for their upward growing stems by twining around an open support system. They weave around the cross pieces of a lattice, or trellis, or fence, virtually tying themselves to it. Nonclingers grow best when the cross members of the supporting structure are 1 inch or less in width, a size that does not challenge the vine's reach as it loops around the cross piece. Be sure to keep in mind the vine's growing habit when choosing a variety and selecting a planting spot. Remember that vines have weight and can cause damage as they mature if their support structure is not adequate.

Chapter Eleven

The checklist of important factors to keep in mind when selecting a planting location for vines are: (1) How much sun does the location receive? Even vines that can tolerate a partly shady spot will always reach for the light. (2) What are the existing plantings and nearby structures? Aggressive vines can overgrow smaller plants and cause damage to buildings, brick mortar, gutters. Be sure you are not planting a vine that will be difficult for you to control. (3) Examine the site's topography and exposure, gathering information about weather, winds, rain, and drainage. This research will help you make the best choice in vines for your planting site and your amount of time to spend in the garden.

These cautions stated, be assured that vines are highly effective landscaping tools. They can quickly block unpleasant views, soften structural lines, increase shade, and help to set apart and enclose seating areas. Many times, vines can accomplish these tasks at far less expense than shrubs, trees, and larger perennial plantings. One tip to consider when first establishing vines is that an annual vine planted in conjunction with a perennial variety will work to create the desired impact during the first growing season. Vines always enliven a landscape; their steadily increasing reach arouses curiosity and admiration. Most lend romantic qualities to a setting through their graceful green windings and often gorgeous flowers. In winter the evergreen varieties sustain us with their color, and those which lose their leaves offer instead a dark tangle of frosted stems lined with sparkling snow.

Boston Ivy

Parthenocissus tricuspidata

Height: 30 feet or more
Flower Color: Pale green
Bloom Period: Early summer
Type: Deciduous perennial
Hardiness Zones: 4 through 8
Color photograph on page 253.

Light Requirements:

Beneficial Characteristic:

B oston ivy is a living wallpaper, and one that is continually transformed by the season. Spreading over a brick or stone wall, or curling around doorways, windows, and archways, it exerts a tremendous visual and aesthetic influence in the landscape. In winter, the ivy's wiry network adheres tightly to the growing surface, offering a mosaic impression, particularly if dusted by snow. In spring, its bare stems give way to emerging reddish foliage that matures to a shiny, dark green, three-pointed leaf. Summer breezes expose the lighter underside of the leaf, creating a movement of light across the cool ivy-covered surface. The flowers hide among the leaves waiting for the wind to pollinate them. Fall is truly the apex season for Boston ivy, when its foliage turns a remarkably vibrant scarlet that mesmerizes passersby.

WHEN TO PLANT

The best time to plant Boston ivy is prior to mid-May or in September through early October.

WHERE TO PLANT

Site Boston ivy at the base of the support structure or randomly if is to be used as a ground cover. This vine requires well-drained soil, either in the sun or shade.

HOW TO PLANT

Regardless of the size of the pot purchased, keep the vine watered prior to planting. Delineate a planting space and remove undesirable plants by digging or with an herbicide. Rototill or spade the soil to a depth of 6 to 8 inches, and blend in a total of 6 inches of organic matter with the existing soil before raking smooth to create a raised bed. If the site is sloped, use erosion netting. Dig a hole twice the width of the pot or a minimum of 12 inches. Carefully remove the plant from the pot, loosen the roots if pot bound, and place the plant in the hole at a depth which is slightly higher than the surrounding ground. Backfill the hole, firm the soil, water the plant thoroughly, and place 1 inch of mulch around the plant.

CARE AND MAINTENANCE

If planted in the spring, feed the vine with a water-soluble fertilizer every 14 to 21 days during the first growing season, with none applied after mid-August. After the first growing season, feed monthly with a well-balanced food beginning in early May until mid-August. Do not allow drought stress to occur and eliminate weeds to prevent competition for nutrients. Once the vine is established, removal is difficult. Its clinging habit will scar the growing surface. Though several diseases and insects may attack, the damage is mostly cosmetic.

ADDITIONAL INFORMATION

This plant's rate of growth is very fast, so expect an impact quickly. Boston ivy is available at garden centers and through mail-order nurseries. The garden centers have plants in 4-inch to 5-gallon containers, and there is no advantage to one size, except that larger plants will have a quicker impact time. If dormant, the plant should have numerous buds on flexible stems; if it is leafed out, look for consistent color and size of leaves in relation to position on the stem. Mail-order plants arrive bareroot wrapped in moss or in smaller pots.

ADDITIONAL SPECIES, CULTIVARS, OR VARIETIES

Varieties with a different leaf are the larger *Parthenocissus tricuspidata* 'Green Showers' or the purplish-tinted *Parthenocissus tricuspidata* 'Purpurea'.

Cardinal Climber

Quamoclit sloteri or *Ipomoea quamoclit*

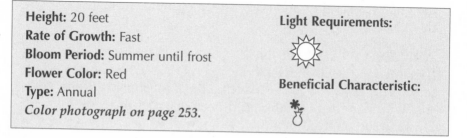

Height: 20 feet
Rate of Growth: Fast
Bloom Period: Summer until frost
Flower Color: Red
Type: Annual
Color photograph on page 253.

Light Requirements:

Beneficial Characteristic:

The brilliant red flowers of the cardinal climber bring a warm feel of the tropics onto your patio or deck, or along a fence. Because this vine is a nonclinging type, a growing framework must be provided for the cardinal to wrap around. The medium green foliage has a fernlike appearance and, with a little encouragement, this vine will mask the entire support system. Direct the vine back toward the trellis, arbor, or fence, until the framework is filled in as much as desired. The scarlet 1 1/2-inch flowers will bloom at intervals along the vine, helping to obscure the support structure, and transforming the setting into a tropical paradise—at least until the fall!

WHEN TO PLANT

In early to mid-April, begin seed germination indoors. Use a seed-starting soilless mix. Plant the seed in cell packs, and use full spectrum lighting and bottom heat. If planting in mid- to late May, you may place the seeds in a folded damp paper towel to germinate overnight, and plant them the next day, 1/2 inch deep, or simply direct sow the seed at the same depth.

WHERE TO PLANT

Plant cardinal climber in an open, sunny, well-drained site, in a prepared bed, at the base of the climbing structure, or in a container that is 14 inches in diameter or larger. The stem is nonclinging, and therefore must be woven through the support structure.

HOW TO PLANT

Delineate a planting space and remove undesirable plants by digging or with an herbicide. Rototill or spade the soil to a depth of 6 to 8 inches, and blend in a total of 6 inches of organic matter with the existing soil before raking smooth to create a raised bed. If the site is sloped, use erosion netting. Punch a hole 1/2 inch deep in the soil, drop in germinated seed, and gently firm the soil around the growth if sprouted. Water thoroughly and place 1/2 inch of mulch over surface. If planting in a container, fill one-quarter full with gravel and then well-drained potting soil.

CARE AND MAINTENANCE

If the seed is germinated prior to installation or once the seed sprouts have broken the soil surface and are 2 to 3 inches long, begin feeding with a water-soluble fertilizer every 2 weeks to get the maximum growth rate. Monitor the soil moisture, and remember that young seedlings may need watering twice daily for the first 7 to 10 days.

ADDITIONAL INFORMATION

Annual vines are sold in almost exclusively seed packets. Purchase the seed from a reputable company, and check the date on the package to ensure freshness. It is possible to gather ripe seeds from the previous year's growth and store them for next year. Always check a few seeds in the early spring for germination potential by using the wet paper towel method described above. If the seed does not germinate, purchase new seed packets.

Did You Know?

The cardinal vine belongs to the morning glory family, but the similarities between these relatives are hard to spot. Vines are grouped into families according to flower parts and numbers. In the tropical areas of Central and South America, this vine grows rampant, covering vast sunny open spaces as a ground cover and climbing wherever it can.

VINES

Hyacinth Bean

Lablab purpureus

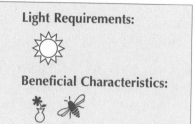

Height: 20 feet

Flower Color: Purple

Bloom Period: Summer until frost

Type: Annual

Color photograph on page 253.

Light Requirements:

Beneficial Characteristics:

When the hyacinth bean is first planted, it looks to be a rather limp and fragile vine. But it quickly develops into a remarkably elegant plant whose dramatic presence lasts throughout the growing season. The large leaves grow up to 7 inches wide and are arranged in an overlapping position along the vine, creating a solid green background for the rich purple sprays of flowers that shoot out from the stems. After the flowering season, the vine produces dark maroon bean pods, which can be used in seasonal arrangements. Once experienced, this vine is hard to do without, and gardeners seldom forget to find a place for it at the front or back door, on the patio trellis, or in a pot sitting on the deck. Keep in mind when selecting a place to plant the hyacinth bean that the flowers are highly attractive to bees.

WHEN TO PLANT

In early to mid-April, begin seed germination indoors. Use a seed-starting soilless mix. Plant the seed in cell packs, and use full spectrum lighting and bottom heat. If planting in mid- to late May, you may place the seeds in a folded damp paper towel to germinate overnight, and plant them the next day, 1/2 inch deep, or simply direct sow the seed at the same depth.

WHERE TO PLANT

Plant hyacinth bean in an open, sunny, well-drained site, in a prepared bed, at the base of the climbing structure, or in a container that is 14 inches in diameter or larger. The stem is nonclinging, and therefore must be woven through the support structure.

HOW TO PLANT

Delineate a planting space and remove undesirable plants by digging or with an herbicide. Rototill or spade the soil to a depth of 6 to

8 inches, and blend in a total of 6 inches of organic matter with the existing soil before raking smooth to create a raised bed. If the site is sloped, use erosion netting. Punch a hole 1/2 inch deep in the soil, drop in germinated seed, and gently firm the soil around the growth if sprouted. Water thoroughly and place 1/2 inch of mulch over surface. If planting in a container, fill one-quarter full with gravel and then well-drained potting soil.

CARE AND MAINTENANCE

If the seed is germinated prior to installation or once the seed sprouts have broken the soil surface and are 2 to 3 inches long, begin feeding with a water-soluble fertilizer every 2 weeks to get the maximum growth rate. Monitor the soil moisture, and remember that young seedlings may need watering twice daily for the first 7 to 10 days.

ADDITIONAL INFORMATION

Annual vines are sold almost exclusively in seed packets. Purchase the seed from a reputable company, and check the date on the package to ensure freshness. It is possible to gather ripe seeds from the previous year's growth and store them for next year. Always check a few seeds in the early spring for germination potential by using the wet paper towel method described above. If the seed does not germinate, purchase new seed packets.

Did You Know?

The hyacinth bean is a member of the bean family, which means it captures some nutrients from the air. The root system stores the minerals, and when the plant's foliage is reworked into the soil—a process called green manuring—it helps improve the soil. In the tropics of Africa, Asia, and India, the hyacinth bean is cultivated for the pods which are harvested for food and forage.

Jackman Clematis

Clematis × jackmanii

Height: 10 feet or more
Flowers Color: Dark purple
Bloom Period: Summer
Type: Deciduous perennial
Hardiness Zones: 3 through 8
Color photograph on page 253.

Light Requirements:

Beneficial Characteristics:

Royal among vines, the Jackman clematis bestows its splendid deep purple blossoms, some as large as 7 inches wide, beginning in June, and with proper care and the right weather may sustain its magnificent show until the early fall. Heavily veined, true green leaves complete the vine's bouquet when the gorgeous flowers explode from small rounded clusters of pointed buds. Clematis stems attach to a facade through the leaflets reaching around and locking together, as if shaking hands. As a group, they are slow to establish, and have a rather stiff demeanor, but the magnificent display they provide is well worth the trouble of observing the proper growing protocol. Show off the clematis on a trellis all its own, use it as a ground cover, or weave it through evergreen shrubs in a sunny location.

WHEN TO PLANT

The best time for planting the Jackman clematis is prior to mid-May or in September through very early October.

WHERE TO PLANT

Site this vine where the root system is shaded and the stem and foliage are in the full sun. An easy way to shade the roots is to place them behind the growing framework; the foliage can then be directed toward sunlight. The stems are a nonclinging type and must be woven through the support structure.

HOW TO PLANT

Regardless of the size of the pot purchased, keep the vine watered prior to planting. Delineate a planting space and remove undesirable plants by digging or with an herbicide. Rototill or spade the planting area, blending in a total of 6 inches of organic matter and a handful of lime with the existing soil before raking smooth to form a raised bed. Dig in the bed an 18-inch-wide by 18-inch-deep hole for each clematis plant. Carefully remove the clematis from the pot, loosen its roots if they are potbound, and place the plant in the hole with the crown 2 inches below the surface. Backfill the hole, firm the soil, water thoroughly, remove existing flowers, and place 1 inch of mulch around plant, keeping it away from the stem.

CARE AND MAINTENANCE

If the vine is installed in the spring, feed it with a water-soluble fertilizer every 14 to 21 days for the first growing season, with none applied after mid-August. After the first season, feed monthly with a well-balanced food, beginning in early May and ending in mid-August. Do not allow drought stress to occur and eliminate weeds to prevent competition for nutrients. Cut back to 6 to 8 inches each fall for the first several years after planting to encourage a fuller, bushier plant. Jackman clematis flowers on the new year's growth, so once it is established it can be cut early each spring to control. Though several diseases and insects may affect this plant, the damage is mostly cosmetic, unless it is improperly planted.

ADDITIONAL INFORMATION

If purchasing dormant plants, look for swollen buds on stiff brown stems. Actively growing plants may be tied to a stick and awkward looking. Check for consistent color and size of foliage. Remove any flowers when planting.

ADDITIONAL SPECIES, CULTIVARS, OR VARIETIES

Clematis vines are grouped according to which pruning practices maximize results for each kind of clematis. Three varieties which belong to different groups than the Jackman clematis are: the white *Candida*, the carmine red *Ville de Lyon,* and the fragrant sweet autumn *Clematis maximowicziana.*

Japanese Wisteria

Wisteria floribunda

Mature Height: 40 feet or more
Flowers Color: Whitish lavender
Bloom Period: Late spring
Type: Deciduous Perennial
Hardiness Zones: 4 through 9
Color photograph on page 253.

Light Requirements:

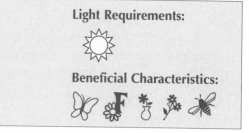

Beneficial Characteristics:

The grand twisting trunk and branches of the wisteria, sometimes so strong they can lift a roof or pull down old gutters, are awe inspiring to behold. And no less remarkable are the pale green leaflets and the blossoms that drop from the branches like pale fragrant bunches of grapes. No vine equals the wisteria for romance when trained over a high arbor to shelter picnics and summer evening sojourns. The flowers are gradually replaced by bean pods that darken with the fall.

WHEN TO PLANT

It is best to plant wisteria prior to mid-May or in September through early October.

WHERE TO PLANT

Site wisteria at the base of a strong support structure, an arbor, trellis, or cyclone fence, where the soil is well drained.

HOW TO PLANT

Regardless of the size of the pot purchased, keep the vine watered prior to planting. Delineate a planting space and remove undesirable plants by digging or with an herbicide. Rototill or spade the planting area, blending in a total of 6 inches of organic matter with the existing soil before raking smooth to form a raised bed. Dig a hole twice the width of the pot a minimum of 12 inches in diameter. Carefully remove the wisteria from the pot, loosen its roots if they are pot bound, and place the plant in the hole. Backfill the hole, firm the soil, water thoroughly, remove existing flowers, and place 1 inch of mulch around plant.

CARE AND MAINTENANCE

If the vine is installed in the spring, feed it with a water-soluble fertilizer every 14 to 21 days for the first growing season, with none applied after mid-August. After the first season, feed monthly with a well-balanced food, beginning in early May and ending in mid-August. Do not allow drought stress to occur and do not prune after late July. Once wisteria is established, removal is difficult because of the massive root system. Though several diseases and insects are potential problems, most have only a cosmetic effect.

ADDITIONAL INFORMATION

The fast-growing wisteria is available at garden centers in 1- to 5- gallon containers. There is no advantage to the larger plants except that they will impact more quickly. If dormant, the plants should have numerous buds on flexible stems; if leafed out, look for consistent color and size of leaves in relation to their position on the stem.

ADDITIONAL SPECIES, CULTIVARS, OR VARIETIES

Many cultivars are listed, with the main distinctions being the size of the flower or a greater fragrance, but most are not available for purchase.

 Did You Know?

This variety is the Japanese wisteria which is native to the temperate regions of Asia. This perennial vine is a member of the bean family. Although the pods or beans are not considered edible, they are quite attractive in floral arrangements. Remember not to plant the wisteria where it can reach any unintended structure.

Moon Flower

Ipomoea alba

Height: 20 feet

Flower Color: White

Bloom Period: Summer until frost

Type: Annual

Color photograph on page 254.

Light Requirements:

Beneficial Characteristic:

The moon vine scents the night air with a pleasant fragrance, making it an ideal candidate for deck or patio plantings. The pointed buds open during the night and become large white funnel-shaped flowers which float on top of the leaves. The stems, which are filled with a milky sap, are nonclinging type and must be woven through the supporting structure. The vine's tremendous number of leaves will entirely mask the top two-thirds of the support framework. Allow adequate space at the bottom for other nonclimbing plantings and you will be able to create a tiers of color and texture.

WHEN TO PLANT

In early to mid-April, begin seed germination indoors. Use a seed-starting soilless mix. Plant the seed in cell packs, and use full spectrum lighting and bottom heat. If planting in mid- to late May, you may place the seeds in a folded damp paper towel overnight, and plant them the next day, 1/2 inch deep, or simply direct sow the seed at the same depth.

WHERE TO PLANT

Plant moon flower in an open, sunny, well-drained site, in a prepared bed, at the base of the climbing structure, or in a container that is 14 inches in diameter or larger. The stem is nonclinging, and therefore must be woven through the support structure.

HOW TO PLANT

Delineate a planting space and remove undesirable plants by digging or with an herbicide. Rototill or spade the soil to a depth of 6 to 8 inches, and blend in a total of 6 inches of organic matter with the existing soil before raking smooth to create a raised bed. If the site is sloped, use erosion netting. Punch a hole 1/2 inch deep in the soil, drop in germinated seed, and gently firm the soil around the growth if sprouted. Water thoroughly and place $1/2$ inch of mulch over surface. If planting in a container, fill one-quarter full with gravel and then well-drained potting soil.

CARE AND MAINTENANCE

If the seed is germinated prior to installation or once the seed sprouts have broken the soil surface and are 2 to 3 inches long, begin feeding with a water-soluble fertilizer every 2 weeks to get the maximum growth rate. Monitor the soil moisture, and remember that young seedlings may need watering twice daily for the first 7 to 10 days. Various insects may chew holes in the leaves, but this is only an aesthetic problem.

ADDITIONAL INFORMATION

Annual vines are sold almost exclusively in seed packets. Purchase the seed from a reputable company, and check the date on the package to ensure freshness. It is possible to gather ripe seeds from the previous year's growth and store them for planting during the next year. Always check a few seeds in the early spring for germination potential by using the wet paper towel method described above. If the seed does not germinate, purchase new seed packets. If moon flower vines are not removed after a killing frost and allowed to remain through the winter, they may self-seed the following year.

ADDITIONAL SPECIES, CULTIVARS, OR VARIETIES

There are none available.

Did You Know?

Moon flower belongs to the morning glory family, which also includes the sweet potato. Native to the tropical regions of Central and South America, it has been in cultivation for hundreds of years. Because moon flower germinates so easily and grows so rapidly, it is an excellent "learning" vine for children.

VINES

Morning Glory

Ipomoea tricolor

Height: 20 feet
Flower Color: Pale red or blue
Bloom Period: Summer until frost
Type: Annual
Color photograph on page 254.

Light Requirements:

The lovely blue or red blossoms of this vine are truly the glory of the morning. The funnel-shaped flowers unfurl soon after sunrise, brightening the summer days with their tranquil beauty. The morning glory vine is easily germinated and spreads rapidly, twining, twisting, and climbing up the fence or trellis where it is planted. The stems conform easily to the growing structure, but must be woven in and out of the framework. When well cared for, this vine produces a large number of flowers and will bloom well into the fall. Plant this vine within view of a window or near a door where you can enjoy its glorious color the first thing in the morning.

WHEN TO PLANT

In early to mid-April, begin seed germination indoors. Use a seed-starting soilless mix. Plant the seed in cell packs, and use full spectrum lighting and bottom heat. If planting in mid- to late May, you may place the seeds in a folded damp paper towel to germinate overnight, and plant them the next day, $1/2$ inch deep, or simply direct sow the seed at the same depth.

WHERE TO PLANT

Plant the morning glory vine in an open, sunny, well-drained site, in a prepared bed, at the base of the climbing structure, or in a container that is 14 inches in diameter or larger. The stem is nonclinging, and therefore must be woven through the support structure.

HOW TO PLANT

Delineate a planting space and remove undesirable plants by digging or with an herbicide. Rototill or spade the soil to a depth of 6 to 8 inches, and blend in a total of 6 inches of organic matter with the existing soil before raking smooth to create a raised bed. If the site is sloped, use erosion netting. Punch a hole 1/2 inch deep in the soil, drop in germinated seed, and gently firm the soil around the growth if sprouted. Water thoroughly and place 1/2 inch of mulch over surface. If planting in a container, fill one-quarter full with gravel and then well-drained potting soil.

CARE AND MAINTENANCE

If the seed is germinated prior to installation or once the seed sprouts have broken the soil surface and are 2 to 3 inches long, begin feeding with a water-soluble fertilizer every 2 weeks to get the maximum growth rate. Monitor the soil moisture, and remember that young seedlings may need watering twice daily for the first 7 to 10 days. Various insects may chew holes in the leaves, but this is only an aesthetic problem.

ADDITIONAL INFORMATION

Annual vines are sold almost exclusively in seed packets. Purchase the seed from a reputable company, and check the date on the package to ensure freshness. It is possible to gather ripe seeds from the previous year's growth and store them for planting during the next year. Always check a few seeds in the early spring for germination potential by using the wet paper towel method described above. If the seed does not germinate, purchase new seed packets. If morning glory vines are not removed after a killing frost and allowed to remain through the winter, they may self-seed the following year.

ADDITIONAL SPECIES, CULTIVARS, OR VARIETIES

There are none available.

Scarlet Runner Bean

Phaseolus coccineus

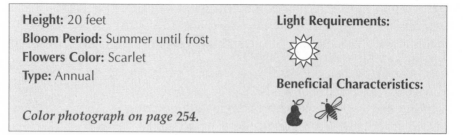

Height: 20 feet
Bloom Period: Summer until frost
Flowers Color: Scarlet
Type: Annual

Light Requirements:

Color photograph on page 254.

Beneficial Characteristics:

In summer, backyard trellises and arbors, patio pots, and fences come alive with the showy scarlet runner bean. Once planted in the warm soil of late May, this vine runs away with the season, its nonclinging stems growing in leaps and bounds as they are gently woven through the growing framework. The 5-inch, heart-shaped flowers frame clusters of 1-inch long, brilliant red flowers. Once pollinated, the flower produces a mottled, dark maroon bean pod that can grow up to 8 inches in length. All in all, another spectacular show by a member of the bean family.

WHEN TO PLANT

In early to mid-April, begin seed germination indoors. Use a seed-starting soilless mix. Plant the seed in cell packs, and use full spectrum lighting and bottom heat. If planting in mid- to late May, you may place the seeds in a folded damp paper towel to germinate overnight, and plant them the next day, 1/2 inch deep, or simply direct sow the seed at the same depth.

WHERE TO PLANT

Plant the scarlet runner bean in an open, sunny, well-drained site, in a prepared bed, at the base of the climbing structure, or in a container that is 14 inches in diameter or larger. The stem is nonclinging, and therefore must be woven through the support structure.

HOW TO PLANT

Delineate a planting space and remove undesirable plants by digging or with an herbicide. Rototill or spade the soil to a depth of 6 to 8 inches, and blend in a total of 6 inches of organic matter with the existing soil before raking smooth to create a raised bed. If the site is sloped, use erosion netting. Punch a hole 1/2 inch deep in the soil, drop in germinated seed, and gently firm the soil around the growth if sprouted. Water thoroughly and place $^1/_2$ inch of mulch over surface. If planting in a container, fill one-quarter full with gravel and then well-drained potting soil.

Care and Maintenance

If the seed is germinated prior to installation or once the seed sprouts have broken the soil surface and are 2 to 3 inches long, begin feeding with a water-soluble fertilizer every 2 weeks to get the maximum growth rate. Monitor the soil moisture, and remember that young seedlings may need watering twice daily for the first 7 to 10 days. Various insects may chew holes in the leaves, but this is only an aesthetic problem.

Additional Information

Annual vines are sold almost exclusively in seed packets. Purchase the seed from a reputable company, and check the date on the package to ensure freshness. It is possible to gather ripe seeds from the previous year's growth and store them for planting during the next year. Always check a few seeds in the early spring for germination potential by using the wet paper towel method described above. If the seed does not germinate, purchase new seed packets. If the scarlet runner bean vine is not removed after a killing frost and allowed to remain through the winter, it may self-seed the following year.

Additional Species, Cultivars, or Varieties

There are none available.

VINES

Silver Lace Vine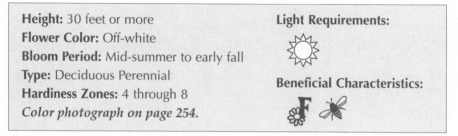

Fallopia baldschuanica

Height: 30 feet or more
Flower Color: Off-white
Bloom Period: Mid-summer to early fall
Type: Deciduous Perennial
Hardiness Zones: 4 through 8
Color photograph on page 254.

Light Requirements:

Beneficial Characteristics:

The warmer days of mid-spring trigger leaf production by the silver lace vine, whose large disk-shaped leaves emerge so quickly that winter is soon forgotten. Then in mid-summer, when many plants are dying off in the brutal heat, this vine suddenly blooms in an abundance, its fine-textured flowers scenting the heavy summer air and lasting into the early fall. The vine's nonclinging stems persist through the winter, and their twisted shape softens the bare outline of the growing structure. Its ability to bloom when the heat is at its worst makes the silver lace vine an ideal candidate for any spot that withers before you are ready to say good-bye to the green of summer.

WHEN TO PLANT

The best time to plant silver lace vine is prior to mid-May or in September through very early October.

WHERE TO PLANT

Site this vine where the root system is shaded and the stem and foliage are in the full sun. An easy way to shade the roots is to place them behind the growing framework; the foliage can then be directed toward sunlight. The stems are a nonclinging type and must be woven through the support structure.

HOW TO PLANT

Regardless of the size of the pot purchased, keep the vine watered prior to planting. Delineate a planting space and remove undesirable plants by digging or with an herbicide. Rototill or spade the planting area, blending in a total of 6 inches of organic matter and a handful of lime with the existing soil before raking smooth to form a raised bed. Dig in the bed an 18-inch wide by 18-inch deep hole for each clematis plant. Carefully remove the vine from the pot, loosen its roots if they are pot bound, and place the plant in the hole with the crown 2 inches below the surface. Backfill the hole, firm the soil, water thoroughly, remove existing flowers, and place 1 inch of mulch around plant, keeping away from the stem.

CARE AND MAINTENANCE

If the vine is installed in the spring, feed it with a water-soluble fertilizer every 14 to 21 days for the first growing season, with none applied after mid-August. After the first season, feed monthly with a well-balanced food, beginning in early May and ending in mid-August. Do not allow drought stress to occur and eliminate weeds to prevent competition for nutrients. Cut back to 6 to 8 inches each fall for the first several years after planting to encourage a fuller, bushier plant. Silver lace vine flowers on the new year's growth, so once it is established it can be cut early each spring to control. Though several diseases and insects may affect this plant, the damage is mostly cosmetic, unless it is improperly planted.

ADDITIONAL INFORMATION

Fast-growing silver lace vine are available at garden centers and through mail-order nurseries. The garden centers have plants in 4-inch to 1-gallon containers; there is no advantage to the larger plants except that they will create a quicker impact. If purchasing dormant plants, look for numerous buds on flexible stems. If the plants are leafed out, check for consistent color and size of leaves in relation to their position on the stem. Mail-order vines arrive bareroot wrapped in moss or in smaller pots.

ADDITIONAL SPECIES, CULTIVARS, OR VARIETIES

There are none available.

Trumpet Honeysuckle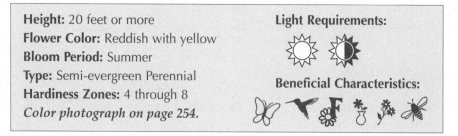

Lonicera sempervirens

Height: 20 feet or more
Flower Color: Reddish with yellow
Bloom Period: Summer
Type: Semi-evergreen Perennial
Hardiness Zones: 4 through 8
Color photograph on page 254.

Light Requirements:

Beneficial Characteristics:

This ambitious vine strives to reach the top regardless of the circumstances. The twining, nonclinging stems of the trumpet honeysuckle reach ever higher, even twisting and climbing on top of themselves to stretch across open spaces. Each year, at mid-spring, this perennial sprouts new leaves which have a purple tint when they first appear and then mature to a shiny bluish green coloration. Clusters of tubular-shaped flowers, red with yellow throats, bloom from May until August. During milder winters, the foliage will persist until it is shed by new growth in the spring. Most growth occurs at the top of the vine, and the bare stems at the bottom are best hidden behind another planting. This vine works well if turned free in a natural or rustic landscape, but will try to colonize neighbors' yards if not watched carefully.

WHEN TO PLANT
The best time to plant trumpet honeysuckle is prior to mid-May and again in September.

WHERE TO PLANT
Honeysuckles require a well-drained soil at the base of a support structure, which has openings for it to weave through.

HOW TO PLANT
Regardless of the size of the pot purchased, keep the vine watered prior to planting. Delineate a planting space and remove undesirable plants by digging or with an herbicide. Rototill or spade the planting area, blending in a total of 6 inches of organic matter and a handful of lime with the existing soil before raking smooth to form a raised bed. Dig in the bed an 18-inch wide by 18-inch deep hole for each plant. Carefully remove the plant from the pot, loosen its roots if they are pot bound, and place the plant in the hole with the crown

2 inches below the surface. Backfill the hole, firm the soil, water thoroughly, remove existing flowers, and place 1 inch of mulch around plant, keeping away from the stem.

CARE AND MAINTENANCE

If the vine is installed in the spring, feed it with a water-soluble fertilizer every 14 to 21 days for the first growing season, with none applied after mid-August. After the first season, feed monthly with a well-balanced food, beginning in early May and ending in mid-August. Do not allow drought stress to occur and eliminate weeds to prevent competition for nutrients. Cut back to 6 to 8 inches each fall for the first several years after planting to encourage a fuller, bushier plant. Insects and diseases are not a problem.

ADDITIONAL INFORMATION

Trumpet honeysuckle is fast-growing and basically an adult as soon it is as planted. It is available at garden centers in 4-inch to 5-gallon containers and will appear as a tangled mess. There is no advantage to the larger plants except that they will create a quicker impact. If dormant or actively growing, look for buds at the base of the leaves which should be consistent in color and size relative to their position on the stem.

ADDITIONAL SPECIES, CULTIVARS, OR VARIETIES

Several types are available, but in reality the advantage is minimal.

🌿 Did You Know?

If you pluck a trumpet honeysuckle flower and suck on the pistil, you'll experience a slightly sweet taste. The flowers' trumpet shape and red and yellow color invite bees and hummingbirds over for a taste as well. They pollinate the flowers while gathering nectar, which leads to the production of red fall fruits that draw many kinds of birds.

Wildflowers

THE WILDFLOWERS THAT THRIVE TODAY in the deep rich
soils of Missouri's flood plains or on the rocky bluffs high above
its rivers were valued by Native Americans for their beauty, and
used in foods and medicines long before the first Europeans crossed
the Mississippi. Those early explorers and settlers discovered a collection of unique flowers, some of which were scattered throughout
the western territory now called Missouri, and others which
bloomed in only one place. Gardeners who want to include wildflowers in a Missouri landscape today face nearly the same
limitations. Many wildflower varieties can thrive in multiple locations, while others never get a foothold and either struggle to endure
or simply die. Wildflowers are hardy, but they are very particular
species, and many thrive only in their own wild homes or in conditions that successfully imitate those homes. These conditions involve
many factors, including weather, soil profile, chemical nature of the
organic soil content, neighboring plants, and moisture circumstances.
Generally speaking, a plant qualifies as a wildflower if it is one that
has grown in an area without the help of human cultivation. The
variety may have evolved over time but, if so, the changes have not
resulted from human intervention. The varieties included here are
true natives of Missouri or plants that have been naturalized for
lengthy periods of time and are hardy in Missouri.

People sometimes have very opposite reactions to plants, and
this is especially true of the group known as wildflowers. Some
see "flower," and they revel in the beauty of the rare specimen clinging to a rocky cliff or an expanse of windswept fields dotted with
countless bright blossoms. Other people see "wild" and groan with
exasperation at the nasty rogue plant that defies the boundaries of a
garden bed or an enemy patch of weeds that threatens to take over a
lawn. It is true that wildflowers generally are not as sensational as
many of their hybridized relatives which are major players in

Chapter Twelve

today's landscapes. But wildflowers offer other characteristics which are just as rewarding. Durable in the right location, subtle in their beauty, and bearing a rich heritage in their native roots, wildflowers are a source of continual pleasure and interest to anyone who gets to know them well.

Just like all perennials and self-seeding annuals, wildflowers are grouped in broad categories, for example, "sun or shade tolerant" and "requiring wet or dry soil." A little research, some planning, and careful attention at the start will help you get the maximum benefit from a wildflower planting. You should determine how much sun a site receives, and at what time of day and in what season. Ask whether there are nearby plantings that will overshadow the wildflowers or aggressively compete for water and nutrients. What kind of exposure does the site have to wind and rain? One of their most attractive qualities is that, once they are established, wildflowers require very little time of the gardener. Unless extreme conditions occur, there is no need to worry about watering them, protecting them from pests and diseases, deadheading them, or cutting back their foliage. Just a little planning and preparatory work are guaranteed to bring rewards in the rainbow of native colors that wildflowers provide and in the nostalgic air they lend to any landscape.

Bee Balm N

Monarda punctata

Height: 2 to 4 feet
Growth Habit: Upright
Bloom Period: Summer
Flower Color: Red or pink
Type: Perennial wildflower
Color photograph on page 254.

Light Requirements:

Beneficial Characteristics:

Bee balm ignites the summer garden with tall stalks crowned by large, showy flowers. The square stem reaches straight up, swelling at the top into a many-fingered calyx that supports a big, bright whorl of flower petals. The plant's overall coarseness and vertical habit are a plus to garden settings regardless of their style. The impact is more pronounced if a mass planting has resulted from naturalizing or initial installation. The large flower heads attract butterflies, bees, and hummingbirds. Bee balm belongs to the mint family, all of whose members are very aggressive. Site this plant where there is plenty of space to spread, or simply dig up clumps and offer your bee balm bounty to gardening friends.

WHEN TO PLANT

Plant bee balm from early fall until the ground freezes, and again from early to late spring.

WHERE TO PLANT

Though adaptable, bee balm performs best in full sun in moist but well-drained soil.

HOW TO PLANT

Delineate the planting area. An area prepared in the spring can be planted with wildflowers in the fall, or an area prepared in the fall can be planted in the spring. Eliminate unwanted plants by digging or with an herbicide. Spread 2 inches of organic matter over the planting area and lightly rototill or hand spade to mix the organic material with the existing soil. Rake the surface smooth and allow the area to sit for 6 months. Water it during this period to germinate weeds, then remove the weeds and install the wildflowers. Dig a hole twice the diameter of the roots. Its depth should allow the plant to sit in the ground no deeper than it previously sat in the pot. Remove the plant from the pot and loosen the roots if they are potbound, place the plant in the hole, backfill, and water thoroughly. Fertilize monthly for the first growing season, using a water-soluble type of fertilizer. Pinch back the flowers and remove weak or dead growth to encourage new growth. If seeding, September through October is best. Scatter the seed, rake lightly for maximum soil contact, and water the area. Keep the soil damp until germination. After that time, water only if drought conditions occur.

CARE AND MAINTENANCE

During the first year after installation, deeply water sun-loving wildflowers only during extreme drought. Do not weed the area until definite identification of the wildflowers is possible. Lightly fertilize newly installed plants monthly for the first growing season. If planting seed, do not use mulch or fertilizer. Wildflowers are available in sod. These are plants grown from seed on fibrous mats, which can be cut into pieces. After the first growing season, water if drought is longer than 10 days, remove weeds or unwanted plants as needed, and do not mulch or fertilize. Remove any weak or dead growth, thin stems to reduce mildew problems, and cut spent flowers to encourage rebloom. Insect problems are minimal.

ADDITIONAL INFORMATION

When buying live plants, purchase only nursery-grown stock; never buy plants gathered from the natural environment. Plants are available as nursery-grown stock, seeds, and seeded sod. If plants are live, check for strong stem and leaves and a healthy overall appearance.

Big Bluestem Grass [N]

Andropogon geradii

Height: 6 feet or more
Growth Habit: Clump
Bloom Period: Summer
Flower Color: Pale purplish white
Type: Native grass
Color photograph on page 254.

Light Requirements:

Beneficial Characteristic:

The stature, texture, animation, and winter presence of big bluestem grass all help it make a true statement in the wildflower garden. It is a multifunctional plant and serves equally well as a focal point, a backdrop, or a mass planting that has dramatic long-distance impact. This grass is a clump grower, which means that new growth emerges from the outer perimeter. The lush green leaves erupt from the ground in a vase shape. Then, as surrounding plants bloom and set their seed, big bluestem's inflorescence waits patiently until the first frost, when suddenly it turns a coppery red color, waving above the now wheat-colored foliage. This native grass is tough and durable, and tolerates wet soil and salt, all of which makes it useful along roadways.

WHEN TO PLANT

Plant big bluestem grass during the spring to allow for acclimation before winter.

WHERE TO PLANT

Plant in a sunny location in soil of nearly any composition. The more organic the content of the soil, the floppier the growth habit.

HOW TO PLANT

Delineate the planting area. Eliminate unwanted plants by digging or with an herbicide. Rototill or spade the soil to a depth of 6 to 8 inches and do not fertilize. Keep the plant moist prior to planting. Dig a hole two times the diameter of the pot, or a minimum of 12 inches. Carefully remove plant from pot, loosen roots if they are potbound, and place plant in hole so that the base is slightly higher than the surrounding ground. Backfill the hole, firm soil, water plant thoroughly, and place 1 inch of mulch around the plant. If adding this plant to a garden with improved soils, mix average soil in the planting spot. Use erosion netting if needed during establishment.

CARE AND MAINTENANCE

Keep newly installed plants well watered during the first growing season. Because of their fibrous root system, grasses are very drought tolerant after the first year, but they will benefit if their soil moisture content is kept constant. Do not mulch over the crown, spread only 1 inch of mulch around the perimeter, and do not create a basin. The foliage remains through the winter to protect the crown of the plant. Cut back in the spring prior to the beginning of new growth. Divide the clump every 4 or 5 years in the spring, discarding any dead portions.

ADDITIONAL INFORMATION

When buying live plants, purchase only nursery-propagated stock; never buy plants gathered from the natural environment. Plants will be available in various sizes of containers. Check for fullness, a strong stem and leaves, and a healthy overall appearance.

WILDFLOWERS

 Did You Know?

Big bluestem grass is found in open areas, all the way from Quebec westward to the Rockies, south into northern Florida, and westward to eastern New Mexico. Even though it is the most widely distributed prairie grass, it is considered royalty because of its height, inflorescence, and overall impact.

Bittersweet Vine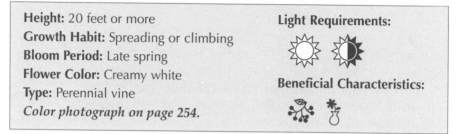

Celastrus scandens

Height: 20 feet or more
Growth Habit: Spreading or climbing
Bloom Period: Late spring
Flower Color: Creamy white
Type: Perennial vine
Color photograph on page 254.

Light Requirements:

Beneficial Characteristics:

Softening a wire fence, reaching through the trees, or gracefully masking the background are some of the ways that bittersweet can frame a wildflower garden. Its tannish brown stem supports dark green glossy leaves which turn yellowish in the fall. The creamy flowers emerge after the leaves and depend on wind for pollination as the male and female flowers are on separate plants. Without a mix of both male and female, no fruit will be produced. One male for every five female plants brings the orange capsules which enclose the fruits. The capsules pop open, exposing a scarlet fruit that is highly prized for fall arrangements.

WHEN TO PLANT

Plant bittersweet prior to mid-May or in September through very early October.

WHERE TO PLANT

Site bittersweet at the base of an arbor, trellis, or fence in full sun to part shade, where the soil is well drained. The vine will grow fastest in rich soil. The stems are a nonclinging type and initially must be woven through the support structure. Bittersweet also works as a groundcover.

HOW TO PLANT

Regardless of the size of the pot purchased, keep the vine watered prior to planting. Delineate the planting area. Remove undesirable plants by digging or with an herbicide. Rototill or spade the soil to a depth of 6 to 8 inches, blending a total of 6 inches of organic matter with the existing soil, and rake smooth, creating a raised bed. Use erosion netting if the site is sloped. Dig a hole twice the width of the pot or a minimum of 12 inches, carefully remove the plant, loosen the roots if they are potbound, and place the plant in the hole so that the base is slightly higher than the surrounding ground. Backfill the hole, firm the soil, water the plant thoroughly, and place 1 inch of mulch around plant.

CARE AND MAINTENANCE

If installing in the spring, feed with a water-soluble fertilizer every 14 to 21 days during the first growing season, with none after mid-August. After the first year, feed monthly with a well-balanced fertilizer, beginning in early May with the last application in mid-August. Do not allow drought stress to occur, and eliminate weeds to prevent competition for nutrients. Prune the male plants back heavily, as they are more aggressive than the females and may soon crowd out the colorful fruit bearers. Once the vine is established, removal is difficult. Though several disease and insects may attack bittersweet, the damage they do is mostly cosmetic.

ADDITIONAL INFORMATION

Bittersweet grows rapidly and makes a quick impact. It is available at garden centers and through mail-order nurseries; be sure to purchase both male and female plants for fruit production. Garden centers have plants in containers from 4-inch to 5-gallon pots, the only advantage to the larger size being that they will have an impact more quickly. If the plants are dormant, look for numerous buds on flexible stems; if leafed out, look for same color and size in relation to position on stem. Mail-order plants arrive bareroot wrapped in moss, or in smaller pots.

Did You Know?

Bittersweet is native to many areas east of the Rockies in Canada and the United States. The species name, scandens, *means "climbing." The roots of this vine have an orange coloration.*

Blue Bells N

Mertensia virginica

Height: 1 to 2 feet
Growth Habit: Upright
Bloom Period: Spring
Flower Color: Blue
Type: Woodland perennial
Color photograph on page 254.

Light Requirements:

Beneficial Characteristic:

Blue bells are found in the rich soils of the woodlands slopes and valleys. The largest display of color on these flowers is a block of pink turning to blue. The coarse texture of the oval-shaped bluish-green leaf should be considered when placing to harmonize other early-spring-flowering perennials and bulbs. The stems support the cluster of 1-inch bell-shaped flowers which hang downward. It is fun to watch bees move in to gather pollen. Remember that blue bells go totally dormant by midsummer. This means that a blank garden space will either have to be overplanted with annuals or intermingled with later-blooming shade wildflowers or perennials.

WHEN TO PLANT
Plant divisions in early spring or fall; plant seed in midsummer.

WHERE TO PLANT
Plant in well-drained organic soil in a site protected from the elements.

HOW TO PLANT
It is best to prepare the garden site at least 6 months prior to planting. Determine the location (not under surface-rooted trees) and remove plants that will not be part of the woodland garden. Apply safe herbicides. Rototill or hand spade to a depth of 6 to 8 inches, blend a total of 6 inches of organic matter with the existing soil, and rake the surface smooth. Water to encourage weed germination; remove weeds as needed and install the wildflowers the following planting season. Dig a hole twice the diameter of the rootball, at a depth that insures the stem will be located no deeper than previously grown. Remove wildflowers from the pot, loosen roots, place the plants in the hole (removing existing flowers), water thoroughly,

and lightly apply a water-soluble fertilizer. Pinch back or remove weak or dead growth. If planting seeds, scatter the seeds and rake lightly for maximum soil contact, and water. Keep the soil damp until germination; continue to water during drought conditions.

CARE AND MAINTENANCE

During the first year after installation, water deeply only during extreme drought. Do not weed the area until positive plant identification is possible. Lightly fertilize newly installed plants monthly for the first growing season. No mulch or fertilizer is necessary if planting seed. After the first growing season, remove weeds or unwanted plants as needed. Remove weak or dead growth as it occurs. Add 1 inch of leaf mold mulch on an as-needed basis; do not cut back stems or seedheads. Insects and disease problems are minimal.

ADDITIONAL INFORMATION

When purchasing live plants, do not buy if gathered from natural environments regardless of the situation. Plants are available as divisions from nursery-grown stock, seeds, or seeded sod. If plants are live, check for a good strong stem and leaves and a healthy over-all appearance.

 Did You Know

Blue bells are native from New York south to Alabama and west to Kansas, with a distant relative found in Europe and Asia. Buds will be pink and turn to blue as they age. The genus name Mertensia *is derived from the name of a German botanist.*

Blue Sage

Salvia azurea

Height: 4 feet or more
Growth Habit: Upright
Bloom Period: Late summer into fall
Flower Color: Blue
Type: Meadow perennial
Color photograph on page 254.

Light Requirements:

Beneficial Characteristics:

Close to the ground, the leaves of blue sage are large and broad, but they grow smaller and more slender as they climb the tall, slim stem, accentuating its graceful stature. Blue sage is native to the southeast and is very tolerant of heat and humidity. This fine-textured plant provides vertical relief to any garden setting. The slender, striking blue clusters of flowers bloom over a month period. Whether repeated as single plants in several spots or planted en masse, blue sage welcomes the eye in the mirror it makes of the blue summer sky.

WHEN TO PLANT

Install container-grown plants and sow seed in the early fall.

WHERE TO PLANT

Plant in average well-drained soil in an area where the flower can be seen easily.

HOW TO PLANT

Delineate the planting area. Eliminate unwanted plants by digging or with an herbicide. Spread 2 inches of organic matter over the planting area and lightly rototill or hand spade to mix organic material with the existing soil. Rake the surface smooth and allow to sit for 6 months, watering the area during this period to germinate weeds. When the growing season arrives, remove weeds and install wildflowers. Dig a hole twice the diameter of the roots, to a depth that ensures the stem is set no deeper in the soil than previously grown. Remove plant from pot and loosen roots if potbound. Place plant in the hole, backfill, and water plant thoroughly. Fertilize monthly for the first growing season, using a water-soluble fertilizer. Pinch back the flowers and remove weak or dead growth. September or October are the best months to plant from seed. Scatter seed, rake lightly for maximum soil contact, water to keep soil damp until germination, and then water only if drought conditions occur.

CARE AND MAINTENANCE

During the first year after installation, deeply water sun-loving wildflowers only during extreme drought. Do not weed the area until definite identification of the wildflowers is possible. Lightly fertilize newly installed plants monthly for the first growing season. If planting seed, do not use mulch or fertilizer. Wildflowers are available in sod. These are plants grown from seed on fibrous mats, which can be cut into pieces. After the first growing season, water if drought is longer than 10 days, remove weeds or unwanted plants as needed, and do not mulch or fertilize. Remove any weak or dead growth, thin stems to reduce mildew problems, and cut spent flowers to encourage rebloom. Insect problems are minimal.

ADDITIONAL INFORMATION

When buying live plants, purchase only nursery-propagated stock; never buy plants gathered from the natural environment. Blue sage is available as divisions from nursery-grown stock, seeds, and seeded sod. Check live plants for a strong stem and leaves, and a healthy overall appearance.

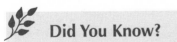

Did You Know?

This member of the mint family is found throughout the central Midwest and south into Arkansas and Texas. Unlike many of the other members of the mint family, blue sage is not an invasive aggressive plant. The species name, azurea, *refers to the sky-blue color of the flowers.*

Blue Star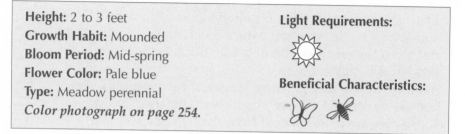

Amsonia illustris

Height: 2 to 3 feet
Growth Habit: Mounded
Bloom Period: Mid-spring
Flower Color: Pale blue
Type: Meadow perennial
Color photograph on page 254.

Light Requirements:

Beneficial Characteristics:

What is most eye-catching about this low-growing mound is the glossy quality of its very fine-textured foliage. Planted in a mass along the front edge of a garden, blue star sometimes looks like a small cloud of captured ground fog. Blue star's growing habit, shiny quality, and pale blue flowers all make it useful in garden transitions. It dramatically sets off different plant shapes and flower colors, and also softly links these various garden pieces.

WHEN TO PLANT
Install container-grown plants or disperse seed in spring or fall.

WHERE TO PLANT
Blue star does well in an evenly moist, well-drained soil that can have a considerable amount of rock content.

HOW TO PLANT
Delineate the planting area. Eliminate unwanted plants by digging or with an herbicide. Spread 2 inches of organic matter over the planting area and lightly rototill or hand spade to mix organic material with the existing soil. Rake the surface smooth and allow to sit for 6 months, watering the area during this period to germinate weeds. When the growing season arrives, remove weeds and install wildflowers. Dig a hole twice the diameter of the roots, to a depth that ensures the stem is set no deeper in the soil than previously grown. Remove plant from pot and loosen roots if potbound. Place plant in the hole, backfill, and water plant thoroughly. Fertilize once or twice with a water-soluble fertilizer. Pinch back the flowers and remove weak or dead growth. September or October are the best months to plant from seed. Scatter seed, rake lightly for maximum soil contact,

water to keep soil damp until germination, and then water only if drought conditions occur.

CARE AND MAINTENANCE

During the first year after installation, deeply water sun-loving wildflowers only during extreme drought. Do not weed the area until definite identification of the wildflowers is possible. Lightly fertilize newly installed plants monthly for the first growing season. If planting seed, do not use mulch or fertilizer. Blue star is available in sod. These are plants grown from seed on fibrous mats, which can be cut into pieces. After the first growing season, water if drought is longer than 10 days, remove weeds or unwanted plants as needed, and do not mulch or fertilize. Remove any weak or dead growth, thin stems to reduce mildew problems, and cut spent flowers to encourage rebloom. Insect problems are minimal.

ADDITIONAL INFORMATION

When buying live plants, purchase only nursery-propagated stock. Never buy plants gathered from the natural environment. Blue star is available as divisions from nursery-grown stock, seeds, and seeded sod. Check live plants for a strong stem and leaves, and a healthy overall appearance.

Did You Know?

Blue star belongs to the dogbane family, which includes species that are used in medicines and in the production of some types of rubber. The flowers are attractive to many insects, particularly butterflies. Amsonia is derived from the name of a nineteenth-century Virginian doctor; illustris refers to the shiny quality of blue star's foliage.

Butterfly Plant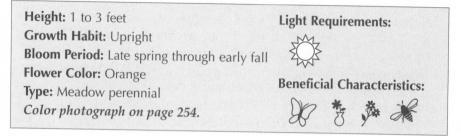

Asclepias tuberosa

Height: 1 to 3 feet
Growth Habit: Upright
Bloom Period: Late spring through early fall
Flower Color: Orange
Type: Meadow perennial
Color photograph on page 254.

Light Requirements:

Beneficial Characteristics:

The showiest milkweed, the orange butterfly plant, sometimes seems to be blooming butterflies. Each of its stems supports alternating 4-inch lance-shaped leaves, arranged in a swirling pattern. The conical flower cluster is made up of small blossoms, each of which looks like two flowers sitting back to back. One group of petals grows upward, the other bends down. The shape of the blossom allows the plant to attract numerous pollinators all at the same time. The pods that result from insect activity burst open, setting free airborne seeds that float and drift on the wind. Butterfly plant works well either as an accent point or planted as a mass of orange delight.

WHEN TO PLANT

Install container-grown plants in the fall; disperse seed in late summer.

WHERE TO PLANT

For peak performance, plant butterfly plant in well-drained soil which is on the dry side.

HOW TO PLANT

Delineate the planting area. Eliminate unwanted plants by digging or with an herbicide. Spread 2 inches of organic matter over planting area and lightly rototill or hand spade to mix organic material with the existing soil. Rake the surface smooth and allow to sit for 6 months, watering the area during this period to germinate weeds. When the growing season arrives, remove weeds and install wild-flowers. Dig a hole twice the diameter of the roots, to a depth that ensures the stem is set no deeper in the soil than previously grown. Remove plant from pot and loosen roots if potbound. Place plant in the hole, backfill, and water plant thoroughly. Fertilize once or twice with a water-soluble fertilizer. Pinch back the flowers and remove weak or dead growth. September or October are the best months to plant from seed. Scatter seed, rake lightly for maximum soil contact, water to keep soil damp until germination, and then water only if drought conditions occur.

CARE AND MAINTENANCE

During the first year after installation, deeply water sun-loving wildflowers only during extreme drought. Do not weed the area until definite identification of the wildflowers is possible. Lightly fertilize newly installed plants monthly for the first growing season. If planting seed, do not use mulch or fertilizer. Wildflowers are available in sod. These are plants grown from seed on fibrous mats, which can be cut into pieces. After the first growing season, water if drought is longer than 10 days, remove weeds or unwanted plants as needed, and do not mulch or fertilize. Remove any weak or dead growth, thin stems to reduce mildew problems, and cut spent flowers to encourage rebloom. Insect problems are minimal.

ADDITIONAL INFORMATION

When buying live plants, purchase only nursery-propagated stock. Never buy plants gathered from the natural environment. Butterfly plants are available as divisions from nursery-grown stock, seeds, and seeded sod. Check live plants for a strong stem and leaves, and a healthy overall appearance.

Did You Know?

The milkweed family is named for the whitish sap that flows in the veins of all green parts. Asclepias *is derived from* Aesculapius, *the Greek god of medicine, and honors the medicinal properties of butterfly plant's dried root. The species name,* tuberosa, *is Latin for "swelling" and refers to the bloating of portions of the butterfly plant's root system.*

WILDFLOWERS

Canadian Columbine

Aquilegia canadensis

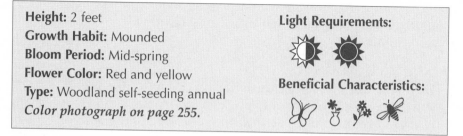

Height: 2 feet
Growth Habit: Mounded
Bloom Period: Mid-spring
Flower Color: Red and yellow
Type: Woodland self-seeding annual
Color photograph on page 255.

Light Requirements:

Beneficial Characteristics:

The columbine is a multi-textured plant. For coarseness, its rounded basal rosette of tri-partite leaves has an almost stonelike appearance. In contrast, its delicate flowers open atop slim stems that rise well above the leaves. This contrasting quality allows for multiple uses in the landscape, from large colonies to single plants which are dotted among shorter, coarser plantings. The olive-green color of the foliage accentuates the bobbing of the sprays of flowers above. This tough wildflower can be used almost anywhere, from sheer rock outcroppings to deeply organic soils under the canopy of trees.

WHEN TO PLANT

Plant columbine seed in the summer, and actively growing plants in the spring.

WHERE TO PLANT

Columbine adapts to many locations, from rock outcroppings to deeply organic gardens, but it is happiest on the edge of shaded areas, where the soil is rich and well drained.

HOW TO PLANT

It is best to prepare the site at least 6 months prior to planting. Do not locate columbine under surface-rooted trees, and remove from the site any plants that are not typical of the woodland garden by digging or with safe herbicides. Rototill or hand spade to a depth of 6 to 8 inches, blending a total of 6 inches of organic matter with the existing soil, and rake the surface smooth. Water during the next 6 months to encourage weed germination. At the next planting season, remove weeds as needed and install wildflowers. Dig a hole twice the diameter of the rootball and to a depth that ensures the stem is set no deeper in the soil than previously grown. Remove wildflowers from pot and loosen roots if they are potbound. Place plant in hole and backfill, pinch back existing flowers, water thoroughly, and fertilize lightly using a water-soluble fertilizer. Remove weak or dead growth as the plant matures. If seeding, scatter seed, rake lightly for maximum soil contact, water to keep soil damp until germination, and then water to prevent drought conditions.

CARE AND MAINTENANCE

During the first year after installation, deeply water part-shade- to shade-loving wildflowers only during extreme drought. Do not weed the area until definite identification of the wildflowers is possible. If planting seed, do not use mulch or fertilizer. After the first growing season, remove weeds or unwanted plants as needed. Remove any weak or dead growth as it occurs. Seed the heads and do not cut back stems. True insect and disease problems are minimal, although some cosmetic problems will occur.

ADDITIONAL INFORMATION

When buying live plants, purchase only nursery-grown stock. Never buy plants gathered from the natural environment. Columbines are available as divisions from nursery-grown stock, seeds, and seeded sod. Check live plants for a strong stem and leaves, and a healthy overall appearance. *A. canadensis* is more resistant to leaf miners, a common plague of columbines.

Did You Know?

Columbines are native to eastern Canada south to Florida and west to Missouri. Mother plants may last three years with a huge amount of seed production each spring guaranteeing future plants. The plant's Latin name, Aquilegia, *means "eagle" and refers to the shape of the flower.*

Celandine Poppy

Stylorphorum diphyllum

Height: 1 to 1½ feet
Growth Habit: Mounded
Bloom Period: Early to late spring
Flower Color: Yellow
Type: Woodland perennial
Color photograph on page 255.

Light Requirements:

Beneficial Characteristic:

The celandine poppy draws attention not only for its bright yellow, four-petaled, 2-inch-wide flower, but also for its unusual foliage. The bluish green leaves have up to seven cutouts and a nearly white underside that winks whenever a breeze passes through the shady garden. The flower produces a bloated seedpod when pollinated, which holds a phenomenal number of small dark seeds and guarantees a rapidly increasing colony of poppies every year. Celandine poppies may enjoy an extended bloom period some years, displaying their yellow brilliance for many weeks.

WHEN TO PLANT

Plant seed or divisions in the early fall.

WHERE TO PLANT

Plant celandine poppies in a consistently moist, highly organic soil with no standing water and with protection from any midday sun.

HOW TO PLANT

It is best to prepare the site at least 6 months prior to planting. Do not locate celandine poppies under surface-rooted trees, and remove from the site any plants that are not typical of the woodland garden by digging or with safe herbicides. Rototill or hand spade to a depth of 6 to 8 inches, blending a total of 6 inches of organic matter with the existing soil, and rake the surface smooth. Water during the next 6 months to encourage weed germination. At the next planting season, remove weeds as needed and install wildflowers. Dig a hole twice the diameter of the rootball and to a depth that ensures the stem is set no deeper in the soil than previously grown. Remove wildflowers from pot and loosen roots if they are potbound. Place plant in hole and backfill, pinch back existing flowers, water thoroughly, and fertilize lightly using a water-soluble fertilizer. Remove weak or dead growth as the plant matures. If seeding, scatter seed, rake lightly for maximum soil contact, water to keep soil damp until germination, and then water to prevent drought conditions.

CARE AND MAINTENANCE

Water deeply to prevent any drought stress at any time. Lightly fertilize newly installed plants monthly for the first growing season. Mulch or fertilize plants from May through August. After the first growing season, remove weeds or unwanted plants as needed. Remove weak or dead growth as it occurs. Add 1 inch of leaf mold mulch on an as-needed basis. Seed the heads and do not cut back stems. Insect and disease problems are minimal.

ADDITIONAL INFORMATION

When buying live plants, purchase only nursery-grown stock; never buy plants gathered from the natural environment. Celandine poppies are available as divisions from nursery-propagated stock, seeds, and seeded sod. Check live plants for a strong stem and leaves, and a healthy overall appearance.

 Did You Know?

Celandine poppies belong to the poppy family that is found in moist woodlands throughout the eastern United States, with many relatives found in Asia. Stylorphorum is Greek for "style bearing," and refers to this plant's consistent growth habit and seed production; diphyllum refers to the two leaves which grow on each stem. The sap inside the stems also has a yellow coloration.

WILDFLOWERS

Coneflower

Ratibida pinnata

Height: 3 to 4 feet
Growth Habit: Upright
Bloom Period: Summer to early fall
Flower Color: Yellow
Type: Meadow perennial
Color photograph on page 255.

Light Requirements:

Beneficial Characteristics:

Members of the sunflower family have two different types of flowers: the disk blossom and the ray blossom. The coneflower blossom has a slight variation on the classic ray petals. The yellow ray petals of this fine-textured plant droop, as if tired, and further expose the grayish disk. The tall stalks support alternating slender leaflets. The potential for an extended bloom period makes this variety a true bonus in almost all sunny garden settings.

WHEN TO PLANT

Install container-grown plants and disperse seed in the early fall.

WHERE TO PLANT

Well-drained soil that can range from poor to average is adequate for coneflowers.

HOW TO PLANT

It is best to prepare the site at least 6 months prior to planting. Eliminate any unwanted plants by digging or with an herbicide. Rototill or hand spade to a depth of 2 inches and rake the surface smooth. Water during the next 6 months to encourage weed germination. At the next planting season, remove weeds as needed and install wildflowers. Dig a hole twice the diameter of the rootball and to a depth that ensures the stem is set no deeper in the soil than previously grown. Remove wildflowers from pot and loosen roots if they are potbound. Place plant in hole and backfill, pinch back existing flowers, water thoroughly, and fertilize lightly with a water-soluble fertilizer. Remove weak or dead growth as the plant matures. If seeding, scatter seed in September or October, rake lightly for maximum soil contact, and water to keep soil damp for

2 to 3 weeks or until germination. Some varieties may germinate in the fall, others in the spring.

CARE AND MAINTENANCE

During the first year after installation, deeply water sun-loving wildflowers only during extreme drought. Do not weed the area until definite identification of the wildflowers is possible. Lightly fertilize newly installed plants monthly for the first growing season. If planting seed, do not use mulch or fertilizer. Wildflowers are available in sod. These are plants grown from seed on fibrous mats, which can be cut into pieces. After the first growing season, remove weeds or unwanted plants as needed. Remove any weak or dead growth as it occurs. Do not add any mulch. Cut back the stems, seed the heads, or fertilize. Insect and disease problems are minimal.

ADDITIONAL INFORMATION

When buying live plants, purchase only nursery-grown stock. Never buy plants gathered from the natural environment. Coneflowers are available as divisions from nursery-propagated stock, seeds, and seeded sod. Check live plants for a strong stem and leaves, and a healthy overall appearance.

WILDFLOWERS

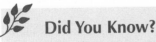 **Did You Know?**

Coneflowers are a familiar wildflower that usually create nostalgia for the summers of childhood. Their low-care requirements are an additional plus. The species name, pinnata, *describes the featherlike quality of the foliage.*

Cranesbill Geranium

Geranium maculatum

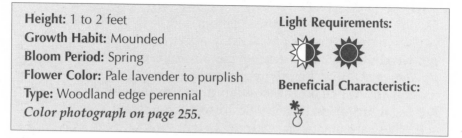

Height: 1 to 2 feet
Growth Habit: Mounded
Bloom Period: Spring
Flower Color: Pale lavender to purplish
Type: Woodland edge perennial
Color photograph on page 255.

Light Requirements:

Beneficial Characteristic:

The finely segmented leaf of the cranesbill and its soft roundish habit make this wildflower an excellent choice for transitions from any other type of landscape into a woodland setting. The medium-green foliage sets off cranesbill's extraordinarily tinted inflorescence. Its 5-petaled flowers are painted with darker highlighting lines radiating from the center. These markings serve as guides to pollen for bees and other pollinators. To create the most impact, plant cranesbill in groups rather than as randomly spaced individual plants.

WHEN TO PLANT

Install containerized plants in early fall; scatter seed when harvested.

WHERE TO PLANT

Plant cranesbill in evenly damp, highly organic, well-drained soil in a location that is protected from midday sun.

HOW TO PLANT

It is best to prepare the site at least 6 months prior to planting. Do not locate cranesbill under surface-rooted trees, and remove from the site any plants that are not typical of the woodland garden by digging or with safe herbicides. Rototill or hand spade to a depth of 6 to 8 inches, blending a total of 6 inches of organic matter with the existing soil, and rake the surface smooth. Dig a hole twice the diameter of the rootball and to a depth that ensures the stem is set no deeper in the soil than previously grown. Remove wildflowers from pot and loosen roots if they are potbound. Place plant in hole and backfill, pinch back existing flowers, water thoroughly, and fertilize lightly using a water-soluble fertilizer. Remove weak or dead growth as the plant matures. If seeding, scatter collected seed, rake lightly for

maximum soil contact, and water to keep soil damp for
2 to 3 weeks or until germination.

CARE AND MAINTENANCE

Do not weed the area until definite identification is
possible. Do not use mulch or fertilizer if planting seed.
After the first growing season, remove weeds or unwanted
plants as needed. Remove weak or dead growth as it
occurs. Add 1 inch of leaf mold mulch on an as-needed
basis. Seed the heads and do not cut back the stems. Insect
and disease problems are minimal.

ADDITIONAL INFORMATION

When buying live plants, purchase only nursery-grown
stock. Never buy plants gathered from the natural
environment. Cranesbills are available as divisions from
nursery-grown stock, seeds, and seeded sod. Check live
plants for a strong stem and leaves, and a healthy overall
appearance.

 Did You Know?

*Cranesbill is a member of the geranium family, and some of its
relatives are used for animal forage while others provide oil that
is essential for perfumes. This species is found on the edge of
woodlands in the eastern United States. The Greek word
Geranium means "crane" or "heron" and refers to the shape
of the unique nose on the seed capsule. Maculatum is Latin
for "spotted."*

False Blue Indigo N

Baptisia australis

Height: 2 to 3 feet
Growth Habit: Upright
Bloom Period: Mid-spring
Flower Color: Blue
Type: Meadow Perennial
Color photograph on page 255.

Light Requirements:

Beneficial Characteristics:

False blue indigo is a familiar face in many kinds of gardens, whether patches of wildflowers, careful perennial arrangements, or formal herb gardens. Its open, spreading, stiffly upright growing habit makes it a dramatic foil for many plants. The almost woody stems support slender pointed leaves made up of multiple leaflets, each up to 2 inches long. The clusters of unusually shaped flowers stand very erect, further accentuating the vertical profile of this wildflower. The blue blossoms attract bees, butterflies, and other insects, and the flower configuration presents a challenge for the eager pollinators. Their efforts are fun for both children and adults to watch. Once fertilized, the flowers become dark thick pods, like bean or pea pods. The pods can remain on the plants for visual enjoyment, or collect them for seasonal arrangements.

WHEN TO PLANT
Install containerized plants in the fall; disperse seeds in the spring.

WHERE TO PLANT
Plant false blue indigo in well-drained soil of average nutrient level; while this plant prefers an alkaline pH, it is not essential.

HOW TO PLANT
It is best to prepare the site at least 6 months prior to planting. Eliminate any unwanted plants by digging or with an herbicide. Rototill or hand spade to a depth of 2 inches and rake the surface smooth. Water during the next 6 months to encourage weed germination. At the next planting season, remove weeds as needed and install wildflowers. Dig a hole twice the diameter of the rootball and to a depth that ensures the stem is set no deeper in the soil than previously grown. Remove wildflowers from pot and loosen roots if they are potbound. Place plant in hole and backfill, pinch back

existing flowers, water thoroughly, and fertilize lightly
using a water-soluble fertilizer. Fertilize monthly for the
first growing season. Remove weak or dead growth as the
plant matures. If seeding, scatter seed in September or
October, rake lightly for maximum soil contact, and
water to keep the soil damp for 2 to 3 weeks or until
germination. Some seeds may germinate in the fall,
others in the spring.

CARE AND MAINTENANCE

During the first year after installation, water sun-loving
wildflowers often enough to keep the soil moist and to
prevent them from wilting. Do not weed the planting area
until definite identification is possible. During the first
growing season, lightly fertilize newly installed plants
monthly. Do not use mulch or fertilizer if planting seed.
Sod is made of plants grown from seed on fibrous mats,
which can be cut into pieces. After the first growing season
remove weeds or unwanted plants as needed. Remove
weak or dead growth as it occurs. Do not add any mulch,
cut back stems, seed the heads, or fertilize. Insect and
disease problems are minimal.

ADDITIONAL INFORMATION

When buying live plants, purchase only nursery-propagated
stock. Never buy plants gathered from the natural environment. False blue indigo is available as divisions from
nursery-propagated stock, seeds, and seeded sod. Check
live plants for a strong stem and leaves, and a healthy
overall appearance.

Did You Know?

*False blue indigo belongs to the pea family, which has many
representatives in various natural environments in Missouri.
The Greek name* Baptisia *means "to dye," and* australis
*means "southern," appropriate since this plant is native to the
limestone glades of southwest and east central Missouri.*

Goat's Beard N

Aruncus dioicus

Height: 4 to 5 feet
Growth Habit: Upright
Bloom Period: Early to midsummer
Flower Color: White
Type: Woodland perennial
Color photograph on page 255.

Light Requirements:

Beneficial Characteristic:

One of the tallest woodland wildflowers, goat's beard introduces vertical excitement and relief in garden settings whether planted as a single freestanding specimen or in larger groupings. Most of the heavily dissected foliage is clustered around the first 2 feet of the stem, but some leaflets do migrate up the flower stalks. A flower shaped like a spear point tops the towering stem, its mass made up of numerous tiny blossoms. Wind or the occasional bee carries pollen from the male flowering plants to the females.

WHEN TO PLANT
Install live plants in the spring or early fall; seed during early fall.

WHERE TO PLANT
Plant goat's beard in evenly moist, well-drained, highly organic soil in an area where there is protection from midday and afternoon sun.

HOW TO PLANT
It is best to prepare the site at least 6 months prior to planting. Do not locate goat's beard under surface-rooted trees, and remove from the site any plants that are not typical of the woodland garden by digging or with safe herbicides. Rototill or hand spade to a depth of 6 to 8 inches, blending a total of 6 inches of organic matter with the existing soil, and rake the surface smooth. Water during the next 6 months to encourage weed germination. At the next planting season, remove weeds as needed and install wildflowers. Dig a hole twice the diameter of the rootball and to a depth that ensures the stem is set no deeper in the soil than previously grown. Remove wildflowers from pot and loosen roots if they are potbound. Place plant in hole and backfill, pinch back existing flowers, water thoroughly, and fertilize lightly using a water-soluble fertilizer. Remove weak or

dead growth as the plant matures. If seeding, scatter collected seed, rake lightly for maximum soil contact, water, and keep soil damp.

CARE AND MAINTENANCE

Water deeply and do not allow any drought stress at any time. Do not weed the area until definite identification is possible. During the first growing season, lightly fertilize newly installed plants monthly. Do not use mulch or fertilizer if planting seed. After the first growing season, remove weeds or unwanted plants as needed. Remove weak or dead growth as it occurs. Add 1 inch of leaf mold mulch on an as-needed basis. Do not cut back stems or seed heads. Insect and disease problems are minimal.

ADDITIONAL INFORMATION

When buying live plants, purchase only nursery-propagated stock. Never buy plants gathered from the natural environment. Goat's beard is available as divisions from nursery-propagated stock, seeds, and seeded sod. Check live plants for a strong stem and leaves, and a healthy overall appearance.

 Did You Know?

Goat's beard is one of the few members of the rose family that is found in woodland environments. Several varieties of wildflowers are called goat's beard, but the name is best suited to this plant. The genus Aruncus is classic Latin for "goat's beard," and dioicus means that there are both male and female plants.

Primrose N

Oenothera missouriensis

Height: 1 foot
Growth Habit: Spreading
Bloom Period: Late spring
Flower Color: Yellow
Type: Meadow Perennial
Color photograph on page 255.

Light Requirements:

Beneficial Characteristics:

Like a small woman who wears a large hat to get attention, the low-growing primrose produces huge yellow flowers, some up to 3½ inches wide. Its lance-shaped leaves alternate from side to side along the entire length of the stem, rising up to the crowning yellow bonnet. As the flowers age, their color fades to a pale orange sunset tint. The capsule-like seeds that they produce have a leathery feel as they mature. Plant primroses as single plants in a rock garden, dotted in perennial and wildflower arrangements, or massed for dramatic color.

WHEN TO PLANT

Install containerized plants in early fall or by mid-spring; seed in later spring.

WHERE TO PLANT

Plant in a location that is very well drained with average or rocky soil.

HOW TO PLANT

It is best to prepare the site at least 6 months prior to planting. Eliminate any unwanted plants by digging or with an herbicide. Rototill or hand spade to a depth of 2 inches and rake the surface smooth. Water during the next 6 months to encourage weed germination. At the next planting season, remove weeds as needed and install wildflowers. Dig a hole twice the diameter of the rootball and to a depth that ensures the stem is set no deeper in the soil than previously grown. Remove wildflowers from pot and loosen roots if they are potbound. Place plant in hole and backfill, pinch back existing flowers, water thoroughly, and fertilize lightly using a water-soluble fertilizer. Apply a slow-release fertilizer at the beginning of the season. Remove weak or dead growth as the plant matures. If seeding, scatter seed in September or October, rake lightly for maximum soil contact, water to keep soil damp for 2 to 3 weeks or until germination. Some varieties may germinate in the fall, others in the spring.

CARE AND MAINTENANCE

Water deeply and do not allow any drought stress at any time. Do not weed the area until definite identification is possible. During the first growing season, lightly fertilize newly installed plants monthly. Do not use mulch or fertilizer if planting seed. Primroses are sold with other wildflowers in sod, which are plants grown from seed on fibrous mats that can be cut into pieces. After the first growing season, remove weeds or unwanted plants as needed. Remove weak or dead growth as it occurs. Do not add mulch, cut back stems or seed heads, or fertilize. Insect and disease problems are minimal.

ADDITIONAL INFORMATION

When buying live plants, purchase only nursery-propagated stock. Never buy plants gathered from the natural environment. Primroses are available as divisions from nursery-propagated stock, seeds, and seeded sod. Check live plants for a strong stem and leaves, and a healthy overall appearance.

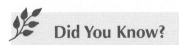

Did You Know?

This member of the evening primrose family is found from Missouri and Kansas south to eastern Texas. Its common name refers to the fact that its flowers open in the evening and close when struck by the morning sun. The bloom will stay open longer on overcast days.

Rose Verbena

Verbena canadensis

Height: Up to 1 foot	**Light Requirements:**
Growth Habit: Spreading	
Bloom Period: Spring to fall	
Flower Color: Pale purple	
Type: Meadow self-seeding annual	**Beneficial Characteristics:**
Color photograph on page 255.	

A low, stiff, bushlike plant, rose verbena adds a coarse texture to garden settings. When viewed from a distance, its rigid moundlike quality mimics the silhouette of smooth rocks and smaller boulders. Close-up inspection reveals a somewhat open growing habit, with considerable space between the 3-inch-long tooth-edged leaves. The small flower clusters, which sit above the foliage, are a striking color and send a strong message to numerous insects looking for nectar. The stems can persist through early winter and are quite beautiful if glazed by a heavy frost or dusted with an early snow.

WHEN TO PLANT

Spread seed or install containerized plants in the early fall or in the spring.

WHERE TO PLANT

Rose verbena does well in almost any type of soil that is well drained. It cannot survive in the shade of nearby taller plants.

HOW TO PLANT

It is best to prepare the site at least 6 months prior to planting. Eliminate any unwanted plants by digging or with an herbicide. Rototill or hand spade to a depth of 2 inches and rake the surface smooth. Water during the next 6 months to encourage weed germination. At the next planting season, remove weeds as needed and install wildflowers. Dig a hole twice the diameter of the rootball and to a depth that ensures the stem is set no deeper in the soil than previously grown. Remove wildflowers from pot and loosen roots if they are potbound. Place plant in hole and backfill, pinch back existing flowers, water thoroughly, and fertilize lightly using a water-soluble fertilizer. Fertilize monthly for the first growing season. Remove weak or dead growth as the plant matures. If seeding, scatter seed in September or October, rake lightly for maximum soil contact, water to keep soil damp for 2 to 3 weeks or until germination. Some varieties may germinate in the fall, others in the spring.

CARE AND MAINTENANCE

During the first year after installation, water deeply only during extreme drought. Do not weed the area until definite identification is possible. During the first growing season, lightly fertilize newly installed plants monthly. Do not use mulch or fertilizer if planting seed. Rose verbena plants are sold in sod, which are plants grown from seed on fibrous mats that can be cut into pieces. After the first growing season, remove weeds or unwanted plants as needed. Remove weak or dead growth as it occurs. Do not add mulch, cut back stems or seed heads, or fertilize. Insect and disease problems are minimal.

ADDITIONAL INFORMATION

When buying live plants, purchase only nursery-propagated stock. Never buy plants gathered from the natural environment. Primroses are available as divisions from nursery-propagated stock, seeds, and seeded sod. Check live plants for a strong stem and leaves, and a healthy overall appearance.

Did You Know?

Rose verbena can be found from Florida to Iowa. Its extended bloom period offers a nearly year-round source of nourishment for pollinating insects. The peak bloom period occurs in the late summer when rose verbena is an excellent choice for a children's garden.

Snakeroot N

Cimicufuga racemosa

Height: 3 to 4 feet
Growth Habit: Upright
Bloom Period: Late summer early fall
Flower Color: White
Type: Woodland perennial
Color photograph on page 255.

Light Requirements:

Beneficial Characteristic:

This woodland plant snakes through the garden in late summer, providing tall, dark green, deeply cut foliage and shining white flowers. Shooting like bottle rockets above the clumps of leaves are the long-stemmed flowers, which dance in the wind offering themselves to later-season insect pollinators. The unusual flowers have no petals; the male part of the flower provides its shape and coloration. When the dry seed heads mature, they make a rattling sound if the stems are shaken or knocked about by stronger winds.

WHEN TO PLANT

Install containerized, actively growing plants in the spring; disperse seeds in the fall.

WHERE TO PLANT

Plant snakeroot in evenly moist, organic soil that is well drained. Place this plant at the base of slopes or in rocky soils with protection from the midday sun.

HOW TO PLANT

It is best to prepare the site at least 6 months prior to planting. Do not locate snakeroot under surface-rooted trees, and remove from the site any plants that are not typical of the woodland garden by digging or with safe herbicides. Rototill or hand spade to a depth of 6 to 8 inches, blending a total of 6 inches of organic matter with the existing soil, and rake the surface smooth. Water during the next 6 months to encourage weed germination. At the next planting season, remove weeds as needed and install wildflowers. Dig a hole twice the diameter of the rootball and to a depth that ensures the stem is set no deeper in the soil than previously grown. Remove wildflowers from pot and loosen roots if they are potbound. Place plant in hole and backfill, pinch back existing flowers, water thoroughly, and fertilize lightly using a water-soluble fertilizer. Remove weak or dead growth as the plant matures. If seeding, scatter seed in September or October, rake lightly for maximum soil contact, water, and keep soil damp for 2 to 3 weeks. Snakeroot may not germinate until the spring.

CARE AND MAINTENANCE

Water deeply and do not allow any drought stress at any time. Do not weed the area until definite identification is possible. During the first growing season, lightly fertilize newly installed plants monthly. Do not use mulch or fertilizer if planting seed. After the first growing season, remove weeds or unwanted plants as needed. Remove weak or dead growth as it occurs. Add 1 inch of leaf mold mulch on an as-needed basis. Do not cut back the stems or seed heads. Insect and disease problems are minimal.

ADDITIONAL INFORMATION

When buying live plants, purchase only nursery-propagated stock. Never buy plants gathered from the natural environment. Primroses are available as divisions from nursery-propagated stock, seeds, and seeded sod. Check live plants for a strong stem and leaves, and a healthy overall appearance.

Did You Know?

Found throughout the eastern United States, this member of the buttercup family is one of the last woodland plants to bloom. Portions of the plant have been used medicinally or as an insect repellent. The common name, snakeroot, refers to the configuration in which the root system grows.

Sneezeweed N

Helenium autumnale

Height: 5 feet or more	**Light Requirements:**
Growth Habit: Upright	
Bloom Period: Late summer through fall	
Flower Color: Yellow	**Beneficial Characteristics:**
Type: Meadow perennial	
Color photograph on page 255.	

Although its common name may at first discourage you from planting sneezeweed, it is an impressive wildflower whose height and late-flowering beauty are hard to resist. Best placed behind other plantings, sneezeweed's height and coarse texture add drama to any garden arrangement. In fall, it towers over the declining garden with bright yellow flowers, drawing insects to gather the last pollen before winter begins. Before flowering, sneezeweed's leaves begin to wither and are almost deciduous, a habit that accentuates the stem's height and the flowers at its apex, but which also encourages planting behind other plants which can mask the browning leaves. At about two-thirds its full height, the stem branches and produces clusters of smaller flowers in an arrangement that looks like a bouquet of sunflowers sitting atop the stalk. Sneezeweed is very much at home in woodland meadows, on the wide-open prairie, streamside, or in streetside plantings.

WHEN TO PLANT

Plant sneezeweed in spring to allow for a full growing season before the fall flowering.

WHERE TO PLANT

Plant sneezeweed in average garden soil, which can range from evenly moist to nearly wet. Because of its height, plant this wildflower behind other specimens; planting in the distance will also help to mask the sometimes unattractive decline of its foliage prior to bloom.

HOW TO PLANT

It is best to prepare the site at least 6 months prior to planting. Eliminate any unwanted plants by digging or using an herbicide.

Rototill or hand spade to a depth of 6 to 8 inches and rake the surface smooth. Water during the next 6 months to encourage weed germination. At the next planting season, remove weeds as needed and install wildflowers. Dig a hole twice the diameter of the rootball and to a depth that ensures the stem is set no deeper in the soil than previously grown. Remove wildflowers from pot and loosen roots if they are potbound. Place plant in hole and backfill, pinch back existing flowers, water thoroughly, and fertilize lightly using a water-soluble fertilizer. Fertilize monthly for the first growing season. Remove weak or dead growth as the plant matures. If seeding, scatter seed in September or October, rake lightly for maximum soil contact, water to keep soil damp for 2 to 3 weeks or until germination. Some varieties may germinate in the fall, others in the spring.

CARE AND MAINTENANCE

During the first year after installation, water deeply only during extreme drought. Do not weed the area until definite identification is possible. During the first growing season, lightly fertilize newly installed plants monthly. Do not use mulch or fertilizer if planting seed. Sneezeweed is sold in sod, which are plants grown from seed on fibrous mats that can be cut into pieces. After the first growing season, remove weeds or unwanted plants as needed. Remove weak or dead growth as it occurs. Do not add mulch, cut back stems or seed heads, or fertilize. Insect and disease problems are minimal.

ADDITIONAL INFORMATION

When buying live plants, purchase only nursery-propagated stock. Never buy plants gathered from the natural environment. Sneezeweed is available as divisions from nursery-propagated stock, seeds, and seeded sod. Check live plants for a strong stem and leaves, and a healthy appearance.

Solomon's Seal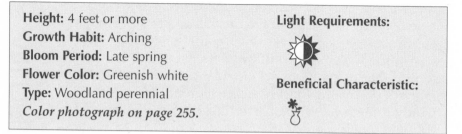

Polygonatum commutatum

Height: 4 feet or more
Growth Habit: Arching
Bloom Period: Late spring
Flower Color: Greenish white
Type: Woodland perennial
Color photograph on page 255.

Light Requirements:

Beneficial Characteristic:

The arching growth habit of Solomon's seal often makes its 6-foot stems appear to be only 3 feet high. This plant is naturally a colonizer, and a massed planting is the way to achieve its best aesthetic effect. The oval-shaped, pale green leaves open opposite each other on the stem and are highlighted by parallel veins. Where the leaf is attached to the stem, a pair of tubular bell-like flowers dangle, offering pollen for low-flying or crawling insects. Pollenization produces a round blue-black fruit which remains attached to the plant well past its bloom.

WHEN TO PLANT
Install containerized plants in the early fall; spread seed in the summer.

WHERE TO PLANT
Plant Solomon's seal in evenly moist, richly organic, well-drained soil located in a spot that is protected from midday sun.

HOW TO PLANT
It is best to prepare the site at least 6 months prior to planting. Do not locate Solomon's seal under surface-rooted trees, and remove from the site any plants that are not typical of the woodland garden by digging or with safe herbicides. Rototill or hand spade to a depth of 6 to 8 inches, blending a total of 6 inches of organic matter with the existing soil, and rake the surface smooth. Water during the next 6 months to encourage weed germination. At the next planting season, remove weeds as needed and install wildflowers. Dig a hole twice the diameter of the rootball and to a depth that ensures the stem is set no deeper in the soil than previously grown. Remove wildflowers from pot and loosen roots if they are potbound. Place plant in hole and backfill, pinch back existing flowers, water thor-

oughly, and fertilize lightly using a water-soluble fertilizer. Remove weak or dead growth as the plant matures. If seeding, scatter seed when ripe, rake lightly for maximum soil contact, water, and keep soil damp for 2 to 3 weeks. Some seeds may germinate in the fall, others in the spring.

CARE AND MAINTENANCE

Water deeply and do not allow any drought stress at any time. Do not weed the area until definite identification is possible. During the first growing season, lightly fertilize newly installed plants monthly. Do not use mulch or fertilizer if planting seed. After the first growing season, remove weeds or unwanted plants as needed. Remove weak or dead growth as it occurs. Add 1 inch of leaf mold mulch on an as-needed basis. Do not cut back stems or seed heads. Insect and disease problems are minimal.

ADDITIONAL INFORMATION

When buying live plants, purchase only nursery-propagated stock. Never buy plants gathered from the natural environment. Primroses are available as divisions from nursery-propagated stock, seeds, and seeded sod. Check live plants for a strong stem and leaves, and a healthy overall appearance.

Did You Know?

Solomon's seal is a member of the lily family that spreads, for the most part, by an underground root system, although some self-seeding may occur. The common name was coined by Dioscorides, who lived in the 1st century A.D., and refers to the scars left on the roots when the stems die off.

Spiderwort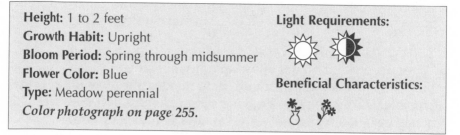

Tradescantia virginiana

Height: 1 to 2 feet
Growth Habit: Upright
Bloom Period: Spring through midsummer
Flower Color: Blue
Type: Meadow perennial
Color photograph on page 255.

Light Requirements:

Beneficial Characteristics:

Spiderwort is a truly adaptable plant that can migrate and take a foothold almost anywhere, even in the cracks of a sidewalk. The fine-textured leaves are long, folded lengthwise, and blue-green in color. The blades appear to reach around and grab the stems, a growing habit that gives spiderwort an open appearance which becomes quite animated in the wind. The three-petaled blue flowers with yellow stamens attract flighted pollinators, and cutting back the plants before seed formation occurs may produce another flush of flowers. Each plant produces a tremendous amount of seed which is transported by water to good germinating spots. Spiderwort looks good randomly placed among other plants or planted in an eye-catching blue mass.

WHEN TO PLANT

Install containerized plants in the early fall; scatter seed as soon as it is gathered.

WHERE TO PLANT

Spiderwort can be planted in almost any type of soil that is well drained, but performs better when planted in a better quality of soil.

HOW TO PLANT

It is best to prepare the site at least 6 months prior to planting. Eliminate any unwanted plants by digging or with an herbicide. Rototill or hand spade to a depth of 2 inches and rake the surface smooth. Water during the next 6 months to encourage weed germination. At the next planting season, remove weeds as needed and install wildflowers. Dig a hole twice the diameter of the rootball and to a depth that ensures the stem is set no deeper in the soil than previously grown. Remove wildflowers from pot and loosen roots if they are pot bound. Place plant in hole and backfill, pinch back existing flowers, water thoroughly, and fertilize lightly using a water-soluble fertilizer. Fertilize monthly for the first growing season. Remove weak or dead growth as the plant matures. If seeding, scatter seed in September or October, rake lightly for maximum soil contact, and water to keep soil damp for 2 to 3 weeks or until germination. Some varieties may germinate in the fall, others in the spring.

CARE AND MAINTENANCE

During the first year after installation, water deeply only during extreme drought. Do not weed the area until definite identification is possible. During the first growing season, lightly fertilize newly installed plants monthly. Do not use mulch or fertilizer if planting seed. Spiderwort is sold in sod, which are plants grown from seed on fibrous mats that can be cut into pieces. After the first growing season, remove weeds or unwanted plants as needed. Remove weak or dead growth as it occurs. Do not add mulch, cut back stems or seed heads, or fertilize. Insect and disease problems are minimal.

ADDITIONAL INFORMATION

When buying live plants, purchase only nursery-propagated stock. Never buy plants gathered from the natural environment. Spiderwort is available as divisions from nursery-propagated stock, seeds, and seeded sod. Check live plants for a strong stem and leaves, and a healthy overall appearance.

Did You Know?

Spiderwort, with its bladelike foliage, belongs to the monocot group of plants, which includes all types of grasses. The "spider" part of its common name refers to the zigzag appearance of its stem which resembles a spider's bent legs and "wort" simply means "a leafy plant."

Sweet William

Phlox divaricata

Height: 1 foot
Growth Habit: Spreading
Bloom Period: Spring
Flower Color: Blue
Type: Woodland perennial
Color photograph on page 256.

Light Requirements:

Beneficial Characteristics:

Sweet William is a colonizing woodland plant. As new growth spreads and comes into contact with the ground, it roots, allowing this wildflower to migrate the woodland floor and even to wrap around the trunks of trees while drawing water and nutrients from roots some distance way. Its 2-inch-long leaves, which resemble delicate spearheads, sit opposite each other along the stems. Rising above the dark green foliage is sea of sweet-smelling, pale violet-blue, 5-petaled flowers. Their color is extremely attractive to early-season bees who venture into the woodlands before the canopy is fully opened.

WHEN TO PLANT

Install live plants in late summer through early fall; disperse seed in the fall.

WHERE TO PLANT

Sweet William prefers evenly moist, richly organic, well-drained soil in a location that is protected from the midday sun.

HOW TO PLANT

It is best to prepare the site at least 6 months prior to planting. Do not locate under surface-rooted trees, and remove from the site any plants that are not typical of the woodland garden by digging or with safe herbicides. Rototill or hand spade to a depth of 6 to 8 inches, blending a total of 6 inches of organic matter with the existing soil, and rake the surface smooth. Water during the next 6 months to encourage weed germination. At the next planting season, remove weeds as needed and install wildflowers. Dig a hole twice the diameter of the rootball and to a depth that ensures the stem is set no deeper in the soil than previously grown. Remove wildflowers from pot and loosen roots if they are potbound. Place plant in hole and backfill, pinch back existing flowers, water thoroughly, and fertilize lightly using a water-soluble fertilizer. Remove weak or dead growth as the plant matures. If seeding, scatter seed in September or October, rake lightly for maximum soil contact, water, and keep soil damp for 2 to 3 weeks or until germination.

CARE AND MAINTENANCE

During the first year after installation, water deeply only during extreme drought. Do not weed the area until definite identification is possible. During the first growing season, lightly fertilize newly installed plants monthly. Do not use mulch or fertilizer if planting seed. After the first growing season, remove weeds or unwanted plants as needed. Remove weak or dead growth as it occurs. Add 1 inch of leaf mold mulch on an as-needed basis. Do not cut back stems or seed heads. Insect and disease problems are minimal.

ADDITIONAL INFORMATION

When buying live plants, purchase only nursery-propagated stock. Never buy plants gathered from the natural environment. Sweet William is available as divisions from nursery- propagated stock, seeds, and seeded sod. Check live plants for a strong stem and leaves, and a healthy overall appearance.

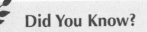 **Did You Know?**

Sweet William is native to the central Midwest, stretching from Canada to northern Alabama. A member of the phlox family, its relatives can be found in Europe, Asia, and South America. Phlox in Greek means "flame;" the Latin divaricata means "spreading" and refers to the flower's branching habit.

Trumpet Vine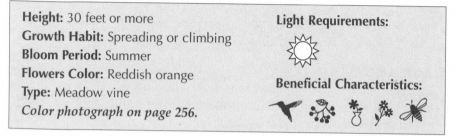

Campsis radicans

Height: 30 feet or more	**Light Requirements:**
Growth Habit: Spreading or climbing	
Bloom Period: Summer	
Flowers Color: Reddish orange	**Beneficial Characteristics:**
Type: Meadow vine	
Color photograph on page 256.	

Trumpet vine's old-fashioned look adds to the nostalgic appeal of any sunny wildflower garden. Its coarse texture makes it a great foil for the finer qualities of many sun and meadow plantings. If not controlled, trumpet vine can become unruly, but simply pruning back the vine on a yearly basis will keep it well managed. Pruning will not reduce flowering, since the 2-inch trumpet-shaped, intensely reddish orange flowers develop on each year's new growth. The flowers persist for a long period of time, reaching out from the leaflets that have up to 11 segments. Once pollinated, the flowers transform into winged capsules that can blow and germinate in distant locations.

WHEN TO PLANT
It is best to plant trumpet vine before mid-May or in September through very early October.

WHERE TO PLANT
Site trumpet vine at the base of an arbor, trellis, or fence in full sun in a well-drained or wetter soil; the richer the planting site, the faster the growth. The stems are generally a nonclinging type, although some aerial rootlets may occur and initially weave through the support structure.

HOW TO PLANT
Regardless of the size of the pot purchased, keep the vine watered prior to planting. Delineate planting space. Remove undesired plants by digging or with an herbicide. Rototill or spade the soil to a depth of 6 to 8 inches, blending in a total of 6 inches of organic matter. Rake the area smooth, creating a raised bed. Use erosion netting if the site is sloped. Dig a hole twice the width of the pot or a mini-

mum of 12 inches. Carefully remove the vine, loosen the roots if potbound, and place vine in the hole so that the base is slightly higher than the surrounding ground. Backfill the hole, firm the soil, water thoroughly, and place 1 inch of mulch around the plant.

Care and Maintenance

If installing in the spring, feed trumpet vine with a water-soluble fertilizer every 14 to 21 days for the first growing season, with none added after mid-August. In following years, feed monthly with a well-balanced food beginning in early May, with the last application in mid-August. Do not allow drought stress to occur, and eliminate weeds to prevent competition for nutrients. Once the vine is established, removal is difficult because of its massive roots and branches. Several diseases may attack, but none warrant chemical application.

Additional Information

Trumpet vine's rate of growth is very fast and it quickly produces an impact. It is available at garden centers and through mail-order nurseries. Garden centers offer plants in 4-inch pots to 5-gallon containers; there is no advantage to size, except that larger plants will create an impact sooner. If dormant, the plant should have numerous buds on flexible stems; if leafed out, the foliage should be the same color and size in relation to its position on the stems. Mail-order plants arrive bareroot wrapped in moss or in smaller pots.

🌿 Did You Know?

Because of its color and the time of year it flowers, the trumpet creeper is very attractive to hummingbirds. Multiple hummingbird feeders hung in the vines offer the opportunity for several hummingbirds to feed at one time.

Gardening Information Sources

Public, Corporate, and Botanical Gardens, Plant Societies and Organizations

The state of Missouri has a tremendous wealth of historical places and state parks within its system. The 79 diverse places, which range in size from small to massive, are administered by the Department of Natural Resources. Each site or park has been maintained in a way that allows visitors to see, feel, and hear the cultural and natural beauty that is part of Missouri's present and past.

These eventful locations can be found in many different places, from the busiest parts of the larger cities to a small trail winding up and through the woods. The names alone create interest and excitement. Think—where else can you visit Elephant Rocks, Roaring River, Prairie State Parks, Ha Ha Tonka, the Trail of Tears, and Taum Sauk? These unusual names stimulate adventurous whims but are actually humbling and awe inspiring. Whether it's a huge meadow of wildflowers, a home planted with a historical garden, cold springs bubbling up at the base of a bluff, or a meandering trail filled with bird and wildlife sounds, the state of Missouri has something for everyone.

The captivating beauty of Missouri's assets has in some circumstances been combined with the many outstanding features and qualities of plants from around the world. This unbelievable blending can be seen, felt, and enjoyed at any of the phenomenal public and corporate parks, college and university campuses, and botanical gardens that exist throughout the state of Missouri.

Botanical and Display Gardens

BETHANY
Edna Cuddy Memorial House
and Garden
1218 W. Main
Bethany, MO 64424-2529
(816) 425-3375

CAPE GIRARDEAU
Rose Display Garden
(at Parkview Drive and
Perry Avenue)
Cape Girardeau, MO 63701

CENTRALIA
Chance Gardens—Centralia
Historical Society
319 E. Sneed Street
Centralia, MO 65240-1341
(573) 682-5711

COLUMBIA
Shelter Insurance Gardens
1817 W. Broadway
Columbia, MO 65203-1107
(573) 445-8441

GRAY SUMMIT
Shaw Arboretum of the Missouri
Botanical Garden
(35 miles west of St. Louis on
Interstate 44)
Gray Summit, MO 63039
(314) 451-3512 or (314) 451-0850

KANSAS CITY AREA
Country Club Plaza
450 Ward Parkway
Kansas City, MO 64112-2101
(816) 753-0100

Loose Park
5200 Pennsylvania Ave.
Kansas City, MO 64112-2384

Powell Botanical Gardens
(30 miles southeast of Kansas City)
Highway 50
Lone Jack, MO 64070
(816) 697-2600

KIRKSVILLE
Sunken Gardens
Truman State University
Kirksville, MO 63501
(660) 785-4000

MOUNTAIN VIEW
Wayside Park Trail
East Highway 60
222 E. 2nd Street
Mountain View, MO
65548-8324

Botanical and Display Gardens (continued)

POINT LOOKOUT
Greenhouse and Arboretum
College of the Ozarks
Point Lookout, MO 65726
(417) 334-6411

SAINTE GENEVIEVE
Bolduc House
125 S. Main Street
Sainte Genevieve, MO 63670-1629
(573) 883-3105

SAINT JOSEPH
Albrecht Kemper Museum of Art
2818 Frederick Ave.
Saint Joseph, MO 64506-2901
(816) 233-7003

Krug Park
(11th Street and King's Park Road)
Saint Joseph, MO 64501

SAINT LOUIS
Missouri Botanical Garden
4344 Shaw Blvd.
St. Louis, MO 63104
(314) 577-5152

St. Louis University
221 N. Grand
St. Louis, MO 63103
(314) 997-2222

St. Louis Zoo
Forest Park
Hampton Ave. and Highway 64/40
St. Louis, MO 63110

Tower Grove Park
4255 Arsenal
St. Louis, MO 63116-1901
(314) 771-2679

Resources

Plant Societies and Organizations

American Hemerocallis Society
3803 Greystone Drive
Austin, TX 78731

American Iris Society
7414 East 60th Street
Tulsa, OK 74145

American Rose Society
P.O. Box 30000
Shreveport, LA 71130

Missouri State Horticultural
  Society
1-60 Agriculture Building
U. of Missouri
Columbia, MO 65211

Perennial Plant Assoc.
Contact: Dr. Steven Still
(614) 771-8431

National Council of State Garden
  Clubs
4401 Magnolia Ave.
St. Louis, MO 63110
(314) 776-7574

International Waterlily Society
Suite 328-G12
1401 Johnson Ferry Road
Marietta, GA 30062-8115
(770) 977-3564

American Community Gardening
  Assoc.
325 Walnut Street
Philadelphia, PA 19106
(215) 988-8785

University of Missouri Outreach
  and Extension
1-98 Agriculture
Columbia, MO 65211
(573) 882-2480

Glossary

Annual: A plant whose life cycle is completed in one growing season.

Biennial: A plant whose life cycle is completed in two years—first year, leaves; second year, flower and seeds.

Bottom heat: Heating cables or mats used under potted plants to stimulate faster new growth (new growth is triggered by soil temperatures).

Deciduous: Describes trees and shrubs that drop leaves yearly in fall.

Deep-root feeding: This technique for feeding trees involves drilling a series of holes around the tree during the winter. Starting one-third of the distance out from the trunk and continuing to the drip line, drill 12-inch-deep holes 2 inches apart encircling the trunk. Fill the holes halfway full with a low-analysis granular fertilizer or organic matter. It is not necessary to backfill the holes with soil.

Drip line: The furthermost extension of a tree's branching.

Evergreen: Trees, shrubs, ground covers, and perennials that maintain their needles or leaves year round. (Needles and leaves do fall or are shed every 2 or 3 years.)

Fertilizers: Organic or inorganic elements that act as nutrients for a plant. Some are needed in large, and others in minute, amounts. When applied properly, fertilizers improve plant health, and should only stimulate natural growth rates. The three numbers that label a fertilizer, for example, 5-5-10, indicate gross quantities in percentages of container weight. The first number gives the percentage of nitrogen, the second indicates phosphorus, and the third potash or potassium. The higher the number, the greater the amount of the mineral element in the fertilizer mixture. Granular types are applied to the ground by hand or spreader and are slower release; water-soluble types are applied to the ground and/or on leaves with a sprayer or watering can and are quickly released to plants.

Herbaceous: Soft-stemmed plants.

Hardscapes: Human-made surface structures, such as driveways, walks, patios, and decks.

Inflorescence: A flower cluster; the budding and unfolding of blossoms.

Resources

IPM: Integrated pest management through the application of physical, mechanical, cultural, or biological controls, with a chemical (the least toxic possible) used as a last resort. These controls are used only when pests are determined to be causing considerable damage and only in the specific places where pests are present.

Mulch: A topdressing applied after planting; it is decorative and it provides a buffer to extremes of temperatures and drought.

Organic matter: Once-living plant materials that have been stockpiled and/or composted and are used for soil improvements and as a very low analysis fertilizer.

Perennial: A plant that returns for more than two years, growing from its root system.

Pinch back: Physically remove soft tissue growth to encourage a shorter, fuller growth.

Propagation: An increase in the plant population through gathering and planting seeds or stem or root cuttings.

Pruning: Mechanically removing portions of a plant to control its overall shape and size. Do not put pruning sealer, which potentially causes more harm than good, over the wound.

Self-seeding: Describes a plant which increases in number with the germination of the previous year's seeds.

Site evaluation: A complete examination of a planting area during the course of an entire year, with attention to sunlight (when and where it falls, how long it lasts), topography (what are the high and low spots), water (from rainfall, down spouts, and run-off), existing plants (their type and health), and building and flat surfaces.

Soil preparation: The process of modifying the existing soil to create better growing conditions (includes adding organic matter to soil).

Variegated: Describes variations in the colors and/or shades of green in the leaves and/or flowers of a plant.

Woody: Describes plants with trunks, stems, and/or branches that remain above ground during winter.

RESOURCES

Bibliography

Cornell University—Staff of Liberty Hyde Bailey Hortorium. *Hortus Third*. Macmillian Publishing Company, Inc., 1976.

Dennison, Edgar. *Missouri Wildflowers*. Missouri Department of Conservation, 1973.

Dirr, Michael A. *Manual of Woody Landscape Plants*. Stipes Publishing Company, 1990.

Eisendrath, Erna R. *Missouri Wildflowers of the St. Louis Area*. Missouri Botanical Garden, 1978.

Grounds for Gardening. University of Missouri-Columbia Extension Publications, 1998.

New Pronouncing Dictionary of Plant Names. Florist Publishing Company, 1967.

INDEX

Index

Index

Index

Index

Index

Index

Index

Index

Index